THE
MAKING
OF
RETURN OF THE JEDI

P9-AOV-341

THE
MAKING
OF
STAR WARS

RETURN OF THE JEDI

™

Edited by John Phillip Peecher

A Del Rey Book

BALLANTINE BOOKS • NEW YORK

A Del Rey Book
Published by Ballantine Books

Copyright © 1983 by Lucasfilm Ltd.

All rights reserved under International and Pan-American Copyright Conventions. Published in the United States by Ballantine Books, a division of Random House, Inc., New York, and simultaneously in Canada by Random House of Canada Limited, Toronto.

Library of Congress Catalog Card Number: 83-90021

ISBN 0-345-31235-X

Manufactured in the United States of America

First Edition: September 1983

Cover illustration supplied by Lucasfilm Ltd.

THE
MAKING
OF
STAR WARS
RETURN OF THE JEDI

CHAPTER 1

Moviegoers, no matter how much they might have liked *The Empire Strikes Back* when it opened on May 21, 1980, were doubtless disappointed that they would have to wait three more years until the next episode—the concluding chapter in the middle *Star Wars* trilogy—would be released. Nineteen eighty-three seemed like a long time away. George Lucas and Howard Kazanjian, who were already deep into preproduction of *Raiders of the Lost Ark* and set to begin shooting at London's EMI Studios on June 30, had already had several meetings about *Return of the Jedi*. And Lucas had already begun work on the first draft screenplay. Kazanjian was set to produce *Jedi*, and even though *Empire* had just opened, they were pretty sure that they would make the third movie. If, for some reason, *Empire* wasn't a hit, then they could simply cancel the project. Kazanjian's handwritten notes, jotted quickly on the back of a page in his production notebook, indicate that Stuart Freeborn, in charge of Make-Up and Special Creature Design for *Empire*, should start work on *Jedi* in the fall of 1980 at the latest. The other notes concern such questions as: Who did they want to edit the movie? Who should do the production designs? When should they notify the cast? When should they begin thinking about a crew? Many of the decisions would have to be put off until January 1981. But all those people who left the movie theaters desperately wondering if Han Solo was going to survive carbon freezing, if Luke and Leia were going to become a twosome, and if Darth Vader was plotting more evil would have to wait still longer. George Lucas and

Howard Kazanjian were making plans (three years in advance) to answer all those questions—and do a lot more besides!

An expensive and complex movie like *Jedi* has to have all the pieces carefully planned and carefully put into place. That is why such a production takes so long. Every detail, from each lasersword effect to R2-D2's "voice" track to the musical score, has to be gauged, broken down into all its component pieces, juggled, and, finally, formed into an overall production schedule. The very last date of the schedule is, of course, the release date. In the early spring of 1981, the date was set—May 1983—more than two years in the future.

Now began the monumental task of filling in all the dates up to that point, and on March 18, 1981, a one-line Revised Tentative Production Schedule was issued on a strict need-to-know basis to a few key people at Lucasfilm and at EMI. Some of the dates were irrevocable, while others would go through several revisions. The schedule looked like this:

REV. 3/18/81

REVENGE OF THE JEDI
(Tentative Schedule)

September-1980	Start Stuart Freeborn
October	Joe Johnston, Ralph McQuarrie
February-28, 1981	George to deliver first draft script
March-3	U.K. production meeting; George Lucas, Howard Kazanjian, Jim Bloom, Robert Watts, Norman Reynolds
April-1	Production/budget meeting; George Lucas, Howard Kazanjian, Jim Bloom, Robert Watts, Norman Reynolds
June-1	George to deliver second draft
July	Model makers begin
July	Director set
September-1	Writer to deliver final script

January-1982	ILM special effects begin shooting
January-13, 1982	Start principal photography in London
April-1	Finish shooting London, move to U.S.
April-21	Begin shooting U.S. locations
June-1	REVENGE bluescreen at ILM
December	ILM finishes all temporary composites
December-1982	LOCK PICTURE. Spot music with John Williams
January-1983	Score music in London
February-1983	Deliver temporary special effects
February-1, 1983	Mix picture at Sprockets
March-1, 1983	ILM finish all special effects
April-1983	Timing, correction prints
May-1,1983	Start making release prints
May-23, 1983	RELEASE

A more careful breakdown and explanation of some of these dates (and a quick look into the future) show that, indeed, the production did stay very close to this tentative schedule.

1981

April-1	United States Production Budget Meeting. (It is a tentative budget since locations and personnel are, at this point, still an educated guess and the final script is not finished.)
June-22	The San Rafael Monster Shop begins. (Stop-motion expert Phil Tippett, after conversations with George Lucas, begins building models of some 60 other-worldly creatures.)

3

July-1 — Director Richard Marquand moves from his London home to San Francisco. (He will stay for two and a half months to get to know the people involved and to work on the final script.)

July-13 — Larry Kasdan script meetings begin. (This is almost certainly the last time that Kasdan will collaborate as just a writer. With his film *Body Heat*, he has now become a successful film director in his own right.)

1982

January-11 — PRINCIPAL PHOTOGRAPHY BEGINS—U.K. (The first day starts with a simulated Tatooine sandstorm, with all the old favorites, except David Prowse, being buffeted by wind machines and fake sand.)

May-15 — PRINCIPAL PHOTOGRAPHY ENDS. (The final date would actually be May 14th.

May-28 — 2nd Unit finishes shooting. (Assistant Director David Tomblin, who had been left in charge of the Crescent City units, called a halt right on time.)

September-1 — Sound Designer begins. (In truth, Ben Burtt began collecting noises months before when, during a preproduction visit to London, he taped the sounds of Big Ben outside the Houses of Parliament and recorded every shake, rattle, and roll of the aging London Underground system.)

4

October-29   ILM finished with all temporary composites. (These interim versions of action scenes and special effects will enable the post-production team to judge the pace of the film while the optical print group corrects the color register.)

November-1   LOCK PICTURE (Apart from very minor adjustments, this should be the final shape of the film, to which sound and music can now be added.)

1983

January-4   London Symphony Orchestra begins under the baton of Mr. John Williams.

January-22   London Symphony Orchestra hold. (After a week of two three-hour sessions per day, a final Saturday is kept in reserve for unexpected emergencies and changes in the recording.)

April-2   SNEAK PREVIEW (The audience will consist of an invited cross section of the general public. Varying age groups from schools and organizations will be asked to view the movie in a San Francisco movie house. The filmmakers, seated in the audience, will gauge the audience's reaction to *Jedi* and, if they feel it is necessary, will make a few final changes in the movie.)

May-27   JEDI RELEASE (The release
              date was brought forward to
              Wednesday, May 25, 1983, to
              coincide exactly with the sixth
              anniversary of the release of *Star
              Wars*.)

By September 1981 Howard Kazanjian was able to issue a two-and-a-half-page, minutely detailed schedule for the film. This schedule, give or take one or two weeks in either direction, became the bible for the making of *Jedi*, and is a perfect example of how careful preproduction planning and incredible attention to detail can pay off for a 32.5 million-dollar movie. (See Appendix #1 for this schedule.)

In the August 1981 issue of *Bantha Tracks*, the official *Star Wars* newsletter, Co-Producer Robert Watts made the prediction that "principal photography, with the cameras filming the actors in a real, full-size set, will begin on January 13, 1982. *Jedi* will be filmed at EMI Elstree in London, on location in Germany and possibly Tunisia."

Behind that assured-sounding statement, however, there were still several large and nagging doubts. Watts and Co-Producer Jim Bloom were flying blind because, at this point, they had no final script. Together with Production Designer Norman Reynolds, they had put in a considerable number of air miles scouting locations contained in the *Jedi* story outline. They needed a vast primeval forest with towering trees to establish the Green Moon of Endor scenes, and the biggest sand dunes in the world to film the Tatooine desert scenes. They wanted virgin sand with no human dwellings or mountain ranges to block the horizon. The Black Forest and Tozeur, Tunisia (an old stamping ground for *Star Wars* and *Raiders*), were distinct possibilities, although there was a strong lobby to transplant the shooting of both exterior scenes back home to North America since the *Star Wars* films had not been shot in the United States before. But without the script it was difficult to choose locations. All they could do was look for locations that they thought might be right.

That August, Robert Watts was also counting down the days until his January start date with the prospect of having nine sound stages—126,950 square feet of prime shooting space—on his hands and the problem of juggling construction crews in order to avoid losing part of his crew to several other big movie productions that were starting up at Pinewood and Shepperton studios.

EMI Elstree Studios, 40 minutes from Piccadilly Circus and 15 minutes from the London airport, had been chosen when *Star Wars* Producer Gary Kurtz and Production Supervisor Robert Watts were looking for a possible long-term home way back in 1975. Robert Watts remembers, "Shepperton—another London facility—was out because they had torn down E, F, and G stages, which effectively turned it from a large studio to only a medium-size studio available to outside renters. I did go to Pinewood—a third studio in the area—but they were unprepared to lease us all the stages. In 1975 the film industry was at a very low ebb, and I think that Pinewood subsequently regretted their decision. *Star Wars* was, from my point of view, a one-shot, so when shooting was over we all left and went our separate ways. The film's success brought us all back together again, and I've been at EMI ever since."

But by September six years later, Robert Watts faced another set of problems altogether. The script had still not arrived from the think tank in California. Now the problem was not studio space, but the lateness of the screenplay.

"The screenplay is the blueprint for everything, and without it you do tend to flounder a bit," Watts recalled. "We'd had indications, we'd had discussions, we'd had drafts, but the final script did come very, very late. It means that sometimes you build things because you cannot wait on certain decisions that are later changed. Then when you get the go-ahead on the final script, you incur an immense amount of overtime, which is expensive, but somehow you make it. It did happen this time, but not to an enormous extent."

On September 10, 1981, over the signature of Production Supervisor Doug Twiddy, a memo went out to all department heads, listing which sets were scheduled for which sound stages. There were, so far, 26 known sets out of at least 52 planned sets. Stage 1, at this point, contained three different small sets, including the polystyrene interior of Yoda's house which Construction Manager Bill Welch had prudently saved from *The Empire Strikes Back*; the Ewok Village composite set was on Stage 3, and the Rebel Cruiser Main Briefing Room was on Stage 5. But the biggest sets were scheduled for the 30,000-square-foot *Star Wars* stage, Stage 6, where the sets for the Interior of the Death Star, the Exterior of Jabba's Palace, and the Rebel Cruiser Main Docking Bay would be built. The use of these three sets represented a careful jigsaw of timing if all three were to be fitted into the 12-week EMI shooting schedule.

If only it were just sets! Robert Watts again: "Costumes have to be designed and manufactured. Props have to be built—you can't just rent *Star Wars* props. So every robot, all the radio-controlled equipment, and all the special-effects gear have to be developed and made well in advance of principal photography."

Special Effects Supervisor Kit West—an Oscar nominee for his work on *Raiders of the Lost Ark*—found himself in a whole new world with the *Star Wars* technology. He and his staff cast around for help in the most unlikely places and began by sending a telex message from London to California.

897932 STWARS G

TO: HOSMER DORRANCE
    CAMPBELL, CALIFORNIA

OCTOBER 15 1981

WE SHOULD BE GRATEFUL IF YOU WOULD SEND US THE DE-

TAILS, SPECIFICATIONS, AND AVAILABILITY OF THE MECHAN-
ICAL PARTS OF YOUR ARTIFICIAL LIMBS.

THANKING YOU IN ANTICIPATION.

JOHN BAKER,
SPECIAL EFFECTS,
CHAPTER 111,
EMI STUDIOS,
BOREHAMWOOD.

(A telex is a means of printed international communication. A message is typed into a typewriterlike machine in
one part of the world, then transmitted electronically and
typed out on a similar machine in another part of the world.
Telexes are less expensive than the telephone, are often
more efficient, and can be sent at any time of the night or
day. The *Jedi* staff in London was in constant telex communication with the staff in California and vice versa, and
this book will contain some of the more memorable ex-
amples of telex art.)

Stuart Freeborn reported for work in the early fall of
1980—right on schedule. He started so early because *Jedi*
would need a new Yoda and a completely new Chewbacca
suit. Both are time-consuming, detailed projects. Freeborn's
Jedi identification tag (issued to him much later) would list
him simply as Make-up Supervisor. That is a low-key name
tag for the man responsible for creating two of the *Star Wars*
stars, Yoda and Chewbacca, along with most of those en-
gaging *Star Wars* Cantina creatures and many, many others.

Toward the end of 1980, over at the Industrial Light and
Magic* building in the Lucasfilm San Rafael headquarters
compound, Visual Effects Art Director Joe Johnston would
be taking down the sketches of *Raiders of the Lost Ark* that
had covered his walls for the past several months in order

---

*Industrial Light and Magic is the special effects division
of Lucasfilm. It is generally referred to as ILM.

to begin the first of many hundreds of sketches for *Jedi*. For both previous *Star Wars* movies, the eminent painter and illustrator Ralph McQuarrie had been responsible for much of the conceptual artwork. Although he was still involved, this time around, the bulk of the conceptualization and visual effects for *Jedi* would start with conversations between Joe Johnston, Nilo Rodis-Jamero, Ralph McQuarrie, and George Lucas. From these conversations would come such creations as Jabba the Hutt, speeder bikes, and Ewoks, many of the costumes, and much of the overall look of the film.

Jedi personnel were also becoming familiar figures on the San Francisco Airport/Heathrow run as the days ticked off toward the start of shooting, and all the travelers were "encouraged" to act as couriers for any urgent *Jedi* freight that needed to be delivered. So Co-Producer Jim Bloom, due in London to make some decisions about the Ewok forest and Tatooine desert locations, found himself vastly overweight with six trunks and two boxes on one of his preproduction flights.

In order to avoid overexciting the customs officers in London, Assistant Production Manager Pat Carr sent a warning telex to the company's British freight agent at Heathrow Airport detailing some of the rather intriguing contents:

TO: ROBIN AT RENOWN
FROM: PAT CARR

OCTOBER 23RD

THE FOLLOWING IS A LIST OF THE ITEMS THAT JIM BLOOM WILL BE BRINGING M.I.B. WHEN HE ARRIVES ON FLIGHT PAN AM 124 TOMORROW SATURDAY 24TH OCTOBER:

TRUNK 1:
STORMTROOPER:
1 BLACK DICKIE, 390 BLACK COTTON HOODS

TRUNK 4:
WOOKIEE

2 HAIR BODY SUIT 1 HAIR HEAD 2 PRS HANDS 2 HAIR FEET
BEN KENOBI KIMONO AND SASH

BOX 1:
2 PRS GREEN HANDS
2 GREEN HEADS WITH RED EYES
1 BEIGE HEAD
1 GREY HEAD
1 DARK HEAD WITH HORNS

ALSO IN TRUNK 5 I THINK IS A QUANTITY OF BABY FOOD!

OUR PROPVAN WILL BE WAITING IN THE COACH PARK TO LOAD
WHEN THESE ARE CLEARED.

THANKS AND LUV

PAT

To judge by Box 1, either the creatures of Jabba's Court would be something to behold or an incredible Halloween party was planned for October 31.

Pat Carr is a 1975 charter member of the Lucasfilm team. Now, she can send a telex on just about any subject to any part of the world and manage to remain calm. She remembers, however, the early days of the trilogy quite well. "For *Star Wars*, in fact, we didn't have an office to start with; we had the corner of a corridor on the ground floor at 20th Century-Fox. There was a small construction unit and an art department at Lee Studios, and they were modeling the original R2-D2 out of wood. Fox wasn't sure they wanted to go ahead with the project. In November we were expecting a board meeting decision about the movie and had a directive saying, 'Don't spend any more money.' So we more or less ceased operations and waited for a phone call.

"When I first started, Robert Watts said to me, 'Patricia, look at it this way: I'm unit father and you are the unit mother!' I've never forgotten that!"

Now, of course, she is very used to the *Star Wars* ways, but in the beginning there were some adjustments to make.

"George was unlike any director I had ever met. Having worked with people like Fred Zinnemann and George Cukor and seen the way they interviewed actors, it was quite amazing to watch George. Peter Firth was one of about a dozen possible actors up for the part of Luke Skywalker. He went into George's office and came out within, I think, about 60 seconds. He looked at me and said, 'What was that all about?'

"When we had to get work permits for the American actors, I remember we cooked up the wording 'the characters in this film will have to appeal to a prepubescent international audience.' We look back and laugh now.

"Mark Hamill evidently appeals to that audience, judging by the fan mail from fourteen-year-olds that smell of perfume and have hearts and flowers all over them. Harrison gets much older ladies writing to him with other suggestions, and then there are the weird ones—people in love with R2-D2 or Darth Vader.

"I would think 80 percent of the crew of the original movie thought it was a load of rubbish and said so at the time—including some very high-up people who should have known better who were overheard on the set saying that Gary Kurtz and George Lucas didn't know what they were doing."

Is Pat responsible for some of the tight security that is kept up around the movies?

"The secrecy started with *Empire*. They felt they had been ripped off by *Battlestar Galactica*, and because, in another instance, certain stills and models were stolen, we had to keep everything under wraps. I walked around like a wardress, with an enormous ring of about 20 keys. That's when I invented, at George's request, a special way of coding scripts. The shredders only came in on *Jedi*.

During his London stay, as the preproduction pieces began to fit together, Jim Bloom often sent overnight telexes to the staff at Industrial Light and Magic and to his Monster Shop workers to let them know of recent changes. The messages often had a rather cryptic quality:

ATTN: PHIL TIPPETT + PATTY BLAU
FROM: JIM BLOOM

RANCOR KEEPER THAT CRIES WILL NOW BE A HUMAN.
DO NOT ARTICULATE WOOOF TO CRY.

JIM
30TH OCTOBER 1981

LFLPRM 897932 STWARS G

By now, Tunisia and Germany were out, and Yuma, Arizona, and Crescent City, California, had become almost virtual certainties as location sites for the Tatooine desert Sail Barge sequence and the climactic Battle of the Rebels and the Ewoks on the Green Moon of Endor, but one final look was in order.

Tuesday, November 3

The publicity department is off to a cautious start.

For an ordinary movie, the publicity department's job is to beat the drum, blow the horn, and, in general, stir up as much attention as possible for the movie in production. Normally, this would include a wooing of all the news media and a real effort to get blurbs in the newspapers and magazines, articles written about the movie, and interviews with the stars wherever and whenever the publicist can arrange them. No matter how brief, or occasionally even ridiculous, requests for information about the movie are processed and generally granted. This is all done in order to make the public aware of the movie and to try to create a desire in the public to go and see the movie when it is released—to pay to go and see the movie.

Because of the intense interest in anything to do with *Star Wars* and because of the new characters, plot twists, and production elements that must be kept under wraps for

Jedi, the function of the publicity department, in this case, will be the reverse of its traditional function. Now the publicist will politely and as efficiently as possible fend off most of the requests from people who are interested in the movie. So, rather than make the world aware of the fact that the movie is under way, the *Jedi* folks will be just as happy if hardly anyone knows that the movie has started. The objective of the department is to be as low-key and to keep as low a profile as possible about one of the most anticipated movies of all time. It is a unique turnabout for a publicity department and is, in many ways, a much harder job than the good, old-fashioned drum beating. Much of the thrust of the department actually will be preparation for the formal marketing campaign that will really start to simmer about four months before the release of the picture.

The department is allocated Room 103 and its antechamber, Room 103a. It is a famous place. George Lucas roomed there for *Star Wars*; more recently, Stanley Kubrick was the tenant during production of *The Shining*. Foursquare against one wall of the office, there is a small, white, mysterious, and immovable safe. It is locked. Casual visitors that first day guessed its contents as: George Lucas' first royalty check; the Force; or even the Ark of the Covenant. (It turned out, unfortunately, to contain none of these treasures!)

Tuesday, November 3, 10:30 A.M.

Heads-of-departments meeting. Producer Howard Kazanjian in the Chair, Robert Watts in support, Patricia Carr on notebook. Most of the heads are shaking. The problem is still the script—or lack of it. It is less than ten weeks to the wire, for a film that could be as complex as *Star Wars* and *Empire* rolled into one, and there is a whiff of anxiety in the air. A strike force will leave for California in two days, headed by Howard Kazanjian, who closes the meeting with a promise that a bound screenplay will be in everyone's hands in ten days. "If I don't come back with a script, I won't come back," he says, and he is only half joking.

Tomorrow is announced as Ewok Day.

Wednesday, November 4

At first sight, an Ewok turns out to be a blend of cuddly Koala bear and miniature Wookiee. On closer examination, an Ewok is a five-piece suit plus a furry sculptured head. The production needs several dozen "little people" to dress up in the suits and portray Ewoks.

Pat Carr was responsible for most of the Ewok little people search. "We only got four or five applications from the Job Center. Then some reporter from the *Sun* newspaper put the story on page 3 under the picture of a nude, and suddenly we had phone calls from all over the country. About 120 people applied, and we soon had all the people we needed under 4 feet 2 inches tall. Up until then we had thought that Kenny Baker—R2-D2—was the shortest man in Britain. Later on we began asking for even smaller performers so that the Ewok children would look more natural. At that point we had to tell those people more than 4 feet 6 inches tall that they were now too tall. They said on the phone that they had never been told they were too tall in their lives! The shortest was 2 feet 11 inches. He is eleven years old, bright as a button, and his name is Warwick Davis.

"Most of the applicants belong to an Association of Little People, have normal jobs, and lead near normal lives, often in specially adapted houses," Pat continued. "There was a customs official from Southampton Docks who was only 3 feet 1 inch tall, and a lady who worked for the Gas Board. One girl—not eventually used as an Ewok—out of work for two years but highly qualified as a shorthand typist, lost the chance of a job at British Telecom because they feared she might fall into the machinery and hurt herself."

Three little people—John, Gerald, and Josephine—test the Ewok costume mock-ups on videotape. John, getting accustomed to the costume, managed to slice the entire ear off his suit with the first brandish of his Ewok warrrior's weapon. Obviously, many more tests and then rehearsals will be necessary to accustom everyone to his or her Ewok costume. The tapes of the test will be hand-delivered to George Lucas the following day for his comments.

Thursday, November 5

The strike force leaves for the United States today in order to take one final look at the sites in Yuma and in Crescent City which have been chosen for the locations. Everyone is also keeping fingers crossed that they will return with a completed and final script.

Friday, November 6

Pat Carr takes advantage of the temporary lull to drive into Central London and inspect accommodations for the Lucas family, due to arrive in early January. There must be room for Lucas, his wife Marcia, their baby Amanda, and her nanny. Good room service is a must because of the long and erratic hours that Lucas will have to keep at the studio. Pat Carr comes back with two possible hotels, each of which meets the Lucas criteria.

Monday, November 9

The welcome arrival of David Tomblin, First Assistant Director. His job, like a factory foreman, is to make sure that everything and everybody are in the proper place at the proper time. Always. He must judge the pace of the operation carefully and know when to push and when to pull back. A legend in his own galaxy, Tomblin has worked on such films as *A Bridge Too Far*, *Superman*, *The Omen*, and *Gandhi*. For one scene in *Gandhi*, he guided a quarter of a million extras into position for the Panavision cameras. He also worked on both *Empire* and *Raiders*. Always gruff, occasionally grumpy, he usually knows best, and will provide the strong right arm that Director Richard Marquand will need. In his early fifties, with his thick, graying hair worn slightly long, David Tomblin is a solid-looking bear of a man. (It is only later that you discover that he is an old softie on the inside.)

First Assistant Director is a difficult job to define precisely. The First A.D. must take all the kinks out of the director's day and help to foster an atmosphere which will allow the director to roam free creatively, but he must also stop the director gently if he sees him about to turn up a blind alley. He is part benign headmaster and part honor student all at the same time, and when the chips are down—which they frequently are—he is also an ardent student of compromise. When producers hire a First A.D., they are looking for wisdom and stamina; by the time a movie is in production, regular studio visitors can often take a barometric reading of how the movie is going by looking at the demeanor of the First Assistant Director. He is often the first person to arrive at the studio in the morning and, in most cases, the last person to leave at night. Tomblin, who loves the job but hates to talk about it, allows that "I don't sit down much between the time a movie starts production and the time it finishes, and I look at my watch every 11 seconds." He brushes aside any talk of technique with this advice: "When in doubt—mumble; when in trouble—delegate." Then, in case one might believe this humorous piece of advice, he hastily takes it back.

Ultimately, it all boils down to experience, and David Tomblin has plenty of that. At the age of fourteen, he started as a production runner at the old British National Studios in Borehamwood.

By the time he was ushered into George Lucas' temporary office at EMI Elstree in 1975, Tomblin had served a very full apprenticeship in the movies and had worked with an impressive array of people from Stanley Kubrick to Robert Redford. He had also worked on over 500 episodes for 13 different television series. He had spent almost 30 years in the business. That first meeting with Lucas was brief. "I looked at him. He looked at me. And I didn't get the job. I read the original script. I thought it was fascinating and very brave because it all hinged on the believability of the robots." It is the source of some pleasure to Tomblin that, years later, during lunch in Crescent City one day, George Lucas, in casual conversation, intimated he had probably been wrong the first time around.

Through Director Irvin Kershner, with whom Tomblin had worked on the movie *Return of a Man Called Horse*, he joined up with the *Star Wars* team on *The Empire Strikes Back*. Like so many of the Lucasfilm technicians in influential positions, Tomblin is now almost a fixture on the team. After working on *Empire* and *Raiders*, he has had a lot of opportunity to observe the people around him.

"George is obviously a very bright man. He is the most knowledgeable producer I've ever come across. It's a pity he no longer directs pictures.

"Lucas and Spielberg are the best chemistry, the best combination you could find anywhere. George is basically kind, but also tough and single-minded; Steven is basically tough and single-minded. But before and after the production he does have his lighter moments. When we planned *Raiders*, he was determined to do the impossible and shoot it in 73 days, 'even if it kills THEM.' We did it in 70, and it aged me 70 years. Spielberg is something special, purely as a filmmaker; he is in a class of his own. If you read *Raiders*, it's a good script, but only as good as the director. The day after we finished *Jedi*, I saw a preview of *E.T.* Only a sensitive man could make a picture like that. I got soaked by the tears of the people sitting around me.

"What I like about the Lucasfilm outfit is that the organization is so thorough and that there are very high-class technicians on its productions."

Tomblin's last picture, before starting work on *Jedi*, was the Richard Attenborough film biography of *Gandhi*. He still has nightmares over trying to control 250,000 extras, so a few Ewoks seemed like child's play when he was promoted to Second Unit Director. The offer to stay behind and finish off the Ewok action scenes in Crescent City, although they were already carefully planned out, gave him the "freedom to improvise on a theme." He was obliged to steer a middle course, however, between filming only what was drawn in the storyboard sketches and filming small, complete sequences that could be dropped in anywhere for the final cut of the Endor Battle scene. "The camera crews were marvelously cooperative. I'd have a briefing every morning and give each of them their work load. We could stretch our cameras to four units at four different locations, as long as they stayed within commuting distance."

The Ewok action?

"An incredible bunch of people. Pound for pound and inch for inch, they have more humor than anyone. They are hard workers, willing to try anything, and very mischievous."

As if he weren't busy enough, Tomblin began a project in his spare moments and on the nights when he couldn't sleep. It is a 30-minute documentary woven around little Warwick Davis, who plays the Ewok Warrick. (Later, the character was rechristened into Wicket W. Warrick.) It is about Warwick Davis, age twelve, height 2 feet 10 inches, going out into the grown-up world and living out several boyish fantasies before being cast as an Ewok in *Jedi*.

"It all began when Warwick walked in the door for his audition and smiled," Tomblin says ruefully. "That smile cost me all my lunch hours and most of my days off."

It is Tomblin's rueful view of the world and his sense of warmth and solidness that help him handle, on one hand, directors who are wonderful with actors but don't know a zoom lens from an 85 filter, and on the other hand, those directors who can rewrite camera manuals in their sleep but can't direct an actor to the restroom. He is also very good with actors and actresses. With an air of confidentiality, he says, "There is a basic insecurity about actors. In my experience it works if you are firm and give them a distinct direction to go in—even if you're completely wrong!

"I don't find most artists difficult to handle. Harrison Ford and Sean Connery are the most down-to-earth. They are extremely professional, always on time, and they know what they are up to."

His next project? He's linking up with Kershner and Connery again for the new James Bond movie.

There is no evidence of a clause in a First Assistant Director's contract mentioning the right to a private life. David Tomblin and his wife have four children. "So I must have had four days off somewhere," he says with a big grin. "No, wait, three. Two of my kids are twins..."

Construction Storeman Dave Middleton, known as "discount Dave" to some people, is responsible for getting the gear together. His job is to pay the very best price for everything needed without holding up the production. "They ask for some crazy things," he says. "I know where to get 90 percent of it. What I don't know, I just look up in the bible—my books and phone numbers—and see what I can find." One should not be fooled by the "All-Right-Guv"-cockney-cloth-cap-and-muffler image that Dave shows. He is a canny and sharp-eyed shopper and can bargain with the best of them. He found the correct fur samples for the Ewoks down in the garment district and for almost a year now has been scouting for *Jedi* supplies, beginning with two bags of crystacal plaster, so that Stuart Freeborn could get up to his old tricks once more.

The East End of London is still his best hunting ground, he says. "Scrapyard Mafia, yeh. You can always find somebody to talk to—'I don't know, but Charlie will; give Charlie a ring,' someone will say. It's where I come from originally—in a way." He was brought up among the street markets and has been working since he was ten years old. "In the North End Road, getting a couple of quid. Reasonable education. My applied math is good—if you like.

"The first *Star Wars*? They didn't know what they had until they put it together. Who did? I suppose George Lucas did. I'd like to know what his secret is. Clever in his way—I'm clever in my way.

"George Lucas is a nice man, but I work for the construction manager. All Right Guv!" He is up, signaling the end of the talk, anxious to get back to work. There are bargains to be struck and weird and wonderful supplies to be tracked down in strange corners of London and the world.

Tuesday, November 10

The Crescent City crowd was actually in Yuma, Arizona, instead of Northern California, according to an early morning phone call to the Elstree art department from Norman Reynolds. Norman had been out of bed since 4 A.M., Los Angeles time. Either they were leaving very early for their location scouting or Norman's anxiety was showing. Possibly both.

Reynolds missed his routine morning studio inspection tour, but if he had been in England, he would have been pleased at the intense activity going on everywhere. Sketch artist Roy Carnon, a visualizer for *Raiders of the Lost Ark*, is working hard on a series of very detailed color story-boards, while farther along the corridor C-3PO's "keeper," Brian "Toby" Lofthouse, is burnishing a new set of golden-hued-robot suits.

Over on Stage 2, an Ewok Village overspill is taking up most of the space. Redwood trees that would normally take a thousand years to grow are being cut from polystyrene and artificially aged in a matter of a few hours. The finished trees could fool a squirrel at ten paces—or an Ewok! The finished set will be built 20 feet off the ground because the Ewoks build their villages high in the massive trees.

On Stage 8, Jabba the Hutt's Throne Room is beginning to take shape. This sequence is strongly rumored to be one of the early sequences, although the official shooting schedule has not yet been published. Here the new creatures will do their thing. One of the more humanlike creatures is named Bib Fortuna, a huge-headed character, who will be Jabba's Major-domo. From the gossip around the studio, the redoubtable Jabba sounds like an intergalactic godfather, but with none of Don Corleone's redeeming features.

Sand is being poured onto the floor of Stage 6, the *Star Wars* stage. It is an exterior version of Jabba's Palace gate, replete with a heavy metal drawbridge door and a sweeping, dimly lit vestibule.

Sound Stage 5 is dominated by the circular walls of the Rebel Cruiser Briefing Room set. Use of Number 5 is to be avoided, if possible, because the soundproofing is rudimentary, and it is just not in very good shape. Generally the stage is used for construction and storage and any production function other than that of a main stage, but *Jedi* needs all the space it can command, and Number 5 has reluctantly been pressed into service.

Construction Manager Bill Welch is keeping a very careful watch on all the stages and all the building activity for *Jedi*. Now he sits in his spartan office surrounded by the trappings of his job: blueprints, hard hat, rubber boots, and a green racing bicycle that he uses to pedal around the sound stages for his inspection tours. He remembers his feeling about the first movie. "Early on in *Star Wars*, I got very involved because it was just a handful of people."

That same feeling does not seem to be present on the set of *Jedi*. Perhaps it is because the production has grown so large, perhaps because there is so much pressure on everyone to get the movie going, or perhaps because there is three times as much money involved, but the same esprit de corps is impossible to recapture. Welch says, honestly, that he "thought *Star Wars* was the biggest load of rubbish I'd ever worked on. Not the sets—scriptwise. I couldn't see it making it. I was very, very surprised and very pleased when the film was so successful. Being involved in an award winner—it's a credit to you.

"*Raiders* I enjoyed very much. It was one of the toughest pictures I've ever done because of the time factor. I think most construction managers would like more preparation, smaller crews, and not so many hours." As soon as he says this, however, he knows it is an impossible wish in the movie business and smiles.

"I enjoyed getting away from pictures like *Star Wars* and *Alien*—very much space—and into architectural things again, into building airplanes and submarines, Egyptian stuff—it was a lovely variation on the sets." Speaking of sets, he looks as if it is once again time for him to climb on his bicycle and do a turn of inspection.

Friday the Thirteenth

In spite of the date, the omens are good. As the venerable Jedi Master might say, "Exists the script"; the touring company is to return from California by the weekend. It is now clear that Jabba the Hutt will be the "Man" on this production. Stuart Freeborn almost lives on the premises these days. In two months' time Jabba must be ready to "wobble, wink, and display fine furies," according to Freeborn.

Monday, November 16

It is wet and windy in Borehamwood. The strike force has returned from San Rafael, and Robert Watts, jet-lagged and tired, is back on the job. Norman Reynolds, testing possible camera positions for the Stage 5 Rebel Briefing Room scene, thought that the trip was successful. But he does wish that it had taken place three months ago! A George Lucas quote from the *Star Wars* days, about starting a movie without a completed script, comes to mind: "It's like riding a freight train at about 120 mph and having the guys trying to build the track in front of you as you go." Luckily, *Jedi* does not have that problem now.

Just three copies of the finished script are made. Every page is coded individually. *Jedi* may be the only script in living memory to have its own shredding machine close by the copying machine.

Tuesday, November 17

Richard Marquand reappears. In his absence there has been much progress on the building of the sets. His first impression of the vast size of the sets is one of awe. On the *Star Wars* stage, Jabba's Palace, whose 45-foot-high entrance extends from floor to ceiling, is now finished. It will be used for only three or four shots and seems like an awfully big door for such a short scene.

In the only free corner of Stage 6 sits five tons of undercarriage which will be used to support a full-size Imperial shuttle. Bill Welch would dearly like to know where the craft will be located on the set for the Imperial Docking Bay that will eventually be built here. It is not a question to ask any director seven weeks before shooting begins, but Welch needs to drive four-foot holes into solid concrete just to hold up the shuttle.

The Ewok Village is almost completed. The main square of the Village will be treated like a location, and the studio floor below will disappear into shards of special-effects mist. The Ewoks, for the more precarious shots, will wear protective wire harnesses. In order to reach the two-story-high set, regular forklift service will be available for everyone. The dressing rooms, or portacabins, for the Ewoks will be located right on the sound stage. It is difficult for most little people to get around easily, simply because of their size and their builds. When they are enclosed in an Ewok costume, mobility is even more difficult, so every effort is being put forth to make life as easy as possible for them during the shooting.

Wednesday, November 18

Jabba is being molded in special ovens built into the Freeborn make-up laboratories. The workmen must wear masks, helmets, breathing apparatus, and voluminous white suits, and must work very carefully with the strong, poisonous chemicals. One of the big questions is: Will Jabba be ready on time?

Friday, November 20

For Gary Kurtz, producer of *Star Wars* and *The Empire Strikes Back*, but not involved with Lucasfilm on *Jedi*, there is a moment of nostalgia as he stands on the doorstep of Stage 2 to watch an X-Wing Fighter and parts of the original *Millennium Falcon* winched into place. When Lucas and

Company were strapped for cash during the filming of *Star Wars* and Fox was dithering about funding a "science-fiction" film, Kurtz suggested that EMI take a piece of the *Star Wars* profits in lieu of stage rent. They declined—a decision he is sure that they regret.

Monday, November 23

Last night Richard Marquand, in a transatlantic telephone conversation with George Lucas, suggested that one portion of the script was still a little flat. This suggestion pushed the correct Lucas button, and out tumbled an instant idea that stunned the director. Today, Marquand is still marveling over it: "He keeps the whole *Star Wars* mythology in his head—interrelationships, attitudes, everything—the whole visual cascade."

Wednesday, November 25

There are Ewoks abroad. They are in Black Park in rural Buckinghamshire, to be precise—not far from the studio. News that they were to perform in Black Park on a cold and frosty morning came as a shock to the three little people who arrived for work early this morning. The first to show up declined a cup of coffee because he suspected that going to the bathroom would be difficult in his costume.

Once in the woods, the three Ewoks caper for an audience composed of Richard Marquand, about 20 very interested technicians, and a brace of rather blasé forest rangers who long ago learned to tolerate film people and their funny ways. Using a long lens, the cameramen shoot the Ewoks running through the underbrush, running backward, running toward the camera, turning, dancing, sitting, standing, looking at the camera—all the movements they will be required to make in the movie.

These tests demonstrated that several aspects of the Ewok suits would have to be modified. First, the plastic eyes misted up immediately. Stuart Freeborn partially solved this problem by punching small holes all around the piece of plastic in order to let the heat out—and some more air in.

Second, the little people must be able to get the Ewok heads off quicker in order to rest—the only solution is to split each head down the back. How to cover the seam? Easy. All the Ewoks will now wear leather helmets, which previously only a few of them were going to wear. The costume shop in San Rafael is alerted to produce several dozen more leather helmets for all the Ewoks.

Third, the Ewok fur. It looks saggy around the waist and thighs, and it wrinkles in places. The problem is solved by having the characters wear belts that hold their knives or pouches, or wear straps across their chests, which will help disguise the sags and wrinkles. Richard Marquand and his crew make a note to pay special attention to the look of the Ewok costumes during the actual filming. The leather helmets and the belts and chest straps will also add characterization and texture to these little forest creatures.

Cinematographer Alan Hume is photographing the capering Ewoks with a new, fast-exposure Kodak film, Number 5793—a 400 ASA film. Howard Kazanjian lobbied strongly for the production to use a faster film stock; in fact, ILM in San Rafael has been testing one developed by Fuji. But after seeing the test with the Kodak film, everyone agrees that the Kodak stock is the best. The other big question has been whether Kodak will be able to supply enough film by the January start date. They can and will, so Kodak 5793, 400 ASA, it will be.

The camera being used is a BL3 camera with a series of lenses developed by an Englishman named Joe Dunton. Richard Marquand talked about the final decision on which camera to use on *Jedi*: "Everyone was inclined to go with Panavision since that company gives great service, but Panavision is monumentally expensive. You're not allowed to buy a Panavision camera—you have to rent it. The production team and George were toying with the idea of going with the BL3, which is a very solid camera—sturdy, very useful—and they were interested in buying a camera rather than renting a Panavision camera." The camera also passed the test, and Lucasfilm will now buy one BL3 camera and rent another for use on *Jedi*.

Thursday, November 26

The one-line shooting schedule is finally delivered today. (See Appendix #3 for a copy of the one-line schedule.)

It is now time for the Monster Shop in California to think about transferring its children from California to their new home on Stage 8 at EMI. The man chosen to coordinate the transatlantic move of the creature costumes and operate as team coach during the filming of the studio interiors is a highly qualified, thirty-two-year-old engineer from Fairfax, California. One of the slightly "off center" *Jedi* talents and a true eccentric—Mr. Stuart Irwin Ziff.

To help Ziff with the move, to clear a path through customs, and to give the director an inkling of the care package heading his way, Patty Blau sent a rundown on the courtiers for Jabba's Throne Room:

ATTN: RICHARD MARQUAND
FROM: PATTY BLAU
CC: HOWARD KAZANJIAN

THESE ARE THE CREATURES WE ARE SENDING FOR THE PALACE SCENE: BIBLE NUMBER/NAME

1	REE YEES
3	TOOTHFACE
4	THE MOLE

6	SQUIDHEAD
10	WOL CABASSHITE
14	GAMORREAN GUARDS—3 OF THEM
17	BUBO
21	RED BALL JETT
24	SIC SIX
26	HERMI ODLE—HIS HEIGHT IS 88 INCHES WHEN ON A SIX FOOT PERSON. DO YOU NEED CIRCUMFERENCE? CIRCUMFERENCE IS 123 INCHES AND WIDTH IS 40 INCHES.
28	SNOOTY
31	YAK FACE
34	DROOPY
36	HEADHUNTER
37	EPHANT MON
37A	SALACIOUS CRUMB
38	CANE ADISS
39	ROCK WART
40	HOOVER
41	TOADSTOOL TERROR
42	YUZZUM
44	OOLA'S APPLIANCES
45	NIKTO NUMBER 3 AND 4
49	WOOOF NUMBER 2 AND 3
55	WIEBBA-WIEBBA'S APPLIANCES

PATTY
LFLPROD SRFL

Three days later, in case anyone felt the animals would need feeding over the Christmas break, Patty Blau sent another message:

ATTN: RICHARD MARQUAND
FROM: PATTY BLAU

DO NOT, REPEAT, DO NOT OPEN ANY OF THE CREATURE CRATES WITH THE ONE AND ONLY EXCEPTION OF CRATE 19 (PIG GUARD FOR RICHARD TO TRY) UNTIL PHIL TIPPETT AND COMPANY ARRIVE IN JANUARY. THIS IS VERY IMPORTANT. IF THESE

CRATES ARE OPENED AND THE CREATURES DISTURBED, IT COULD COST US A LOT OF TIME AND MONEY. BESIDES, THEY BITE.

While most of the rest of the world agonized over last-minute Christmas shopping, the *Jedi* tempo on both sides of the Atlantic was rising to a crescendo. And more than human passengers were being bumped from overcrowded flights:

PBCE18.03
897932 STWARS G
KEY + 230172605
LFGLPROD
897932 STWARS G
ATTN: LATA RYAN
FROM: PAT CARR
DECEMBER 21 1981

RE: TWO LARGE CRATES CONTAINING MODEL OF SARLACC PIT

THIS WAS DUE TO FLY OUT OF LONDON LAST SATURDAY—WAS TAKEN OFF THE PLANE COS THEY WERE OVERLOADED WITH PASSENGERS AND FIRST CLASS MAIL.

The holiday rush has never been a respecter of individuals—or of a Sarlacc Pit—whoever or whatever that might be!

The Sarlacc model eventually arrived in California with no untoward damage, although, of course, he wasn't home for Christmas. The Christmas and New Year's holidays did cause a bit of a slowdown around the studio, but things continued to percolate. The movie is going to start shooting in a few short days, and even with the spirit of the holidays, there is already an air of anticipation about the studio, a sense of "Yes, we can make it, but, as always, it is going to be close." The anxiety and the frenzy typical of that last, impossibly busy, oftentimes insane final week will begin on Monday, January 4.

CHAPTER 2

The week before the start of production is often one of the worst weeks in the schedule of any movie. It seems as if there are simply too many things left to be done, or that too many important things have accidentally been over-looked and must be picked up; all of which will, of course, require much more than a week to be put right. Everyone is pushing to hit the deadline, and tempers get short, eyes get red from lack of sleep, and the start date gets closer.

There is an element of all this for *Jedi*. But many of the people here are veterans of both *Star Wars* and *Empire* and many also worked on *Raiders*, so they know what they are doing and they know what they are facing. There is a strong sense of work and a real edge of seriousness about making this movie. The movie will, undoubtedly, be lots of fun on the screen, but getting it there is going to be lots of hard, difficult work.

Monday, January 4

D-Day minus 7, and there is total silence from San Rafael. Torrential rains, landslides, and four-foot floods have closed Golden Gate Bridge and knocked out telephone and telex cables. Thankfully, service is soon restored.

Luckily, Los Angeles flights are not affected by the weather. Carrie Fisher slipped into town on Sunday. She is going to stay at Lee Remick's house in St. John's Wood—a simple 20-minute trip to the studio at her time of day—usually an early morning call!

Today might be called Medical Monday. Mike Carter, the actor playing Bib Fortuna, is due at the optician for a fitting for his special contact lenses, Richard Marquand and Anthony Daniels have appointments to visit a doctor in Belgravia for their insurance check-ups, and Carrie Fisher is due at the dentist.

Mark Hamill and his family have arrived safely in the country with a minimum of fuss. So has Billy Dee Williams. The airport run has become almost a reflex action after three films shot at EMI. One problem: Harrison Ford did not appear for his plane. He has, it turns out, a bad back from lifting a heavy suitcase while on vacation in Hawaii. He will arrive tomorrow.

Howard Kazanjian was in his office at 7:30 this morning; he is an early bird, and his 12-hour days usually begin before 8 A.M. Looking at his calendar, he notes that he has been in London for 71 days already. Like a general anxious for battle, he is counting down the days until the beginning of the picture.

Tuesday, January 5

Harrison Ford touches down—in a wheelchair! Could Han Solo possibly be suffering from the effects of carbon freezing? Nope. Just his temporary back pain.

Creature Chief Phil Tippett and two of his key personnel arrived waterlogged from San Rafael.

Kazanjian and Watts met with the insurance people today to finalize the insurance coverage for the movie. They had to block out such questions as: If the film stock is bad, what does the insurance cover? If there is a fire at the studio, what does the insurance cover? This is a somewhat macabre subject, but such things have to be taken into account. Kazanjian said that the worst he figured could happen would be that a block of stages would burn, say Stages 1 through 4 or Stages 7 through 9, or that an individual stage might burn down. Certainly not the whole studio. In his usual no-nonsense approach to the problem at hand, and with his usual eye on the budget, Kazanjian was able to negotiate the insurance fee down to a cost of slightly over a million!

At 2:30 this afternoon, everyone gathered to see the test of the sandstorm which was done last week. The first day of filming on Monday will be a Tatooine sandstorm, and wisely, they decided to do a test before actually beginning production. Kazanjian explains: "The set is on Stage 2 and is a 360-degree cyclorama which is painted a medium beige color. The color gets lighter toward the top and fades into a very pale blue. This cyc was hand-painted for the scene."

Richard Marquand talks about the test: "We tested everything. We tested the look, the color, the quality of the sand, what we needed to make it look like sand, the fans, what the problems were in terms of everything. The sand is a mixture composed of small balls of styrofoam and a blending of talcum powder. The talcum powder is terrible. I hope to God it's not carcinogenic, because it certainly gets everywhere. The powder is used to give some thickness in the background. We didn't use sand. I mean, hey, why would you use sand in a sandstorm? This is the movies!

"We came up with the idea that we should probably get these sort of blankety-looking, cloaklike things and some goggles for the actors to wear, just in case. So I telexed back to San Rafael and asked Aggie [Aggie Rodgers, Costume Designer] to make some terrific, spacy-goggly-type things and cloaks which the heroes could have picked off the skiffs. It was at this point that she brilliantly suggested that we give some of the skiffguards some of these things so it will all tie in. They could have grabbed them as they ran, and then that would make some sense."

At 6 P.M. in the Administration Theater at EMI Elstree, a screening of *Star Wars* took place for those needing to refresh their memories.

Wednesday, January 6

There was a major rehearsal today for the 41 minor and the 6 principal Ewoks on Stage 3, after their usual warm-up exercises with Choreographer Gillian Gregory. A film test was also made of the Ewoks, even though they wouldn't be needed until the second week of filming. Kazanjian said, "We wanted to see what the Ewoks would look like now and how they were walking and how their costumes were shaping up." Today's test was the culmination of weeks and weeks of Ewok work. After all the little people were chosen, the painstaking job of making the molds for their costumes began. Impressions were taken of all their hands and feet so that the Ewok gloves and boots would fit each little person perfectly. Then the heads, and finally the bodies, were put together. Next came the arduous task of fitting each complete costume to each person, making the fit as comfortable and as realistic-looking as possible. "After the costumes were finished, we brought them all in together and they all started learning how to walk.

"At first, in the workouts, they couldn't even walk on the ground. They would trip—they couldn't see, because the eyes kept fogging up. Some of them would bump into one another because they couldn't see over their bellies. You know, if you suddenly stood up and you had this protruding belly . . . it's very weird; you can't see your feet. It's a whole new education.

"So the choreographer was teaching them not only how to walk but how to walk like an Ewok walks and to mimic these small animals we were creating. She also taught them ballet movements and various exercises in order to limber them up. Remember, we are dealing with dwarfs and some midgets; and a lot of these guys haven't had much exercise, they don't have the greatest stamina, and they don't normally perform from 8:00 in the morning to 6:00 at night in a heavy, hot costume.

"They are some of the hardest-working people I've ever been associated with. I thought after the first day none of them would come back for the second day—but they were there every morning. They all were, every single one.

"Finally, they learned how to walk on the ground, on a flat floor. Then we took them up high onto the set, where they were walking on the log-type flooring. And that's when we discovered that the soles of the boots were too hard. So we had to change all the soles to softer material. Once on the set, which is 20 feet off the ground, we had to be very careful so no one would fall off the edge. Wherever there was a place that they could fall off, we had to put boxes, and mattresses and nets so anyone—crew or cast—would land in this net."

The other reason for the Ewok test today is to check on how the costumes look on film once again. Are there wrinkles in the fur that are very obvious and can be avoided? What kinds of problems should Marquand and the crew watch out for during the actual filming? The final reason for the test is to check the lighting. As Kazanjian says, "You can't shoot in broad daylight because the Ewok costumes are going to look like costumes, so we want to make it dark enough in the Ewok forest to help disguise some of that costume look."

The grand opening of the creature crates by Phil Tippett also took place today. All his creature children seem to have survived the transatlantic flight in grand form and will be up and cavorting very soon!

Mark, Billy Dee, and Carrie are in the studio today for make-up tests and final costume fittings. Kazanjian explains that all the costumes are designed and made in San Rafael;

all the actors had already been up to the Lucasfilm head-quarters once or twice to see the costumes, try them on, and comment on them. When one of the actors was in a complete outfit, Lucas, Kazanjian, and Marquand would come from whatever part of the studio they were in and take a close look at the total effect.

Kazanjian explains the costume process: "By now most of the sets are finished or, if they're not finished, we know pretty much what they are going to look like. And we know the details of each set. The actor's props are finished and since we know how each actor or character in a scene is going to be costumed, we have an overall view of how everything will fit together. Take Billy Dee, for example. He would have a complete outfit on and George, who is specially good at this, would say, 'No, it isn't quite right yet. Try it with the cape on.' Or, for another character, one of us might say, 'Don't wear the vest, or, wear the vest—but take the coat off. Or, wear the vest *and* the coat but halfway into the scene, take the coat off.' This was the only way that we could really determine how all the colors would finally weave together." The process was slow and occasionally tedious for the actors, but the costumes are now ready to go—one more element is in place as the countdown continues.

The telex wires are also jammed with urgent, last-minute requests.

ATTN: JIM BLOOM
FROM: PAT CARR

KIT WEST HAS BEEN LET DOWN BY A SUPPLIER OF ELECTRIC LIGHT BULBS HERE. HE URGENTLY NEEDS THE FOLLOWING ITEMS TO COME OVER AIR FREIGHT OR ACCOMPANIED BAGGAGE:

1000 (ONE THOUSAND) SYLVANIA FLASHBULBS—CLASS 'S' NO: 3 SLOW PEAK

PLEASE ADVISE

This evening, same time, same place, there will be a screening of *The Empire Strikes Back* for those who can make it.

Thursday, January 7

There will be a little more testing on film today with the Ewoks to check out some small problems that showed up on yesterday's test.

Each day this week, Kazanjian has made it a point to have lunch with a different group of people involved in the production. Today, he and Robert Watts lunched with Norman Reynolds and Bill Welch. This is a more relaxed way to talk over the progress and any problems and make sure that everything is proceeding on schedule.

Lucas arrived, very quietly, at the studio around 3:00 this afternoon, and he and Howard Kazanjian walked the sets. "Walked the sets" is Kazanjian's phrase for his daily hike through all the sound stages and all the departments. It gives him an opportunity to see everyone, say hello, and keep tabs on what is being built, what is being worked on— be it a set, a costume, or a special effect—at the entire studio. Today Kazanjian gave the boss the super tour, no charge.

Friday, January 8

Just 72 hours to go. George Lucas demonstrates his usual attention to detail by closely supervising the haircuts given to Mark Hamill and Harrison Ford. Lucas' intention is to stay for about three weeks, but some believe he will probably find it difficult to leave, what with the Ewok sequence and the Jabba Palace sequences well up in the first half of the schedule and very much unknown quantities at this point. Richard Marquand has mixed feelings about the proprietor living on the premises. On one hand, he feels a second opinion can be helpful, but on the other hand, as Marquand admitted in a recent conversation, "It is rather like trying to direct *King Lear*—with Shakespeare in the next room!" Stuart Ziff is beginning to stock up his temporary creature workshops, which are located above and behind the Jabba Throne Room set. There are also a couple of domestic queries to settle for his crew before the weekend, and a telex is zipped off to California.

LFL SRFL
897932 STWARS G

ATTN: PATTY BLAU
FROM: STUART ZIFF
1/8

YOUR TELEX 1/7

TWO QUARTS OF RED RED OK INSTEAD OF VARIOUS SHADES, PLEASE INCREASE ORDER AS FOLLOWS:

ONE PINT MORE OF ALL COLOURS
TWO PINTS MORE OF BLACK AND WHITE
ONE QUART OF BILL TUTTLE'S MAKEUP REMOVER FOR THE ABOVE

WE BOUGHT 'EVOSTICK.' IT IS LIKE BARGE CEMENT AND IS ACCEPTABLE.

SNOWING, I'M WALKING BETWEEN THE STAGES LEAVING FOUR-INCH-DEEP FOOTPRINTS, SINGING CHANUKAH CAROLS

DAVE WONDERS WHY THE DEPOSITED CHECK IS SO SMALL? TIM WORRIED ABOUT GETTING HIS YODA EARS HAT.

LFL SRFL
897932 STWARS G

In the afternoon, in a dark corner of Stage 8, an enormous Gamorrean Guard auditioned for Creature Supervisor Phil Tippett. The man inside the large and complex costume was having trouble mastering the way a Pig Guard would walk, since his synthetic feet were more than twice the size of human feet. Sensing Tippett's impatience, the man called out in a muffled voice from inside the grotesque headpiece: "It's coming. I'm thinking Ernest Borgnine!"

Kazanjian took his last preproduction walk of the sets today. Beginning on Monday, all the planning that he and the staff and crew have done over the past year and a half will come into play. If the planning has been as accurate and as methodical as it appears to have been, then the filming of one of the most expensive and technically complex movies ever made will run smoothly for the next 78 days—as smoothly, that is, as any movie in production can run.

From his comfortable but spare corner office in the Front Administration building (see map of EMI, Appendix #2), Kazanjian has a clear view of the Special Effects (SP. F.X.) building across the way. Occasionally he would see something going into the Special Effects building and, unable to recognize it, would walk over to inquire. "Special effects is an area where you can go way over budget, so as I would see things going in there, I would go over and say, 'What is this? What are we doing?' and I would occasionally have to say, 'No, we don't need that.' Then I'd talk to Norman or to someone else and get it stopped. That didn't happen very often, but it did happen."

In passing, Kazanjian mentions that in the mornings the staff will view the dailies in the Preview Theater Number 3, which is over near Stage 8; in the evenings they will use Preview Theater Number 1 in the Front Administration building.

Stage Number 1 is the first stop on Kazanjian's walk of the sets. (This block of stages, Numbers 1 through 4, is, at a guess, roughly 100 feet wide by about 120 feet long.) "For the opening of the picture," Kazanjian explains, "there are a lot of smaller sets here. Over there is Darth Vader's Destroyer Bridge; over there they are working on the skiffs for the Tatooine desert scene. Right now, this is primarily construction and smaller sets." The building is humming with the sounds of workmen and equipment, and everyone seems to know what he is doing. Since this is the third *Star Wars* movie to be shot at EMI, it would probably be difficult to shock—or even startle—a carpenter with the explanation that he is working on an anti-gravity skiff that will skim above the desert floor or that he is carrying part of a spaceship that can fly at the speed of light.

Kazanjian explains what will happen on Stage Number 1 next: "After we take out the Star Destroyer Bridge, we will put the full-size Rancor Pit in here. There will be three different Rancor Pits; the full-size one will be built here. We needed a 'real' set because we will have Mark running around inside it, with guards and a door and two smaller doors and the Rancor keeper's bay and all that. The second pit will be maybe about 12 feet by 16 feet in size, and it will have a man in a Rancor suit and a toy model of Mark. Finally, there will be the stop-motion Rancor, which will be about 18 inches tall, and he will have a set built to scale. That, of course, will be done at ILM in California."

These sound stages are not connected from the inside, so Kazanjian leaves Stage 1, goes outside, and enters Stage 2—the Tatooine desert. There is a 360-degree, painted cyclorama which surrounds the entire inside of the building. High overhead, Luke's X-Wing Fighter is suspended from the rafters. It will be lowered onto the floor for the scene where Luke takes leave of his friends in the sandstorm and heads for his final meeting with Yoda. On one side, a part of the *Millennium Falcon* is already in place, just waiting for our heroes to climb aboard and head for sanctuary. Several large wind machines are standing silent now, and large banks of lights also suspended from the ceiling will simulate desert light.

What is coming to Stage 2 when the sandstorm sequence is finished on Monday? "Dagobah," Kazanjian says. "The swamp and Yoda's home. There are a few cutout trees left over from the Dagobah set we built for *Empire*—they were flat, so they were easily stored—but the whole swamp will be rebuilt here from scratch. The original trees were so heavy that they had to be chain-sawed out of the original set. We will build three new huge trees, bring in the set dressing—vines and branches—and then flood the swamp. This set will not be the same size as it was for *Empire*— that was wall-to-wall—but it will be pretty good-sized." Kazanjian also explains that Luke's X-Wing Fighter, which is already here, will be used in the Dagobah scenes.

Stage Number 3 houses the Ewok forest set. Number 3 was the stage that burned while Kubrick was filming *The Shining*, and consequently some of the shooting on *Empire* had to be postponed. The first use of Stage 3, after it was rebuilt, was as The Well of the Souls and the Catacombs set for the shooting of *Raiders of the Lost Ark*. Now, however, a complete Ewok Village with thatched huts, wooden walkways, and the trunks of giant redwoods that loom toward the dimly lit ceiling resides here. The whole thing is built 20 feet off the floor. Kazanjian says, "This set is very close to being finished. The roofs are almost done, and over there they are beginning to bring on some of the greens and vines. That," he says, pointing, "is a live tree—many of the smaller trees are live."

The hand-painted, 360-degree cyclorama that surrounds the Ewok Village comes very close to duplicating the real redwood country skies. Right now, because of the harsh work lights and the commotion, the set looks a little flat; but when the proper lighting is in place and three dozen Ewoks are scampering about, it should come to life. Since most of the scenes in the Ewok Village are set either at night or at dusk, the production won't have to worry too much about trying to match the real lighting of the forest in Crescent City. According to the one-line shooting schedule, the company will spend five days on the Ewok Village Square and two days in the interior of the Ewok Chief's Hut. They are scheduled to move to Stage 3 next Thursday and start with Scene Number 78, the scene where our heroes

41

have been captured and taken back to the Ewok Village. "After we finish with the Ewok Village," Kazanjian says, "we will strike the set and bring in the Imperial Landing Platform for the other scenes that are set in the forest on the Green Moon of Endor. We'll be able to reuse some of these trees and part of the set."

Kazanjian has taken this walk so often already that he could probably do it with his eyes closed. He enters Stage Number 4, which is mostly construction right now. Here, the workmen are modeling the Tatooine desert skiffs out of clay. They are making the sides and bottoms and molding all the exterior details. Next step, Kazanjian explains, will be casting the clay models in fiberglass. Once a life-size fiberglass model is made, the skiff will be moved to another stage and the special effects people will begin building the steel undercarriage that will support the skiff. The undercarriage will, for the filming, be attached to two steel I-beams which will be sunk deep into the Yuma sand in order to support the skiff. Either the desert scenes will be shot so that the I-beams will not show, or else ILM will take them out later.

One of the skiffs has to be specially rigged so that it will rock on its side when, during our heroes' escape from Jabba the Hutt, it is hit by cannon fire. When it is hit by the cannon, it will tip about 30 degrees to one side, a part of the railing will fall off, and a breakaway hole, concealed in the side, will open up.

In another corner, giant pieces of styrofoam are being cut into tree trunks for the Ewok Village and the Landing Platform. Two methods are used for cutting the styrofoam: either a piece of hot wire slices through the foam, like a string through butter, or the workmen use chain saws.

Next stop, past the Sound Department building, is the plaster shop. There are about 30 people busily engaged here. Kazanjian motions toward a bunch of plaster pieces that look like architectural ornamentation. "Things we would do in America in wood are done in plaster in England," he says. "Details, moldings, filagree—all of that is plaster.

These are details for the interior of Jabba's barge, and over there are Ewok hands and feet for the American Ewoks. A whole new set of Ewoks was hired for work in Crescent City, but all their costumes were made in England.

"Things are beginning to taper off some already," he remarks, "because they've been working here for six months." Counting about 200 people who are on staff, probably 750 people are working on *Jedi*.

On Stage 5, Kazanjian continues his tour. "This is really a ratty stage and is being used mostly for construction and prefabrication of other sets. Or we will store sets here until they're needed on another stage. It is almost impossible, once production begins, to go in, strike a set, and build a new set from scratch—that's why we're prefabricating some of them here. Eventually, however, we will use about half the stage for Admiral Ackbar's Frigate—for the big scene that is set in the Rebel Briefing Room."

Stage Number 6 is the *Star Wars* stage. It is immense. At 248 feet long and 120 feet wide and 45 feet high, it is truly the biggest sound stage in Europe. (For a comparison, a football field is 300 feet long by 159 feet wide.) "On two walls are the side walls of the Imperial Docking Bay in the new Death Star, a gigantic set that will be almost as big as the stage itself. In the corner stands the shuttle, which will eventually be moved to about the center of the Docking Bay and will stay there throughout most of the production. In the middle of the stage are Jabba's main gate and the corridor inside. Right after we shoot the sandstorm on Monday, we will come here on Tuesday and shoot the scene of the two droids approaching the exterior of Jabba's Palace and the scenes in the corridor. Then we will strike that set out of the middle of the stage as quickly as possible and finish building the Docking Bay." How much will the set for the Docking Bay cost? "Including the shuttle, I think about $800,000. The set will be used for about four or five minutes of screen time—three different times."

Outside again, Kazanjian points to a large building right next door. "Those are warehouses," he says. "Labeled A,

B, C, and D Dock. That is where we kept parts of the various planes and sets and miscellaneous items from both pictures. Jam-packed."

He walks past the building known as the Scotten Barn and on to the building known as the Timber Rack, "where we are creating much of Jabba the Hutt—the pouring of the molds, the electronics for his eyes, and all of that. Robert Watts and I are both very concerned that Jabba won't be finished in time. Stuart Freeborn has been promising that he will be finished, but it is going to be close."

Kazanjian goes by the building that houses drapes and electricians, and also past the plumbers' building and Stage Number 9. "Nine is just construction," he points out. This block of three stages, Numbers 7 through 9, is the smallest on the lot—about half the size of Stages 1 through 4. Inside Number 8, Jabba the Hutt's Throne Room is being built. Three weeks from Monday, on January 25, the production will move here for a scheduled eight days of filming in the Throne Room. Those are going to be hectic days. Not only will all the principal actors and the two droids be on the set, but Jabba and his crew of weird and wonderful creatures will also be there. And each weird and wonderful creature has one, two, and sometimes three people who are necessary to make him move properly. The Throne Room takes up the entire stage and is being built about six feet off the floor because many of the puppeteers and operators will be concealed under the floor. These are great scenes in the screenplay, but because of the sheer number of people involved, they are going to be difficult, time-consuming scenes to shoot.

The tour continues with Stage 7. Here, the set for Jabba's dungeon and the corridor leading to it is being built. Two days, in the middle of February, are scheduled for shooting scenes here.

Outside once again, Kazanjian says, "Usually, I also go into the carpenters shop, right over there. A great deal of construction is going on there—walls, panels, and some cockpits. After the carpenters shop, I generally go into the art department. It is a big department. I go in to visit Norman Reynolds and sit and talk with him. We look at models, or miniatures, sometimes blueprints, and talk over any problems. Joe Johnston and Nilo Rodis-Jamero will still send over designs, but now that George is here, most anything new will be generated here. George will still talk to Joe and Nilo about things which will take place almost exclusively at ILM.

"After the art department, I go past the power house, which is around the corner, and enter the dressing rooms building, which is attached to the sound stages," he explains. The second floor of this building is the costume department for the Ewoks. There are probably five rooms up here that are devoted exclusively to making and building Ewok suits. There are people sewing pieces of fur into the costumes, other people molding foam rubber into pudgy little bellies or into leg shapes, and others brushing and steaming the fur to make it lie properly.

Kazanjian exits the Ewok shop and heads back to the Administration building. Is he looking forward to the start of production? "Yes. I can hardly wait until the first day of shooting because then we will be in motion; there will be no way for somebody to come to me and say they need another two weeks' time; there is no way for anyone to stall. We will be locked in, except for certain construction-type things. We will have the same crew, the same cameras; we will know that tomorrow we are going to be on a certain set and that we are going to film a certain scene. Now I can really start analyzing the production and start trimming certain areas and pull in extra monies from other areas to make sure that when we finish, we will be on budget. Right now, we're $1.5 million over budget because of extra construction and a couple of other things, but I know I can get us back on budget once we start."

It is the end of his daily walk of the sets. Beginning on Monday, *Jedi* moves from preproduction to production, and the focus of all the people working at EMI will shift from getting the movie started to getting it finished.

"Once you start," Kazanjian continues, "you are in motion. The train is going down the track and there is no way you can stop it. Absolutely no way."

CHAPTER 3

They are all back: Han, Luke, Leia, Lando, Chewie, Threepio, and Artoo. And for their reunion they will spend the day being blasted by an unpleasant blend of fake sand. The first scene to be shot on the first day of *Jedi* is Scene 44, Exterior Tatooine Desert Sandstorm. Our heroes, after a fierce battle, have escaped from the desert Sail Barge and skiffs of Jabba the Hutt, and several things have happened: Chewie is wounded—the call sheet reminds props and make-up to prepare a bandage; C-3PO has had some trouble with one of his eyes—props is reminded that the C-3PO head should have the eye *in*; and wardrobe is reminded to provide a black glove for Luke, whose hand has been damaged slightly.

The call sheet for today, put together and signed by First Assistant Director David Tomblin, had been hand-delivered to the principals' homes on Friday night, after they had been called and reminded of their pickup times. In order to be at the studio and in make-up bright and early, they all were picked up at home sometime this morning between 6:30 and 7:15. Anyone else with even the remotest chance of being involved in the first day of filming had also received a call sheet.

A call sheet is a workmanlike, straightforward document that imparts a great deal of information in a brisk and efficient manner. It reminds everyone from the actors to the catering crew where he is supposed to be, how he should prepare, and what he should expect. The call sheet is an outline for a day of shooting; later it becomes a record of that day. The call sheet for the first day looks like this:

THE MAKING OF THE RETURN OF THE JEDI

DIRECTOR: RICHARD MARQUAND   DATE: Monday, 11th January, 1982.

SET: EXT. TATOOINE SANDSTORM   UNIT CALL: 8.30 a.m.

SC. NO: 44   STAGE: 2

ARTISTE:	CHARACTER:		D/R:	M/UP:	ON SET:
HARRISON FORD	HAN SOLO		86	8.00 a.m.	8.30 a.m.
MARK HAMILL	LUKE		82	8.00 a.m.	8.30 a.m.
CARRIE FISHER	LEIA		78	7.30 a.m.	8.30 a.m.
BILLY DEE WILLIAMS	LANDO		92	7.30 a.m.	8.30 a.m.
TONY DANIELS	THREEPIO		90	8.00 a.m.	8.30 a.m.
PETER MAYHEW	CHEWIE		129	7.45 a.m.	8.30 a.m.
KENNY BAKER	ARTOO		IF REQUIRED FROM STAGE 3		
STAND-INS:					
JACK DEARLOVE	for	Mr. Ford		8.00 a.m.	8.30 a.m.
JOE GIBSON		Mr. Hamill		8.00 a.m.	8.30 a.m.
ERICA SIMMONDS		Ms. Fisher		8.00 a.m.	8.30 a.m.
QUENTIN PIERRE		Mr. Williams		8.00 a.m.	8.30 a.m.
ALAN HARRIS		Mr. Daniels		8.00 a.m.	8.30 a.m.
STEVEN MEEKS		Mr. Mayhew		8.00 a.m.	8.30 a.m.

PROPS: Luke's sword, weapons for actors, remote switch for ramp, rag bandage for
         Chewie, 3PO costume reqd. with eye in.

CAMERA: As per Alan Hume + Hustler, etc.

ELECTRICAL: As per Bobby Bremner + radios reqd.

SFX: Sandstorm fx. Wind machines. Radios + headphones reqd.
          R2 unit reqd.

ART DEPT: Practical ramp required. 8.30 a.m.

MAKEUP: Chewie wounded.   Rag bandage. Luke's damaged hand.

WARDROBE: Black glove for Luke. Goggles, capes, scarves etc. for actors.

CATERING: 2 trolley at 10 a.m. for 80 people + 1 Urn or orange juice.

            2 trolleys P.M. for 80 people

            2 trolleys for 60 people AM & PM on Stage 3.

CONSTRUCTION: STANDBY to remove Y-Wing and position X-Wing.

.../contd.

THE MAKING OF THE RETURN OF THE JEDI

TRANSPORT:

Car 1:   P/UP Mr. Ford at   7.15 a.m.   to studio by 8.00 a.m.
Car 2:   P/UP Mr. Hamill at   7.15 a.m.   to studio by 8.00 a.m.
Car 3:   P/UP Ms. Fisher at   6.30 a.m.   to studio by 7.30 a.m.
Car 4:   P/UP Mr. Williams at 6.45 a.m.   to studio by 7.30 a.m.
Car 5:   P/UP Mr. Daniels at   7.30 a.m.   to arrive studio 8 a.m.
Car 6:   P/UP Mr. Mayhew at   6.30a.m.   to studio by 7.45 a.m.

PRODUCTION:

1. Nurse reqd. on Stage 3 for Ewok rehearsal.
2. 12 prs. of headphones for SFX., AD's radios reqd.
3. 3 x Mobile Dr./rooms reqd. for 8 a.m.
4. Protective clothing, etc. can be drawn from props dept., from 7.30 a.m. Monday
    11/1 onwards.

STAGE 3 Ewok Rehearsal continues

KENNY BAKER .... Wicket   .... 9 a.m. studio
JACK PURVIS .... Teebo
MIKE EDMONDS .... Logray
JANE BUSBY .... Chief Chirpa
MIKE COTTRELL........ Principal Warrior
MALCOLM DIXON .... Principal Warrior

Crowd:
39 mixed Ewoks   9 a.m. studio

CHOREOGRAPHER: S/BY from 9 a.m. onwards.

NURSE: Required from 8.30 a.m.

STUNT DEPT: Peter Diamond required from 8.30 a.m.

DAVID TOMBLIN

PIG GUARD FITTING: (Phil Tippett & Ron Beck)

1. TONY STAR   )
2. ISAAC GRAND   )   9 a.m. Studio
3. BARRY ROBERTSON   )
4. GEORGE MILLER   )

But why start with a sandstorm? Several days previously, Associate Producer Robert Watts had bowed to the inevitable and made the decision. "You get to a point where you have nowhere to go—it's a non-decision. I looked at the schedule and I saw the sandstorm, I saw a couple of little sets that had been okayed, and I saw the big sets of the Ewok Village and Jabba's Palace—difficult, week-long shoots—all staring us in the face. And, well, a sandstorm is a sandstorm—an unpleasant way to start the very first day—but if you shoot it in one day, it means you can strike the set and get another set up pretty quickly. As you know, the Dagobah bog planet goes in there next, and it would be good to get started building that. So it seemed like a great idea to get all the difficult stuff out of the way first." (Much later he was glad, but it was a very rough way to start.)

Chief Electrician Bobby Bremner's staff was to be issued two-way radios for working up in the gantry while the simulated sandstorm raged below; a construction gang was to be standing by to move in at exactly the right moment and swap the full-size Y-Wing Fighter for the X-Wing Fighter that had been suspended under the rafters just out of camera range. The crew had already re-erected the full-size *Millennium Falcon* (originally built for *The Empire Strikes Back* by dockyard engineers many miles away and trucked in 16 sections to EMI Elstree). Scene 44 was to be the last time the full-size *Falcon* would be used. The model makers at ILM still had *Falcons* ranging in size from a couple of inches to several feet long, all of which would be used in the Air Battle sequences to come. So the full-size version, which had defied the Empire for so long, would now shortly end up in the scrapyard.

Roy Button, Second Assistant Director for *Jedi*, who had also worked on *Empire* and *Raiders*, was an old acquaintance, so the actors knew they were in good hands. Once they were safely tucked away in make-up or their dressing rooms, he could check the progress of the other happenings of the day—the Ewok troupe was due to limber up again, under the direction of Gillian Gregory on Stage 3.

Still Photographer Albert Clark had learned a thing or two about sand while on location in North Africa for *Raiders*. He elected to use two fixed-lens Nikon cameras and to clamp them in boxlike protective "blimps," which would be cumbersome to use; but, fingers crossed, the cameras would only need to be blown out with compressed air at the end of the day to dislodge all the abrasive sand particles, instead of needing a major overhaul. He decided on this course of action after reading pages 37 to 39 inclusive of a script bearing the coding "Roj+ 019 + Dec 81."

EXT. TATOOINE DESERT—LANDING AREA

A ferocious sandstorm blocks our view. Then, through the roar, we HEAR the VOICES of our heroes. They emerge slowly from the veil of sand, pressing on against the wind. First come R-2 and 3-PO followed by Leia, guiding Han, then Luke and Lando come into view, each supporting one side of the towering Chewbacca, who hobbles from his wound. Soon they can make out some large vague shapes in the blowing sand. It is the Millennium Falcon and, parked beside it, Luke's trusty X-Wing and a two-seated Y-Wing. They must shout to be heard.

HAN:
. . . I don't know. All I can see is a lot of blowing sand.

He wasn't the only one!
To calculate the density of the sand and balance the lighting for the scene, Cinematographer Alan Hume and Special Effects Chief Kit West had worked out, during the tests, the exact positions and revolution count of the double tier of wind machines needed to make Stage 2 resemble a bona fide storm. Hume settled on a lightweight Hustler crane to be used for a railed tracking shot. Like everyone else, he drew his set of industrial goggles and a one-piece, hooded,

full-figure white suit from props in order to weather the bombardment.

It was a small miracle that everyone actually arrived in good order, because the early January weather had turned vicious and cold. There were, however, two bits of London news worth mentioning: police, the fire department, and an ambulance were called to unstick a man whose lips had frozen fast to his car as he attempted to give the kiss of life to an iced-up door lock; later that morning, the ceremonial Changing of the Guard at Buckingham Palace was canceled—an event almost unheard of in peacetime England.

For the first half hour of Day One, there were a lot of handshakes and greetings as three years of accumulated gossip was exchanged. Members of the cast also had their share of surprises. Carrie Fisher had sidestepped a potential drama when the heating system at her rented house started to blow back toxic gas fumes, and Mark Hamill's driver's car had been stolen overnight, so Mark had hitched a last-minute ride to the studio with Harrison Ford. The good news for Hamill was that a gray jacket he thought he had lost during the filming of *Empire* had turned up at the Borehamwood High Street Dry Cleaners. "If I had gone in this morning to ask for it, they would probably have said: 'It'll be ready sometime Thursday!'"

Tony Daniels was delighted to see a canvas chair with his name on the back. During the making of *Star Wars*, when he was still unable to climb out of his C-3PO costume between takes and no one knew exactly who was in there anyway, his chair had disappeared. When Daniels inquired gently of a stagehand where it had gone, he was told confidentially: "We gave it to the studio security guard. That Anthony Daniels, he just never showed up, y'know."

Finally, everything was ready for the first shot.

10:18 A.M.

David Tomblin calls, "Turn over," on his radio and loud-speaker. Director Marquand roars, "Action." All systems go? Not exactly. R2-D2 veers off course and careens into a rock. The first camera team doesn't hear the "action" command over the noise of the wind machines and is still waiting to start. And finally, the sand blow is so successful it obscures almost everything anyway.

10:40 A.M.

Take 2 came and went without a hitch. "But can you see the actors?" Marquand inquires anxiously. The two camera operators deem the blow "just the right texture." "Print both cameras," Marquand says. There is a smattering of applause, and orange juice is served all around. *Jedi* is off and rolling.

Around lunchtime on the first day of shooting for *Jedi*, Sidney Ganis, Lucasfilm's Senior Vice-President of Marketing and Publicity, arrived in London. He was the bearer of glad tidings with the news that *Raiders* was still taking in around $1 million a day at the box office and holding well. Others on overnight flights from California usually had the chance to acclimate for a day, but Ganis was whisked off to the studio and suited up just in time to experience some of the sandstorm. Later, in conversation with Lucas and Kazanjian in the producer's office, he suggested a brief start of a production publicity announcement about the

A LOOK INTO THE PAST

Monday, March 22, 1976

First day in Tozeur for *Star Wars*. Forty-two trucks and automobiles, including eight army trucks full of equipment, pulled away from the Oasis Hotel at 6 A.M. Prop man Phil "Maxie" Macdonald had strict instructions to follow R2-D2 and C-3PO everywhere in the fierce heat with the emergency bottle of oxygen. The location caterer had been primed to give everyone tea on arrival to make him feel at home and then to organize lunch with A.M. and P.M. breaks for 130 people. The first shot was completed at 9:35 A.M. under the direction of George Lucas.

Monday, March 5, 1979

First day in Finse, Norway, for *The Empire Strikes Back*. There was snow, low clouds, and heavy winds. Out in the middle of the ice field, the *Empire* team, soon cut off from civilization by avalanches, had their first taste of facial frostbite, ate lunch outdoors in a temperature so cold that the food almost froze while still on the fork, and needed no second warning that it was dangerous to wander away from the shooting area. Nevertheless, within 65 minutes of assembling, they managed the first shot to Director Irvin Kershner's satisfaction.

movie—a sort of "say something, tell nothing" statement. Much of the information about *Jedi* must be kept under wraps, of course, so a purely informational press release was written.

LUCASFILM
LTD.

FOR RELEASE MONDAY, JANUARY 11, 1982

Contact: Sidney Ganis
Susan Trembly

Principal photography begins today (11) on RE-VENGE OF THE JEDI, the third film of the STAR WARS saga, at EMI Elstree Studios on the outskirts of London.

Once more the STAR WARS team has taken all nine sound stages at EMI Elstree, which was also the studio shooting base for both previous productions.

Principal cast and key technical crew are a mixture of old friends and new faces. Luke Skywalker, Han Solo, Princess Leia, Lando Calrissian, C-3PO, R2-D2, Chewbacca, Yoda, and the dreaded Darth Vader are all back in action as the Rebel Alliance again attempts to outwit and outstrike the dark forces of the Empire.

REVENGE OF THE JEDI is a Chapter III Production, produced by Howard Kazanjian and directed by Richard Marquand. George Lucas is executive producer, with Robert Watts and Jim Bloom serving as co-producers.

The film stars Mark Hamill, Harrison Ford, Carrie Fisher, Billy Dee Williams, and Anthony Daniels, with David Prowse, Kenny Baker, Peter Mayhew, and Frank Oz in co-starring roles.

REVENGE OF THE JEDI will be released by Twentieth Century-Fox with a May 25, 1983, opening scheduled in the United States and Canada.

By midafternoon, Producer Howard Kazanjian felt good enough about the progress of the film so far to send an official telex to Lucasfilm's President and Chief Executive Officer Robert Greber in San Rafael.

ATTN: BOB GREBER
FROM: HOWARD KAZANJIAN

PLEASE BE ADVISED THAT PRINCIPAL PHOTOGRAPHY HAS COMMENCED TODAY JANUARY 11TH, 1982 ON 'RETURN OF THE JEDI'

The telex served as an official record of the start of production and fulfilled Lucasfilm's contractual obligation to 20th Century-Fox, the distributor of the movie, to let them know formally that *Jedi* had begun.

It was only Day One of a projected 78-day total shooting schedule, but behind the scenes others continued working on future problems. Location shooting in the United States wasn't planned to begin until April, but Robert Watts maintained a long running dialogue with various federal agencies on both sides of the Atlantic about importing the key production technicians into the United States for the location filming in Yuma and Crescent City. "You get into a situation where you've got a British film presently shooting in a British studio which, when we move to America, is going to be a hybrid. The company will be composed of a majority of American technicians with a smattering of British technicians required for continuity and the smooth running of the operation. I'm no Anglo chauvinist. It would have made my life a lot easier to dump all the British crew and pick up a whole new crew in America, but one has to look at it from a point of view of the film. In England, if you are a bona fide film company coming in for location filming, you can bring in everybody you need. In the United States, however, there isn't the machinery within the immigration service to make this kind of operational thing move smoothly.

On the advice of immigration attorneys in Los Angeles, we ended up bringing in the British crew as a group—rather like the Royal Ballet or the London Symphony Orchestra—so that it was a block of people rather than a group of individuals." The location shooting in America was not going to take place until April, but a good Associate Producer is always looking ahead.

Toward the end of Scene 44, at the conclusion of an uncomfortable first day, Billy Dee Williams, as Baron Lando Calrissian, now firmly on the side of the Rebels, had to shout a line that appealed to everyone:

"Come on, let's get off this miserable dirt ball."

Mark Hamill was the last to be released, preserving his record of being the only actor to perform throughout the first day of all three pictures. Seventeen camera setups had been completed in a total of nine working hours. That amounted to less than a minute and a half of screen time for a movie that would be about 120 minutes long. And 3,210 feet of Eastman Kodak film, Number 5247, had been exposed. The production company had ordered 400,000 feet of film through Rank Laboratories—in order to get the best trade discount—you have to save a cent or two wherever you can!

Pat Carr's files showed that out in Tozeur, *Star Wars* had toiled for 12 hours and 50 minutes for a handsome 2 minutes and 43 seconds of finished film. Her records also showed that a Tunisian midget named Mahjoub had worked a 14-hour day as a local adult Jawa and received 8,500 dinars for his trouble; and an English actor named Anthony Daniels, still getting used to his droid suit, had been forced to take his nourishment through a straw.

In Finse, Norway, on *The Empire Strikes Back* location, a white-out had stopped shooting for 25 minutes in the afternoon, but the frozen crew had completed nine shots, which would account for a minute and a half of screentime. Mark Hamill had worked throughout the 10-hour-and-50-minute day.

Coach Stuart Ziff, whose Monster Shop creature team wouldn't be needed until Monday, January 25, when shooting would move to the interior of Jabba's Throne Room, nevertheless dutifully reported in to San Rafael on the first day of filming:

897932 STWARS G

ATTN: PATTY BLAU
FROM: STUART ZIFF

JANUARY 11 1982

NO OVERTIME TO REPORT

PLEASE ASK CINDY (THE NITE SECURITY GUARD) IF MY CAT IS STILL ALIVE. IF NOT, PUT IT IN THE FREEZER.

THANKS
STUART

LFLSRFL
10UDEW STWARS G

Director Richard Marquand, after a long first day of shooting, paused for a few minutes to talk about his reactions to directing *Jedi*.

"We were preseeding some of the locations today. We had to determine quickly things like whether Chewie was wounded in his leg or his arm. Remember, the actual wounding is a sequence we haven't yet shot. So I said, 'Hey, let's make it the leg and then it won't be in close-ups, but it will be in long shots.' I had to think, well, it's Chewbacca...he's going to be on a skiff and he's going to be wounded, so if he goes down, then his leg will be in a sort of loose-ish shot. You have to think about those kinds of things. So that was a commitment."

How does he feel about making those decisions?

"You've got to do them. You could be wrong, but you've got to do them. You cannot hang back or expect anyone else to—you *dare* not get anyone else to make them for you because if you do, then you've lost your crew. I've realized, through making some terrifically fast decisions in television, that actually, if you make a decision you are better off. You can second-guess yourself for the rest of your life, but actually, what it boils down to is, you've just got to make the decision. Moviemaking is simply too expensive. We don't have the money any more. This is now the age of the guys who can think fast and move fast.

"I was determined not to go over time today because I said to myself all the world is watching. If we go over the first day, I've lost . . . and we didn't." Marquand must head home for a quiet dinner and time with his script, preparing for tomorrow's scenes and then a session of preplanning for some future scenes.

After a night of reflection on the first day of filming and an 8 A.M. look at the previous day's rushes with Marquand, Kazanjian, and their inner cabinet, George Lucas apparently decided that a few sections of the screenplay still needed some changes. Pat Carr sent the following telex Tuesday morning from EMI to Lucas' Executive Assistant Jane Bay and American Production Coordinator Lata Ryan—probably the only *Jedi* staff members permitted to make copies of the scripts.

TO: JANE BAY AND LATA RYAN
FROM: PAT CARR

1/12

I HAVE SPOKEN TO GEORGE AND THE FOLLOWING HAS BEEN DECIDED AS THE SEQUENCE OF COLORS FOR SCRIPT REVISIONS:

ORIGINAL WHITE WILL GO INTO YELLOW

YELLOW WILL BECOME GREEN IF REWRITTEN

PINK WILL BECOME GREEN IF REWRITTEN

AS YOU KNOW BLUE IS FOR SPECIAL USE.

REGARDS

PAT

The copies of the final shooting script for a movie are printed on white paper. If changes are made in that final script, they are printed on another color of paper. This is so that the production will have an immediate and visual record of the changes that have been made. Each page is also dated with the day of the changes. So the first changes on the *Jedi* script will be printed on yellow paper. If changes are made in the yellow pages, they will be printed on pink paper; if still more revisions are made, they will be printed on green paper.

"Blue is for special use" would have lit up like an electric sign to some of those *Star Wars* fans who avidly follow the making of the movie. There have been lots of stories about secret script pages containing plot twists of which even the principal actors were unaware; in fact, only three people on the production of *Jedi* actually possessed copies of the scenes which are printed on blue paper: Lucas, Kazanjian, and Marquand. Only when it is time for a special scene to be filmed do the actors become involved in that scene given the blue pages. One secret plot revelation was already scheduled to be shot next week, but that was next week, and right now everybody was thinking primarily about tomorrow.

David Tomblin once again was preparing tomorrow's call sheet, but Douglas Twiddy was still working on today. At the end of each day of filming, it is his job to fill out the Daily Production Progress Report. This is a much more technical report than the call sheet. It lists the number of takes completed, the amount of screen time filmed, the total amount of film stock exposed, and other important data. The Daily Production Report for Monday, January 11, 1982, looks like this:

DAILY PRODUCTION PROGRESS REPORT

PRODUCTION : "REVENGE OF THE JEDI"

Monday,
DATE : 11/1/82

REPORT No **1**

TIME		DIRECTOR R. MARQUAND	PRODUCER H. KAZANJIAN
CALL	08.30	LOCATION OF WORK/SET EMI ELSTREE STUDIOS	
1st SHOT	10.12		
1st MEAL FROM: 13.45 TO: 14.45		STAGE (2): EXT. TATOOINE SANDSTORM	
1st SHOT AFTER MEAL	15.20		
UNIT DISMISSED	18.30		
TOTAL HOURS	(9 + 1)		

SCRIPT/SCREEN TIME RATIO

	SET-UPS	PAGES	SCRIPT SCENES	EXTRA SCENES	R/T	SCREEN TIME			
							START DATE 11.1.1982.		
							FINISHING DATE (U.K.) April 1'82		
							SCHEDULED DAYS: -		92
							TO DATE		1
TAKEN TODAY	12 + 5		1			1m.20s	REMAINING		91
PREVIOUSLY TAKEN	Nil		–			Nil	DAYS OVER ON SCHEDULE		
TOTAL TO DATE	17		1			1m.20s	UNDER		
TO BE TAKEN			131			118.40	DAILY AVERAGES		
TOTAL SCHEDULED			132			120.00	SET–UPS	1s.	SCREENTIME
							17		20s.

CONTRACT ARTISTS

NAME	W	S/B	RE	CALL	ARR.	DIS.
HARRISON FORD	1			08.00	08.00	17.15
MARK HAMILL	1			08.00	08.00	18.30
CARRIE FISHER	1			07.30	07.30	17.15
BILLY DEE WILLIAMS	1			07.30	07.30	17.15
TONY DANIELS	1			08.00	08.00	17.15
PETER MAYHEW	1			07.45	07.45	17.15

Please see separate
page for details of
Ewok rehearsals

STUNTS

NAME	W	ARR.	DIS.
P. Diamond	Cont	08.00	18.00
C. Skeaping	Dly	08.00	18.00

CROWDS & S/INS	NUMBER	RATE
As per Call Sheet		
No: 1 - from		
8 a.m. to Wrap		
Also Pig Guard Fitting as per		
Call Sheet (4 Crowd)		

ACTION PROPS & EFFECTS

Walkie-talkies from Audiolink
3 Mobile D/Rms.
Catering as per call sheet
Hustler dolly

SLATE NUMBERS

44. 44A.
44B. 44C. 44D.
44F. 44G. 44H.
44J. 44K. 44L.
Also Wild Tracks for
44A. 44E. 44F.

SCENE NUMBERS

Scene 44
(completed apart
from pickups)

INVENTORY OF FULL ROLLS		TBA (See Note)				S/ENDS	TBA			

FILM FOOTAGES						SOUND		STILLS		
RES & NG	PRINT	TOTAL EXPOSED	IDENT.	WASTE	S/ENDS	SOUND	PLATES	B & W	COLOUR	
1340	1870	3210	TODAY	510	TBA	2 rls.	–	8	5	
*	*	*	PREVIOUS	*		–		–	–	
1340	1870	3210	TOTAL	510		2 rls.		8	5	

(Please see attached page for details
of test footage shot. New running
totals start from today.)

REMARKS

1. FIRST DAY OF PRINCIPAL PHOTOGRAPHY ON "REVENGE OF THE JEDI" TODAY.

2. 1st and 2nd camera units working on this set today.

3. 400,000 ft. of Kodak Eastmancolour 5247 stock were ordered (via Rank labs
   to achieve discount). Some of this was used on the pre-production test,
   but some of the film for testing were short ends owned by the company.
   A full inventory will be given as soon as possible.

THE MAKING OF THE RETURN OF THE JEDI

4.   SID GANIS arrived in London today from Los Angeles.

5.   Total footage used on testing on 'JEDI' between 24th November, 1981 and
     8th January, 1982 is as follows:

     WASTE: 500
     RES. & N.G.: 1210
     PRINT: 6830
     TOTAL: 8540

6.   Daily rates for Mon. 11/1:
     Sue Clarkson - Nurse -
     S. Bide & S. Morris - Makeup -
     Sfx. J. Fitt, G. Clifford, D. Beavis
     Harness making asst. S. Miles.

7.   Crowd payments for Mon. 11/1:
     1 x S/In at £51.41 (1 day)
     1 x Crd. at £30.49 (1 day)

8.   Extra equipment on daily basis:
     Makeup truck and 2 caravans.
     JCB from 1 p.m. for snow clearing.

9.   Electrical crew per Lee Electrics.

                                      Douglas Twiddy
                                      DOUGLAS TWIDDY
                                      Production Supervisor

(NOTE: November 18, 1982, San Rafael, California.) Today word went out quietly in the company that they were dropping the entire sandstorm sequence from the movie. It was surprising news, and there was some speculation that the film simply had not turned out properly—that it was murky and too hard to see the scene. Howard Kazanjian strongly denied that speculation and gave the following reasons, which are purely thematic and important to the flow of the movie:

"The big reason we are dropping the sequence is that right now, in terms of the action, we have just gone through a great experience with the Sarlacc Pit and all of our characters escaping from Jabba. And it ends with a great big bang—Jabba's barge exploding, literally, in the desert—and then you cut to this blinding sandstorm. Well, you've already got the audience going 'Whew,' and breathing a huge sigh of relief, and perhaps even giving the heroes a round of applause—and you go right into this blinding sandstorm... where it is very difficult to see people—which is okay—but the noise, and probably the music, will have been up very strong, and you've simply got to bring the audience down. You've got to give them a breather.

"So we eliminate the sequence. Let's pull it out, but we still need some of the information, a very little of the information, that's in the scene to explain some things to the audience. And that's primarily Luke's hand. Luke's hand in the last picture was severed. Remember? And he was given a bionic hand. Now in the barge fight scene, a laser hits his hand and does damage to the top of it, which is where the controls are. It's just minor damage, but he is off to Dagobah, so he slips a glove on—a black glove. He kind of pushes the wires and skin down and slips the black glove on, and we see him wearing a glove on one hand through the rest of the picture. Well, if you don't know what happens—if you don't know why he is wearing a glove in the rest of the picture, and if you don't explain somewhere along the line that it is a bionic hand, then people who didn't see *Empire* are not going to understand about his hand.

"Furthermore, the transition from the sandstorm scene to Luke going off to Dagobah and the other group going off in a different direction is a little abrupt. In the last movie we saw him flying in his X-Wing to Dagobah, so we will probably substitute a new scene in the cockpit—the scene has not been written yet—when he's flying to Dagobah. And the dialogue, probably between him and Artoo, supplies the audience with the information we want to give them. It also allows us a better pacing on the transition. This scene finishes Act I and moves Luke in one direction and moves the other group in another direction.

"It wasn't that the sandstorm footage didn't work. It was simply that when it was all put together, it was too much of a sequence. We needed a breather and we needed a little more explanation about Luke's bionic hand.

"Mark Hamill is coming back for one day of shooting later this month [November] to do the scene where he builds his new lasersword, and we will shoot this new scene explaining his glove and hand at that time."

CHAPTER 4

How do you pick a director to direct *The Return of the Jedi*? George Lucas: "First of all, you get a list of the directors who are available. Sometimes you know their work, sometimes you don't. You eliminate the ones who aren't available. Then you go and ask the rest if they would like to do the movie, and half of those drop out because they don't want to do a *Star Wars* movie. Who knows what personal reasons they have? You get a whole mass dropping out. So you are left with a group of, say, 20 to 30. Then the producer—Howard in this case—interviews them. He sees more of their films, talks to people who have worked with them before. I read the reports and say okay, these seem to be appropriate, these don't. You take 30 and knock it down to 15. I do a quick interview with them and then knock it back to five or three. I see everything they've ever done in terms of work and then I have long interviews.

"I spend the day with them. Come over to my house, talk, go back and forth, and finally it's—you know—instinct. I'm looking for a lot of things. Somebody who has a lot of technical expertise. Who gets the job done, has had enough experience to handle something this big. It's not an easy kind of movie to make, so that's a prerequisite. You'd be surprised how many directors aren't professional enough to handle something this complicated.

"The next thing you look for in a *Star Wars* director is somebody who doesn't just think it's kid's junk. Who understands what's going on. A lot of people don't understand, they think it's just some quick and easy kind of thing you throw out, not much behind it. But the truth of it is, there's a lot going on behind it, and the director has to have that sensibility."

Producer Howard Kazanjian and Co-Producers Robert Watts and Jim Bloom are like members of the same family. They have, in fact, probably watched more movies together, waited in more airport lounges together, eaten more meals together, and driven more miles together than they have with some of their immediate kith and kin. George Lucas, of course, is also a member of that family.

While in London in January 1981, Kazanjian was devoting a small portion of his time to the search for a director. He remembers that time well:

"When I went to London for the scoring session for *Raiders*, I met quite a few of the English directors. I had been meeting Americans here and some English, some Australians, but we had talked with, or I had looked at, directors for over a year. I had been looking at features that various directors had directed and their second features and their television shows. We were also, at the same time, looking for writers—and were reading many scripts."

British or American writers?

"Both British and American writers, but mostly American writers. So when I was in London in March, I met probably a dozen directors. I made copious notes—tried to get into their brains to see where they were coming from— and came back to the United States, took my information, and ranked everybody A, B, or C. I had an A list, a B list, and a total reject, or C, list. We weren't looking for a big-name director. We were looking for a good, sharp, rather young director who had a mind of his own, who could go out and direct his picture, but at the same time would do it the way that had been established twice before."

In the early summer of 1981, Richard Marquand was asked to direct *Jedi*. He accepted. The movie would go into production in about six months.

George Lucas was sure enough of his man to say in interviews almost immediately that: "So far I've had terrific relationships with all the directors I've worked with ... Occasionally, in the beginning you get a little bit of 'Oh, my God, he's going to cut my movie. What's going to happen?' But after about two weeks, when they see what I can do to make the film better, then we become great partners. I'm like the editor. The director still sits over my shoulder and tells me, 'This is what I had in mind,' or, 'That is what I wanted to do ...' Plus the fact that if one hires people who don't have huge egos and don't want to be artists, but who simply want to do a very good job and who understand that other people can make contributions, then it becomes a very satisfying working relationship.

"When I was trying to do everything myself, and everything was always going wrong, it was killing me to sort of drag everybody along and get the movie made. I was absolutely responsible for the vision. And now I'm not. I'm just sort of the overseer. I mean, I try my best to see that all the films conform to one another. I try to see that the production moves along and gets finished on schedule. I have more control over special effects and that sort of thing, simply because I've been involved with all that longer; that is my main contribution. But generally, my participation is maybe one-tenth of what it would be if I were directing. People don't understand why I can be so relaxed at this stage. I can go out to dinner, take weekends off. It's such a different life from when I'm directing a movie."

Richard Marquand, the man who is directing *Return of the Jedi*, has that sense of humor that Lucas was seeking. He smiles broadly, sits up straight in his chair, and says: "Here I am in my middle years, getting enormous pleasure and self-satisfaction out of a job where all I do is go about shouting at people ... telling them where to stand and what to do. For me, the whole thing is magic. Absolute magic."

Richard Marquand was born in Wales but he grew up and attended college in England. "At Cambridge I studied languages and acted all the time. But I loved rehearsals and hated performances—which didn't help."

After college, he decided not to pursue acting and not

to pursue another degree. Instead, he joined the Royal Air Force and was stationed in Hong Kong. While in Hong Kong, Marquand began doing television news commentary and commercials for the local television station and eventually had his own movie-related show.

When he left the service, he moved back to England and was offered a job at the BBC 2 television channel. After doing a variety of jobs there, he began directing. "The BBC training is fantastic. I had a go at everything. I directed four cameras on tape, four cameras live. I learned how to think very quickly on my feet—how to make a film sequence work and how to put things together fast."

The years that he spent in television were a fertile period for Marquand. His television documentary, "The Search for the Nile," was the first BBC documentary to be given a full American commercial network airing when it was shown on NBC. From this period, he won two Emmys and was nominated two other times.

His first feature film, *The Legacy*, starred Katherine Ross and Sam Elliott. His next film, produced in 1979, was called *The Birth of The Beatles*; it chronicled the rise of the Fab Four in the early sixties in England. Next was the big budget feature *The Eye of The Needle*, which starred Donald Sutherland and Kate Nelligan. Marquand was praised for his direction of this movie, and it put him on the map, so to speak, as a feature film director.

"When did *Return of the Jedi* rear its head?"

"*Jedi* was first mentioned in a conversation I had with my agent in October of 1980. I said, 'No, it's impossible. I wouldn't think of it.' It wasn't until I met George Lucas and heard what he thought of my films that I realized I was probably up to it. He was looking for energy, sparkle, the ability to work with actors, and also the ability to understand him. Somebody who he would like, not necessarily someone he wanted as a friend, but certainly someone who wouldn't be a sycophant.

"We met in an office in London, where I was doing a

rough cut of *Eye of the Needle*, and we connected immediately. I know he was feeling me out, because this was long before he needed to decide who his director was going to be. We just talked about how the hell—in the allotted time and with the money that somebody gives you—you get a movie to look so real that the audience is convinced.

"I was bowled over by *Star Wars*. It's pure storytelling on film. What made me hesitate about directing *Jedi* was the fact that anybody would consider *me* for such a picture. If anything, I'm overly sensitive, overly intellectual as a filmmaker, which is why I work well with actors. That was, I suspect, what George wanted, as well as someone who could get on with it and do the job. Someone who would arrive on the set at 8:15 in the morning and have an idea of what the first 16 setups were going to be that day and maybe, just maybe, be able to put in another five after that.

"One of the reasons *Star Wars* is so terrific is because it's absolutely real. I realize that *Jedi*, which possibly goes off into potential realms of unreality more than the other two, has got to keep its feet firmly on the ground. George always says—and it's drummed into everybody, whether it involves R2-D2 or Jabba the Hutt—it has, above all, to be real. Real relationships and real action that stem from real emotions."

What was working with George Lucas like?

"It's fair to say I'm conducting a 120-piece orchestra and I've got the composer in the front row. I'm playing his music, and he's perfectly entitled to speak if he wants. Tends not to. But he's here, so I can turn to him and say, 'Look, this bar doesn't make any sense. Do you really want it?' If he says yes, play it that way. If you feel it can go faster or slower, there's always the cadenza where you get your chance. But it is *his* music—he wrote it.

"I think I work much better with a strong producer than I do with a script I can change. George is an ex-director, he's been through far more hell and high water than I have; he's experienced much more studio pressure and agony than

I have. George has also directed two incredibly successful pictures himself, which I have not; therefore, to have the man at my side was fantastic. He was in London much longer than he planned because I wanted him there; I would have been crazy not to.

"George's magic is to see you along. I really felt it was necessary to encourage him to be around so that I could say, 'I've got real problems with this scene. I don't understand why she says this line and he says that back.' George explains why, it makes sense, and then I know how to work it out."

What about the creatures in *Jedi*? Were they difficult to work with?

"This was the first time, I think, that anyone has dealt with creatures as something you can direct rather than manipulate in stop motion action. In a way, I was breaking new ground. I discovered the way to work with the creatures was exactly the same as working with actors. I had to understand why they couldn't do certain things. I would sometimes shout and lose my temper, other times cajole and ask for retakes. I'm not so sure about the creature language. That's a post-production battle that still has to be fought and won—one way or the other.

"However, the most difficult *thing* to work with that was created by special effects was R2-D2. I'm talking about the robot now. It will rehearse and be perfectly charming, then, when you want to do a take with it, it'll explode or go off the set and not come back for the rest of the day. And it can get away with such things; you can't dock its salary.

"I was given a lot of leeway as far as the other actors were concerned; in fact, I cast them—the Emperor, Bib, that crowd. I inherited most of the experience and ability that make this film work in terms of special effects, the art direction, props, costumes, and that sort of thing; but if I had any problems, I was allowed to have my say.

"The only people I did want to bring in—and George agreed immediately—were Alan Hume, the Director of Photography, and his crew. I've made all my films with

Alan Hume and my own editorial team; if Alan is my right hand, Sean Barton, the editor, is my left.

"Alan Hume didn't really go through the selection board process, because he stands or falls on a large volume of work, which could be seen quite clearly in the three films I showed George Lucas. Then you meet Alan and find he's sharp, energetic, hilarious—a hard-working, crazy guy."

What is it that Marquand likes about Hume's work?

"Alan is adaptable, he doesn't have to put his stamp on everything. The same with Sean. What is so lovely—the three of us can have rows, turn around and walk away, then come back and carry on. It's like a family in that way. Alan Hume's camera team is made up of people I like, and we are all able to walk a very narrow line between friendship and a certain amount of respect."

What about all the special effects and the technically difficult shots that the movie requires?

"Unlike younger cameramen, Alan really did know about the bluescreen process. He is not one for mystique. Basically, what he says is, 'I'll just bash some light on and it'll be all right,' which is not true, but he has a way of cutting through most of the bullshit, which is very nice. Sean doesn't have the same experience, but his attitude is, 'There are a lot of new techniques here and I'm not going to kick against them. There are new ways of doing clapper boards, new ways of cutting film, new machines. Great. I'll figure out how everything works.'"

What was it like working with such a large crew? Difficult?

"I do really miss the old thing of just rushing out with a cameraman, an assistant, and two sound people to shoot some film—it's a shame we can't do it like that. It is difficult to stay in touch with the movie when it is large. You can press two buttons and have your shot list, press two more buttons and there is the shot, press two more, and you have made the cut of the piece of film. The technology will divorce you from the physical business of doing what you normally do, and the final work can suffer. This is a very subtle thing. It bothers me that there is going to be a hard barrier—a beautiful gleaming surface of lights and buttons—between me and the job.

"I'm just a filmmaker, but when you think about it, *Jedi* is sort of the last of the major, major epics. It synthesizes the other two movies, puts all the pieces together. In this film you finally find out all the relationships—and it's being directed by a little Welshman from the valleys!"

Alan Hume was already at work in the film industry before George Lucas was born. He is a stalwart of the old Ealing, Denham, and Beraconsfield studios. He also lit fifteen of the successful British *Carry On* series. Years of shooting in tight corners on even tighter budgets have given him a very down-to-earth attitude. While everything around him is in flux, he has learned the hard way to make it simple.

"Richard got the job as director, and I was fortunate enough that he asked for me. Then they saw the James Bond picture I'd done and agreed to have me on *Jedi*. I was absolutely tickled pink. In June or July 1981, I got a postcard from Crescent City from Richard Marquand, saying, very hush-hush, 'I'm in this part of the world where some location shooting may be done, and this is what it's got to look like.' That was my first brief for the film.

"Working on *Jedi* became a job of trying to dig into George's mind, walking around the sets to see how he wanted them to look. He has got very definite ideas, and, after all, he is Mr. Star Wars. Although I always make it my business to work for the director rather than the producer, on this occasion the producer—even Richard would agree with this—was very much part director."

How did Hume approach the lighting on the movie?

"The sets that Norman Reynolds builds and the colors are such that they don't make my work that difficult. I've just got to follow the style. Everything is photographed rather low-key but well up in the printing area of the film stock. Darth Vader is dressed in black—you can't get any more low-key than black—but it's amazing how black stands out and becomes very dominant on the *Jedi* set.

"I was able to do a bit of my own thing on the Ewok test we shot in Black Park with the new fast film. Richard thought, at that point, that the Ewoks should look like his dog after a two-hour walk in the country on a wet day. Then, when we went into the studio, I lit the set like that because they had liked the way they looked in the test. When George saw it, he said he didn't like it, which knocked me a bit one-sided. He said it was too glossy and nice.

"But seeing Crescent City, I realize that he was totally right, and thank God he told me to make it flat, dull, and real. When we filmed with four cameras, the job became much easier to shoot from all angles with flat lighting.

"On this film a lot of the sequences have lent themselves to the use of multiple cameras. On a scene like the laserbeam fights, it helps when you shoot simultaneously on three or four different lenses. You get total matching action and can cut from shot to shot in the same take.

"I've been fortunate. I've made a lot of good films over the years. Thirty-nine years in the business to date—so I've got a few setups behind me. It's not that the task gets any easier, but you have done it before, so you are not afraid to have a go. It's just a matter of trying your darnedest to be as creative as you can, given the set of circumstances with which you are working. I can be looking at some beautiful shot surrounding me, but the camera is staring at something bloody awful. But I've got to do it because that's what we are all standing there to shoot."

Does he yearn to direct?

"I don't want to direct, never, ever, thank you very much. I'm happy to be where I am—lucky to be where I am. Only every now and then I think, Oh, Christ, I wish I could put the camera where I want it. But I wouldn't want to be a director; it's too hard."

Sean Barton is in his late thirties, tall and lanky, with neatly cut light brown hair; he had worked with Richard Marquand on two previous films.

"I was interviewed out of the blue for *The Birth of the Beatles*. I didn't know Richard Marquand at all. I think we see eye to eye, however. He's often pleased with my editing, and I'm very impressed by his style as a director. Because we get on well, he gets better work out of me than somebody else might.

"I remember that when *Jedi* was announced in England, people were saying, 'But Marquand doesn't know anything about special effects.' It seems to me that if I were George Lucas, the last thing I would want is a director who did. Richard is a good storyteller visually, he gets good performances from the actors, and he ties everything up very tidily. Put that together with all the wonderful special effects, and then you really have something. The auditioning for *Jedi*, I think, was mostly done behind the scenes. I did meet George Lucas. His main interest was that Richard have the key staff he wanted. His other concern was whether he would get on with me. He's very shy and I'm quite shy, so initially we hardly said a word to each other, which seemed to be what he wanted!

"For *Jedi* we have a director's cut, and after that George will do whatever he wants. The advantage is that normally producers do this cut and they frequently don't know a great deal about film and filmmaking, which can be very heartbreaking. In this case, it's quite a relief to know that the person who is going to make the decision in the end is someone whose technique and taste one admires. I can't imagine that the cut will differ too much, since we are cutting the movie very tight. The film will be fast, very fast—packed with stuff. I think it's got more story, more plot, more action, more monsters, better monsters—much more like *Raiders* in space.

"I was a commercials editor at twenty-three. I used to do three commercials a week—an average of about 150 a year—year in and year out. I worked with quite a few interesting directors—such as Ridley Scott—early on. I think my background makes me quite a bit quicker, so it is not such hard work to put the first cut together.

"At one point I thought, I'm not going to do this film—merely because it was so important. In the back of my mind I thought, One doesn't get treated this nicely, things aren't that easy. I was very apprehensive—I usually am on films—rather paranoid for the first few months. I relaxed a lot once I arrived in America and thought, If they have bothered to get me over here, they mean it.

"It's the best opportunity, certainly this year, for anybody!"

CHAPTER 5

HOWARD KAZANJIAN

"How would I define a producer? As an arbitrator, creator, negotiator, psychologist, psychiatrist, developer, budget manager..."

Howard Kazanjian is all of the above—and more—but it is in the area of overseeing the movie's budget that he is especially skilled. It is his job to know where every cent spent on *Jedi* goes, and with a quick look at his record books, he can tell you.

Just under six feet tall, with medium-length dark hair and dark eyes, Kazanjian always dresses in casual-looking clothes—corduroy pants, quiet plaid cotton shirts, and an occasional sweater. Most of the time, he looks like a businessman who is relaxing for the weekend.

Leaning back in his office chair, Kazanjian talks about his family and his beginnings in the movie business.

"The name Kazanjian means coppersmith. I suppose my great, great somebody or other used to make large copper kettles—but not in recent memory. I was born and raised in Pasadena, with an older sister and a younger brother. I was very much the black sheep for going into show business—at that time very, very much so. I think going into the movies was one of the hardest decisions I ever had to make in my life.

"My mother was good about it. Her attitude was, go out and make your success. I think my father's feeling was perhaps more, I hate to use the phrase, 'old country.' A European would understand better. He wanted me to go into his business, learn his trade, carry on the name."

How, then, did Kazanjian decide on film school?

"My sister was at the University of Southern California. I'm sure that was influential, you know—alma mater time. There were only a few schools that had cinema classes: UCLA, USC, Yale. And NYU, I believe, but I didn't want to move to New York.

"USC students were basically those who either had parents who gave them a lot of money to attend or, for some of us, had to earn part of that money to pay our way. We did study harder, I think; we did discipline ourselves. We were more serious about what we were there to learn. It certainly has helped make me a better producer—discipline is very important in the film business. I was at USC at a time when experimental filmmaking was fashionable. Doug Cox, head honcho in the department, really was pushing avant-garde filmmaking: all juxtaposed positions, people popping in and out of the frame, blurry, streaked, out of focus; that was the emphasis. There were only a couple of us in my class—George arrived a year later—who wanted to make Hollywood films. I wanted to make something with a beginning, a middle, and an end. I found the better instructors were the ones who had the choice of teaching school or going into film. The unsatisfactory ones were those who couldn't get into the business—and thought they had all the answers.

"After USC, I gave myself a year. I didn't want to bum around the rest of my life, trying to get into film. I remember going to Universal and meeting lots of people—old-timers, new-timers. I must have met 150 different people, all of whom had different advice. One guy told me that the Directors Guild was starting a training program and suggested I call and find out about it, which I did. I went down for the interview one evening. Four others were waiting outside; two were directors' sons. The interviews were to last maybe 15 or 20 minutes. After a while, they asked, 'How are your legs? We see from your medical report that you have a bad back. We don't want to hire anyone who might get drafted.' I said I had been told by my doctors I would be 4F... Their only reply was, 'Do you realize that Assistant Directors have to stand around on their feet all day long, walk about, never sit down? It is tiring and very grueling. If you can't stand on your feet and have a bad back, then this isn't the job for you.' I just looked at them, got up, and left. I was one of the ten selected."

Later, Kazanjian enrolled in the Hollywood Directors Guild and worked as an A.D. on such traditional Hollywood movies as: *Camelot*, directed by Joshua Logan; *Finnigan's Rainbow*, directed by Francis Ford Coppola; *The Wild Bunch*, directed by Sam Peckinpah; *The Arrangement*, directed by Elia Kazan; *The Hindenburg*, directed by Robert Wise; and *Family Plot*, directed by Alfred Hitchcock.

"At the end of the Hitchcock picture, I'd reached a sort of pinnacle. I told the studio production manager I wouldn't go on; I wasn't going to stay an assistant director until I was fifty-five years old!

"I was a production manager myself for about a year's time, then associate producer on the movie *Rollercoaster*, which was released by Universal. Universal asked me to come back to work on one of the movies they were having problems with. I said, 'I'm not going to take a studio job, but I'll come back and help you out for two months.' Just as I said that, George Lucas came in and asked, 'Hey, how would you like to produce *More American Graffiti*?'

"A lot of people say *More American Graffiti* didn't work because of the form, the screen sizes—the multiple-screen images. I disagree. I don't think it was the story either, or the fact that Richard Dreyfuss wasn't in it. Distributors loved the movie, exhibitors loved it. But we died. I wish somebody would say, 'Howard, you were a lousy producer,' or, 'You had bad actors,' or, 'The script stunk.' Maybe the script could have been better. I'll tell you this, a lot of people thought it was the same movie. We had re-released *American Graffiti* just two or three months earlier. Universal wanted to do it; Lucasfilm didn't. Maybe the word 'More' was wrong. It should have been *American Graffiti II*. It's possible. I don't know . . . I wish somebody would tell me."

As the producer, how did he react to the choice of Yuma for the desert scene?

"We scouted Denver, we scouted near Vegas, we scouted in Spain, and, of course, we had already been to Tunisia before. Yuma was more expensive than some of those other locations might have been, but George knew what he wanted, and we have to go with his eye—his filmmaker's eye. After a decision like that has been made, it is my job to figure out the best and the least expensive way to get the scenes shot. I will argue with George occasionally, but I don't come into a meeting and scream and yell; rather, I try to offer suggestions and come up with the best solutions."

What about the problem of having offices for the movie in England and America?

"Shipping is always a problem, and communications are a little difficult because of the eight-or nine-hour time difference. But with telexes and telephones, nowadays it's workable. We certainly had to have multiple crews, two art departments, a double set of construction personnel—more supervisors, more unit managers, location managers, assistant directors. For the location shooting, we had a teamster captain and two co-captains, one in Yuma, one in Crescent City. There were two production offices, two auditing offices, and the staff to run them. And with top star technicians flying back and forth, we had hundreds of airplane trips.

"There are crews and there are crews. We happened to have picked a very good crew, which has been working for us now for four pictures in Europe. We all speak English, but sometimes we don't all speak the same English."

Kazanjian will be with *Jedi* well into its international release. He will work through the fall of 1983, supervising the dubbing of the foreign versions of the movie and helping coordinate all the foreign markets. By the time he is finished with *Jedi*, he will have spent over three and a half years working on it and will be a long way from the day he and George Lucas first sat down to talk about the third movie in the trilogy.

ROBERT WATTS

Robert Watts is the co-producer of *Jedi*. This is his fourth picture with Lucasfilm Ltd. He started on *Star Wars*, worked on *Empire*, *Raiders*, and now *Jedi*. Someone once described him as "English gruff," although, translated, that means businesslike and straightforward. He was educated at Marlborough College in England and at the University of Grenoble in France and served his hitch in the armed services with The Frontier Force in Nigeria. He specialized in modern languages at school and speaks French and Spanish quite well. "And German not so *gut*," as he says. "I've worked abroad a lot, because I've worked abroad a lot. Having the languages isn't really necessary, just useful."

As co-producer on *Jedi*, Watts spent almost all of his time in England keeping an eye on the production at EMI while Jim Bloom, the other co-producer, stayed in California. Robert Watts is firmly dedicated to the premise that what gets up on that 60-foot screen is much more important than what it takes to get it there. So sending case-hardened technicians out into temperatures that fluctuate from 20 below to 120 above—and scheduling a sandstorm for the very first day of filming—has become sort of second nature to him.

How did he first get involved with the movie business?

"I started in 1960 at the age of twenty-two, after having done my National Service. My grandfather had been at Ealing Studios. He was many things, but he was also a scriptwriter. I got my first job, when I left the Army, through a production man brought into the film industry by my grandfather, so you can call it nepotism—to an extent.

"I was an assistant 'goffer' on a Boulting Brothers picture called *The French Mistress*. I did that on three movies in the first year, decided there wasn't a great deal of future in it, and got a job making commercials. In two and a half years, I went from being the runner to being a kind of production manager. It gave me a broad grasp of film production in a very condensed area because we shot for one day. You didn't have a crew around, so you did all the preproduction yourself. Because of that, I was given all sorts of jobs, even going to the labs to help grade the prints, although most of the commercials then were still done in black and white.

"In 1963, having got my union ticket, I came back into feature films as a Second Assistant Director. My first film back in the business was at EMI—at ABPC, as it was called then—*The Winston Affair*. I did a picture at MGM up the road—that studio is now closed—with a very ritzy cast. Polanski's first production outside Poland, *Repulsion*. A small English film, *Darling*, which won three Hollywood Oscars. Two James Bonds—*Thunderball*, and *You Only Live Twice*—gave me my first crack as location manager: Paris, Miami, Nassau, Japan."

Watts also worked with Director Stanley Kubrick on 2001.

"If you want the differential between shooting *Star Wars* and *2001*, Stanley—if he's going into outer space—wants experts from NASA working on the film, and he has the ability to assimilate technical knowledge so quickly that he knows more than the NASA people by the time you get to do the thing and ask them for their advice. *Star Wars*, on the other hand, because we are not dealing with actual technology, has the freedom to say anything can happen in those days. Therefore, you don't have to explain that Landspeeders or Sail Barges work on an anti-gravitational system. There's no relationship to Earth.

"In *Star Wars* people can walk around in a weightless condition. For *2001*, we had to be very careful—the only time our characters were able to be, as it were, walking on Earth was in the centrifuge."

How did he first get acquainted with the *Star Wars*/Lucas projects?

"About a year after meeting Gary Kurtz in Culver City and talking with him for ten minutes about the subject of working in England, I had a call to send a resume to him since he might be coming to England to make a film. After that, I didn't hear a thing for another two years, not even a 'We'll let you know.' Then, in 1975, he rang again to say he was coming to do *Star Wars*. I went to see him, we got on, and I did the job really as production manager."

How does he like being co-producer?

"I don't think the essence of my job changes that much. I still maintain the elements of control I had on the original *Star Wars*, but view it from a much broader perspective now. The most difficult thing to do in progressing in the job is to learn to delegate, and to trust people to do the things that I was once doing myself.

"With *Star Wars*, we were fortunate in having the very talented John Barry designing the film, using Ralph McQuarrie's production illustrations. We were making a science-fiction picture we all sensed was different—an environment that was lived in, not pristine in the *2001* style. We were making something that was used, old, that leaked and was not infallible. My own feeling at the time was that it was going to be a successful picture in the sense that the James Bond films have been successful, almost as an afterthought. *Star Wars* was a film nobody knew we were making. We weren't dealing with stars, or with any known quantity. We were just getting on with a movie and having a good time.

"With *Empire*, we were following the most successful film in history. It's very difficult to be as cost-conscious following the film that made this incredible amount of money and got such a vast press. I think a lot of people did not realize *Star Wars* was a Fox picture and that a large percentage of the money went to Fox. I tried to make it clear going in that *Empire* was a Lucasfilm production financed by Lucasfilm and that the cash was coming directly out of George's pocket. Therefore, it was incumbent on all of us not to let the thing get out of hand. That's true for any film, but particularly for this one.

"*Empire* was tougher to make and not as much fun. It was a grind at times, a real grind."

What about *Raiders of the Lost Ark*?

"*Raiders* came right out of the blue. I got a phone call

during the last week of *Empire*, saying, 'We've got this new film and we'd like to do a quick budget to see if it would possibly work in England, as against the States.' I got the script literally two days after we finished *Empire*. I went to the South of France and read it lying on the beach. It was a breath of fresh air, good old action-adventure stuff. We just kicked off right into it, really. Back-to-back, without a break. So little time to get the film ready; then Steven [Spielberg], when he got into it, shot it with such speed, verve, and enthusiasm that it carried everyone along.

"We were shooting out in the open, as opposed to being on stages. There were fewer cockpits and bluescreens — and all of that. But the film wasn't without its problems. It was tough because in three years we made two big movies, but it was exhilarating too."

Now, what about *Jedi*?

"*Jedi* was different again. In the first place, we had an English director — something we hadn't had on any of the others. Howard Kazanjian, who produced this film, was a pleasure to work with, so I was solidly backed up all the way. Howard and I have the same sort of background, which is a good grounding in production. We understand each other. He would always give me an immediate decision on any problem, which is important. And I think Richard Marquand took on a heavy task coming into this show. It is so much a creation of George's that it's to Richard's credit he obviously managed to put his bit into it too!

"Four pictures. Wow! I haven't really thought — it's just happened."

Soon it will be five pictures. Robert Watts is set to act as producer of the next Indiana Jones adventure. So he will continue to be a part of the Lucasfilm family for the next two or three years.

JIM BLOOM

Jim Bloom just turned thirty, yet he has already worked in the movie business for 11 years. A decade of experience has not dimmed his love of the movies — probably because he has worked on some very good movies with some very good people. He's been on three films with George Lucas: *American Graffiti*, *The Empire Strikes Back*, and now *Jedi*.

"Originally I'm from New York. At seventeen, I went West to school at UC Berkeley. I was there on and off for over three years—it took me the first two years to decide to drop out. At the time, my brother had been working in the film business, and he said: 'Go make a movie.'

"When I was a freshman in school, we had the opportunity, in a physics class, to do a non-standard project. Instead of writing a paper, four of us got together and made a small film. Somehow, I managed to direct it and edit it, and the others did the lighting and put the physical content into the narrative. I sort of fell in love with the process.

"I used to follow documentary cameramen around. I'd say, 'I've got a free afternoon. I'll carry boxes for you or cables.' One of the first people I worked for was an Italian filmmaker who had me chauffeur him for two weeks in the San Francisco area. He said he would reimburse me for my gas money, but he never did . . .

"In the summer of my sophomore year I had been trying to contact a lot of people—you know, making calls to Zoetrope, sending out letters. I was getting nowhere. One day I went over to introduce myself to John Korty. I knocked on the door, and the conversation took place over the stoop—he was on the inside, I was on the outside. He said, 'You should call George Lucas; he's making a film in San Rafael called *American Graffiti*. The company's Lucasfilm; look them up in the directory.'

"I called that afternoon and spoke to Bunny, Gary Kurtz's secretary. She said, 'Oh, yeah, we're looking for someone. Why don't you come on over?' That had never happened to me before. I hopped into my car, drove to the office, waited for an hour and a half, and finally got to see Gary. I was nineteen years old. I told him, 'I'll work for nothing. I want the experience. You don't have to pay me. Not even gas money!' He said they should be able to manage a little bit. Maybe $10 a day."

What did he do on *American Graffiti*?

"My job was to handle all the vehicles. Instead of people as extras in the background, we had cars as extras. I cast the cars, prepared four booklets for George to go through—different quality vehicles, from very fancy and flashy to old, early 1960s automobiles, that the teenagers would drive around in.

"After *Graffiti*, my brother arranged a job for me with a documentary filmmaker who was going up to Washington to shoot a picture about Indians. He needed a fourth assistant, someone who had never worked as a cameraman before but would help carry the boxes around. The guy paid me $175 a week—I'd never made so much money. It was fantastic. That man happened to be Tom Smith, now the General Manager at Industrial Light and Magic."

After that, Bloom worked on the television series *The Streets of San Francisco* for two years.

"Through the six-year period, I always maintained contact with George Lucas and Gary ... and would ask their advice on what to do."

Bloom worked, during those years, on some good movies—*Close Encounters* with Steven Spielberg and *Coming Home* and *Bound for Glory* with Hal Ashby. Then back to Lucasfilm again?

"I remember very clearly, it was in December. The phone rang and a voice said, 'It's Bunny. Gary wants to talk to you. Give him a ring. He's in Scandinavia.' I'm used to making international calls now, but then it was a big thing for me to pick up a phone, call Stockholm, and trace Gary Kurtz down in some hotel; but I did. He said, 'I think I would like you to work on the next *Star Wars*; are you interested?'"

What did he do on *Empire*?

"They first hired me as an assistant producer. My responsibilities weren't quite so vast as they are on *Jedi*. When I started, I set up ILM—from the production and business standpoint. I also went to England and stayed there for six months. Robert Watts couldn't go to Norway, so they sent me as sort of production man with Peter MacDonald and that whole group for eight weeks. When I returned to London, I heard from Gary that things weren't going too well back in San Rafael, so I came home early to pull all that together.

"After I finished supervising post-production for ILM and all the other photographic effects on *Empire*, they offered to let me stay on and run the facility. But I said I'd rather not, that I preferred to remain independent, working from picture to picture. So I contacted Tom Smith, whom I had worked with years before. He came in, went through a rigorous screening process, and was hired.

"During this last year Robert Watts and I have become very close friends and working associates. After *Empire*, I took six months off, but before I left, George said: 'Howard Kazanjian is going to make the next *Star Wars*, and I would like you and Robert to act as his co-producers.'

"And here we are."

CHAPTER 6

Everybody has his favorite scene in *Star Wars*. Many people would vote immediately for the *Millennium Falcon*'s shift into hyperspace; many others would argue for the last, climactic raid on the Death Star; and there are many who would, without hesitation, champion the Mos Eisley Cantina scene with all those incredible and unexpected creatures. Luke and Ben Kenobi enter a rather plain-looking building, and suddenly the audience is confronted with an amazing collection of weirdos, a rough-and-ready bunch of lounge lizards, all wandering around in a grubby, space-age saloon. Ben used his lightsaber on one denizen, and Greedo was done in by Han Solo, but most of the creatures just went about their business.

The Empire Strikes Back did not have many creatures, but in early 1981, even though the *Jedi* script was unfinished, there was hard evidence that this film was more than going to make up for that. Phil Tippett had been commissioned to set up a full-scale monster department in rented warehouse space near the San Rafael headquarters while still putting the finishing touches on ILM's creations for the film *Dragonslayer*. Stuart Freeborn, devoting all his time to *Jedi*, had already set up shop at EMI Elstree in a series of connecting cubicles behind the front Administration building. A peek at one of his supply telexes shows that he was, indeed, working very hard on something.

ATTN: LATA RYAN
FROM: PAT CARR

STUART FREEBORN REQUIRES THE FOLLOWING FROM:

CHARLIE SCHRAMM
WINDSOR HILLS MAKE-UP LAB

6 × 5 GALLON PAILS FOAM LATEX
65 × ONE POUND BOTTLES OF SPONGE FOAMING AGENT
40 × ONE POUND JARS OF SPONGE CURING AGENT
20 × ONE POUND BOTTLES JELLING AGENT

PLEASE ADVISE SOONEST WHEN WE CAN EXPECT DELIVERY
COS THIS IS VERY URGENT.

Robert Watts was one of the few people privy to the actual numbers involved. "*Star Wars* had a reasonable quota of monsters; *Empire*, many fewer. This film is THE monster movie—there are so many of them it was impossible to make them all here in London. Stuart Freeborn's main areas of responsibility are Jabba the Hutt and the Ewoks. Phil Tippett took on most of the others plus all the creatures in Jabba's Court—there are a few that are being reprised from *Star Wars*.

"They are terribly difficult because you are breaking new ground each time on each new creature. You never know when they are going to be ready or, when they are ready, if they are going to work. We never did get the articulated Ewoks when we should have had them. But Jabba is a very complex chap, who was ready and worked very well indeed."

A few of the technicians thought they remembered Jabba the Hutt. Dave Middleton, in charge of the construction storerooms, thought he remembered someone named Jabba; Pat Carr, who seldom forgets a name or a face, could have sworn she had issued a casting note on him once before, as she now unpacked the first Jabba design sketches for the 18-foot-long king of the desert underworld.

They were both correct. Back in Tunisia on Friday, April 9, 1976, Jabba the Hutt lived briefly—in the humanoid form of an actor. The film containing Jabba, however, remained on the cutting room floor; so Jabba, however, became a vaguely threatening presence, talked about but never seen. He was the shadowy potentate to whom the carbon-frozen Han Solo had to be delivered. Han, who hadn't paid his debt to Jabba, would then hang in Jabba's Palace trophy room as a warning to others not to forget their debts to the ruler.

Marcia Lucas, who won an Oscar for editing *Star Wars*, was in on the final decision about Jabba in the first movie. She remembers: "Jabba was a big debatable item. George had never liked the scene Jabba was in because he felt that the casting was not strong enough. There was an element, however, that I liked a lot because of the way George had filmed it. Jabba was seen in a long shot and he was yelling, while in the foreground, in a big close-up, Han's body wiped into the left corner of the frame and his hand was on a gun and he said, 'I've been waiting for you, Jabba.' Then we cut to Han's face and Jabba turned around. I thought it was a very virile moment for Han's character; it made him a real macho guy, and Harrison's performance was very good. I lobbied to keep the scene. But Jabba was not terrific, and Jabba's men, who all looked like Greedo, were made of molded green plastic. George thought they looked pretty phony, so he had two reasons for wanting to cut the scene: the appearance of Jabba's men and the pacing of the movie. You have to pick up the pacing in an action movie like *Star Wars*, so ultimately, the scene wasn't necessary."

Lucas himself remembers the incident slightly differently. "The original idea was that he'd be a monster. But then we couldn't make him a monster, so we cast him as a human. I was going to superimpose or matte in a monster over the actor. I asked Fox for extra money for more creatures in the Cantina, to shoot some more stuff in the desert, and also to do this bluescreen Jabba to fit into that scene. I needed about $80,000 to do it all, and Fox said: 'We'll give you 40.' So we actually cut the scene out before we got to the point of shooting the monster part. If I had had the money, I might have shot it anyway. If it still didn't work, I'd probably have cut it out. We had a certain kind of monster then and he sort of evolved to where he is today."

But now, five years later, Jabba was about to appear.

He was the first challenge that Phil Tippett presented to his design team in San Rafael. Phil described Jabba to his staff as "a filthy scum bag. He has a palace and an entourage of other monsters. George, at the time, was fishing for designs and he had told us to see what we could think of. So we started off with a design that was an ugly, wormy creature. George took a look and said, 'Too terrible.' We went to another version with forearms. 'Too human. Try again.' We ended up with this character who is very fat, sluglike, and who needs a lot of assistance from his courtiers."

While Jabba took a long time, others came about very easily. Tippett again: "One character that figures quite prominently in the picture is Admiral Ackbar. He's just one of a hundred different designs George accepted. On a whim George said, 'This is Admiral Ackbar.' So it took just one try to get him right!"

Englishman Stuart Freeborn has been in the business of changing people's appearance with make-up and masks for almost 50 years, but Jabba the Hutt is the biggest thing he has ever attempted. A 1930s protégé of Sir Alexander Korda, he often worked on ten productions at a time for the pioneer, Hungarian-born filmmaker. Since the end of World War II, Freeborn has had his pick of British-based pictures. He has worked on such blockbusters as *Bridge on the River Kwai*, *2001*, and *Superman*. His two trickiest assignments during all that time—two that actually sound quite simple—were taking 20 years off an aging actor and making a false nose for Charlie Chaplin.

The three *Star Wars* movies have made full use of his extensive knowledge of precision engineering, physiognomy, and modern prosthetics. Freeborn underplays the difficulties of his job by saying, "It's just foam rubber or wax pieces. You actually have to stick them to the actor's skin, paint other skins over them, and seal it in. Then you can't see the joins!"

Jabba the Hutt was a bit more difficult. He is 18 feet long from the top of his head to the tip of his tail. He is jellylike, slimy-looking, slavering. Everything moves: nose, eyes, tongue. He must wobble, belly flop, and tail swat. There are three operators working inside the body, each with a television screen inside to tell him what his part of Jabba is doing on the outside. There is one operator for each of Jabba's arms, and a little person inside the tail to operate it. There are also two operators to manipulate Jabba's radio-controlled pupils and eyelids. It takes a total of five humans to make Mr. Hutt as humanlike as possible.

"I'd never even heard of George Lucas back in about 1976 when he suddenly appeared in my lab," Freeborn remembers. "I was making some mechanical dogs for a scene in the first *Omen* when George walked in. He vaguely introduced himself. He was very quiet. I really didn't take much notice because a lot of people were always just wandering in. He said, 'I've heard of what you do and I'd like to see some of the creatures you've made.' I usually keep something of everything I've done. He was proposing to make a film that would need a lot of strange things, and he made me interested enough to think that this was really something." Stuart Freeborn has been an important member of the team ever since.

Only the droids are outside his ken. "They're not a make-up job. I'm only concerned where make-up, movable heads, articulated masks—and sometimes bodies—are involved. For *Star Wars*, Chewie actually didn't take me that long, because I used a lot of my experience from *2001*. On that film I had the enormous problem of turning 60 young boys into man-apes capable of plenty of movement, plus the realistic movement of their mouths and their lips. I realized with Chewbacca I could use everything I knew and had learned, and I went further in developing a mask with full facial mechanisms than I'd ever gone before.

"There was so little time to produce all the Cantina figures," Freeborn remembers. "I had a lot of heads I converted. The character of Greedo that George liked so much was actually based on a peahead from a television commercial years before.

"I don't really come up with anything in the daytime. It's only at night, after I've had about an hour of sleep, I'll suddenly wake up and be absolutely full of ideas. It all becomes a very strong vision. I dash out of bed and write the ideas down as fast as I can—little notes of how to make things operate, the mechanics, how they are going to work. It's so exciting to go into the studio the next day with all this in my mind, with my notes and with my drawings. I always think that when I'm properly awake and read over my notes, they are going to be rubbish, but I'm amazed the next morning to find they make an awful lot of sense. Even with Yoda, I got my best ideas during the night. I've had some fine engineering training, and that's been extremely useful over the past few years. Chemistry—mostly self-taught. I went to night school for all sorts of subjects, and the rest really comes from ideas I've developed myself—dental and rubber work and all that. Materials are changing all the time, better but more expensive. I'm usually in contact with firms like DuPont and ICI, and they're constantly sending me samples of new things. I used to know an expert chemist who specialized in creating by arithmetic, materials that never existed before. He was very interested in theatricals and film work, so I'd spend a day at his factory discussing such things as flesh with him."

Freeborn warms to his subject. "Foam rubber is nothing like flesh. With certain plastics you can get pretty close, but there are still problems with it. In some circumstances you go back to foam rubber, but then you lose the transparency. I got very far with some PVC formulas. It's incredible what you can do with them, but unfortunately, they are very toxic, so I had to keep clear to protect the actors. Jedi, of course, is much bigger than the other two movies. I think, at peak, counting plasterers, engineers, radio-control experts—even some wardrobe staff who were involved in what I was doing—my staff reached about 40.

"There were some magic moments," he says, pausing for a moment. "Yoda, of course, was one of the principal moments of magic. I liked him straightaway. And then the Cantina scene with all the odd things made a tremendous hit."

Is Jabba the Hutt going to be one of those?

"I don't know. It depends how his personality comes through. I tried to run the whole gamut of emotions with him, except being a nice character—that, he never was and never could be. Jabba was my biggest headache, and unfortunately, I didn't get much time to see him on the screen. I think we just about made him work."

Immediately following the shooting of the opening sand-storm sequence, there was a private monster preview on Stage 6. This rehearsal, set in the main hallway of Jabba's Palace which leads down to his Throne Room, was the first time the semihuman Major-domo Bib Fortuna had worked. Bib Fortuna is a tall, hairless creature with a large, oddly shaped head, long fingers, and mesmeric eyes. Actor Nick Carter had left his home in south London at 5:00 in the morning in order to be on time for his three-hour make-up session. He would be required to wear the heavy and uncomfortable Fortuna headgear throughout the day. The only respite would be the removal of his special contact lenses from time to time, under the supervision of an eye doctor.

In the days to follow, he would spend just under three hours every morning getting into the Bib make-up, but only 25 minutes every evening getting out of it.

Another unusual sight that day, which became common-place once the set for Jabba's Throne Room was fully operational, was a Pig Guard with a vacuum cleaner exhaust, set on Cold, thrust up the pants of his costume to cool his body while a blow dryer, also set on Cold, was pressed to his massive snout, cooling the actor's overheated head inside.

The final set dressing was now being completed on Jabba's Throne Room. It resembled a house somewhere between an Arabian Nights pleasure palace and an overdecorated dungeon. From the look of the set, there was no doubt that anyone incurring the master's wrath would be summarily dealt with on the spot and in public view.

Norman Reynolds had let his imagination run free. The room contained everything from a gigantic cooking spit behind the dais on which Jabba reclined to galactic fruit machines to a metal grate set into the center of the stone floor. Below the grate, the insatiable Rancor prowled. "The range of creatures in Jabba's Palace did compound my problems," Norman Reynolds explained, "because it meant that the entire set had to be built up off the floor in order to accommodate the people who would be working the creatures from below. The entire area had to be removable with individual panels—sort of like trapdoors—and that became very expensive. The other problem was the sheer number of people involved—make-up, puppeteers, wardrobe, video engineers. I remember once going in there when we were trying to finish the set and screaming at everyone, 'Get off! Get off!' It was like Piccadilly Circus."

Phil Tippett had done his best to tailor the monsters to their living quarters from 6,000 miles away. "We were in constant touch with Robert Watts and Richard Marquand about what we could expect over in England. I talked to Norman quite a bit about set specifications, and I talked to Richard about the characterizations he expected out of certain of the creatures. We were essentially building these costume figures around our own bodies, since we really didn't have any idea who the performers in England would be. To compensate for that, we made a number of generic-size monsters, from small to medium to large, that would fit the five of us from here who were going over."

How did some of those characterizations come about?

"Some of the creatures kind of suggested their character. Like little Max Rebo. He's a goofy, screwy, funny-looking guy—personality pretty much decided by the design."

Saturday, January 23, was put aside for a final walk-through rehearsal for the creatures—for everyone except the principal actors, that is. The three Jabba operators—Toby Philpott, David Barclay, and tail man Mike Edmonds—spent most of the day inside Jabba, demonstrating his repertoire of movements.

Howard Kazanjian explains more about what Mike Edmonds does inside Jabba's tail. "We have two different tails that do different things. One is kind of curled up, and one undulates... very much like a lizard's tail. (Actually, Edmonds is also an Ewok. He's worked for us in our other films when he has played the part of small people.) The tail is attached to a mechanism that turns it, but it has to be controlled by this individual who handles the apparatus—motors and stuff like that. But he also has a monitor down in the tail, so he can watch the television camera that is placed on Jabba and the tail and see how the tail is moving. He sees the performance from the outside as well. The two guys who are in Jabba's head and body have a TV monitor that they look into as well in order to see how they are moving Jabba's hands."

There were, as expected, problems of lighting, costumes, and overcrowding, plus one piece of set reconstruction that would have to be done over the weekend.

Stuart Ziff, in an evening telex, helped record part of the weekend and the first day in the Throne Room for posterity.

ATTN: PATTY BLAU
FROM: STUART ZIFF

TODAY FIRST DAY OF SHOOTING IN JABBA THRONE ROOM.
OVERTIME:
PLEASE REPORT MY WEEKEND HOURS TO MARGARET IN 'B' BUILDING, STUART SAT 23 JAN 10 HOURS
JEANNE, TIM ROSE, DAVE C, WORKED 10-1/2 HOURS

EVERYONE HAS OR IS GETTING COLDS. PLEASE SEND SUDIFEDS—SEVERAL BOXES. AND WITH NEXT SHIPMENT A 6-PACK DOCTOR PEPPER.

THANK YOU FOR YOUR SPEEDY SUPPORT. MANY HERE AMAZED HOW WE CAN GET THINGS FASTER FROM THE UNITED STATES THAN FROM LOCAL SUPPLIERS IN ENGLAND.

OF COURSE THIS IS A THIRD WORLD COUNTRY. BUT I FEAR REAGONOMICS WILL MAKE THAT SHORT LIVED AND WE WILL PASS THEM IN THIS DIRECTION.

SMILING SAM

LFLPROD SRFL
897932 STWARS G

It hadn't been so very long ago that Phil Tippett's creature crates had passed through British customs. At the time, the contents were very bizarre. A sampling:

Crate 5, belonging to a Mr. Hermi Odle, contained, among other things, one main body with costume attached and one fake skeleton.

Crate 6, in addition to containing a pair of arms with hands attached, boasted six pieces of aluminum tubing and two more lengths of solid steel rod.

Crate 11 contained Hoover the hand puppet with Yuzzum the marionette for company, plus ten feet of pipe for Yuzzum's operation. The box also contained a spear with skulls and hair, belonging to one Amanaman.

Mr. Ephant Mon needed two whole containers to himself, one for his body costume and another for 100 feet of two-inch vinyl air hose.

Phil Tippett reflected on where all this had begun. "When we began doing some of the design work on *Jedi*, we were halfway into the most critical phase of work on *Dragonslayer*, so we started making weird and wonderful monsters in our spare moments. A lot of us watched horror movies when we were children and we therefore had a pretty good foundation in what had been done already and what we didn't want to do.

"Most of us are from optical effects backgrounds, having worked at ILM, so we've all been pretty much involved in doing stop-motion photography work and post-production insert camera work rather than in making creatures. Rick Baker on *Star Wars* was our mentor, teaching us a lot about how to build these things, because we really had never done it before. In our production schedule there was a list of approximately ten different steps that you have to go through. Steps such as design, sculpture, moldmaking, rubber running, trimming, painting, and then all the final tweaking in order to get them as real-looking as possible. When we begin construction, we first make very rough mock-ups of the characters. We also do extensive video tests all the way along."

What is the first step?

"We tend to like to work in three dimensions since most of us are sculptors. The first designs are basically models for George to accept or turn down. We have a rejection pile that is made up of probably 50 or 60 monsters, whereas the acceptances are 25 to 30, so that makes it roughly two models for each one that is accepted and goes on to be built in a larger form.

"We have three basic ways of operating a creature. One puts the actual performer inside a costume. Many times that is supplemented by a cable running into the creature, winding its way up his back, then running via the mask to the eyes. Cable grips, operated by another person by hand off camera, are synchronized in order to make the eyes blink. Also, we have air bladders and tubes that are attached to bellows, so that when an operator presses a bladder, the lips or the cheeks on a creature will pooch out a bit."

What about the Gamorrean Guards?

"The Gamorrean Guards are used quite prominently in the Throne Room sequence. For most of the sequences, where they are just running around, there will be pullover masks on their heads. However, when you have to go in for a close-up, or if the Pig Guard is required to have some facial expression, the cable-assisted mask will be put on. Using the handgrips attached to the cables, an operating crew will make the eyebrows raise, or the mouth open, or the nose snarl, depending upon what kind of reaction Richard Marquand wants."

What about Jabba's musical trio?

"Although they occupy only one line of the script, something like 'And then the band started up . . .' we have put as much animation and life into the band as possible. We also did extensive video tests with them. The creatures are incredibly complicated, and the video tests allowed us to see if we really were on the right track. They are more way out than most of the costume creatures, which are, essentially, just men in masks.

"There are three band members: Max Rebo, a two-legged blues keyboard player; Droopy McCool, a pudgy little saxophonist; and Sy Snootles, dancer and lead vocalist. The two instrumentalists have people inside costumes, with extra movement supplied by cables and bladders. Snooty the singer, because of her configuration, however, is both a marionette operated from above and a rod puppet manipulated from below. That was the only way to accomplish all of her gyrations. In addition, there is a considerable amount of cable-controlled movement to get her lips to look as if she is singing into a microphone.

"George brought in a tape of some music he wanted to use as a temporary track to give us an idea of the music the band would be playing. The band members are not horrible creatures who take themselves very seriously. Rather, they are kind of quasi-comical, so the music is fun, kind of uptempo. From this temp track John Williams made up a much more elaborate version for playback that we practiced with when we got to England."

The result of Phil Tippett's hard work was definitely paying off, as evidenced by one of Mr. Z's communiqués.

ATTN: PATTY
FROM: STUART

PEPPY PATTY

YOUR EFFICIENCY IS OVERWHELMING. WE FOUND DROOPY'S
FOOT BELLOWS. NO NEED TO SEND MORE.

SALACIOUS STEALING SHOW—BUBO HOT—HERMI, YAK FACE,
SQUID, MOLE AND TOOTH FACE ALSO SHOT. PUPPETEERS AND
MIMES ARE EXCELLENT. JABBA SUPER HOT. HIS EYES ARE EL
PRIMO.
SIX EYE NIXED, BAND SHOT TODAY.

MY THOUGHTS ARE WITH YOU IN A VEGETARIAN RESTAU-
RANT IN MARIN. . . .
WINCING SAM

And more of the Throne Room jamboree from Mr. Z.

ATTN: PATTY
FROM: STUART
1/29

MR. TIPPETT WAS FEATURED ALONG WITH STUART FREEBORN
IN THE CENTER OF A PUBLICITY SHOT WITH ALL OF THE CREA-
TURES, ALIENS, PUPPETS AND JABBA. PLEASE TELL ALL THE
RABBLE THAT THEIR FORMER PHIL IS NOW MR. TIPPETT.

SHOT SNOOTY FULL AND AS A HAND PUPPET. IT GOT AP-
PLAUSE. MIXED BLADDERS ON DROOPY. RED BALL SUPER!

THE GROUP STILL WAS HOT, THIS PIC IS NOT (UNDERLINED)
GOING TO BE TISHA B'AV IN NELLIES-VILLE WHEN IT HITS THE
SILVER SCREEN. THERE IS NO DOUBT IT WILL RACK UP SUPER
BOFFO GROSSES IN THE NABES, OZONERS, YUMPS VILLE AND
THE CONTINENT.

CHOW FOR NOW

MORRY SLINE

By February 1, about midway through the two weeks that it would take to complete the sequence, everyone felt that he could see a light at the end of the tunnel. And a new star was emerging during the shooting. His name is Salacious Crumb. Howard Kazanjian talks about how Mr. Crumb became so popular.

"We never knew he would be the star that he turned out to be. We enlarged his role when we saw him. He is operated as a hand puppet, and he sits right next to Jabba much of the time. We cut a hole in Jabba's throne and put a man under there. But that was added way late. We were fortunate that we were able to cut away some of the underneath structure and put a man in there and lie him down flat and still have the support to carry Jabba and his throne. It looks as if Salacious will speak in Huttese, but much of his performance is laughs and reactions rather than dialogue. What happened was, when we weren't even shooting with him, Phil Tippett—or the puppeteer under the floor who was manipulating him—would be playing with Salacious and would have him do something unexpected, such as peck at somebody's ear, or some other impromptu action, and we couldn't help but fall in love with him. So, gradually, we enlarged his part. At the same time, we would discover that another character would be very cumbersome, or not mobile enough. Or it took too long to dress him, and that creature would just kind of fill a dark spot in the background."

George Lucas took off for a break in Paris and ended up spending the entire weekend sick in his hotel room. He returned to London to spread the alarm of a suspected case of the measles. Everyone breathed a sigh of relief when it turned into a dose of influenza instead.

The Monster Shop, meanwhile, worked on.

ATTN: PATTY
FROM: STUART
2/1

OVERTIME:

STUART, JEANNE AND DAVE 10 HOURS; 4 HOURS DURING WEEK, 6 ON SUNDAY.

TODAY'S QUOTE FROM LADY MACBETH: THINGS WITHOUT ALL REMEDY SHOULD BE WITHOUT REGARD, WHAT IS DONE IS DONE.

THANK YOU ALL FOR THE CARE PACKAGE, EVERYONE IS DELIGHTED WITH THEIR GIFTS. DOSEQUIS BEER, CHIPS COMPASSES AND DR. PEPPER.

WE COOKED SOME OF THE MASA, STARTED TO TURN, BUT STILL GOOD.

HAVING A WONDERFUL TIME, WISH . . .

KILLER
LFLPROD SRFL
897932 STWARS GT

By Thursday, February 11, the team had entered the last phase of the Jabba the Hutt affair and had moved to the interior set of Jabba's Sail Barge. In this scene, our heroes are just about to escape from their captor. These are the scenes that immediately preceded Scene 44, the sandstorm, where filming started last month.

In Los Angeles, February 11 was also Oscar nomination day, and Lucasfilm made a very good showing.

ATTN: HOWARD KAZANJIAN
FROM: IAN BRYCE

RAIDERS NOMINATED FOR THE FOLLOWING ACADEMY AWARDS:
BEST PICTURE
BEST DIRECTOR
BEST VISUAL EFFECTS
BEST ART DIRECTION
BEST EDITING
BEST MUSIC
BEST SOUND
BEST CINEMATOGRAPHY

A TOTAL OF 8 NOMINATIONS. IN ADDITION, BEN BURTT AND
RICHARD ANDERSON HAVE BEEN AWARDED, AND WILL RE-
CEIVE ON OSCAR NIGHT, A SPECIAL ACADEMY AWARD FOR
SOUND EFFECTS EDITING.

CONGRATULATIONS
IAN LFLPROD SRFL

897932 STWARS G
VIA WUI

When the awards were handed out in March, *Raiders*
won Oscars in four of the categories:

Best Visual Effects—Richard Edlund, Kit West, Bruce
Nicholson, and Joe Johnston.

Best Art Direction—Norman Reynolds, Leslie Dilley,
and Michael Ford.

Best Film Editing—Michael Kahn, A.C.E.

Best Sound—Phil Varney, Steve Maslow, Gregg Lan-
daker, and Roy Charman.

Ben Burtt and Richard Anderson also received their special Academy Award for Sound Effects Editing.

Four of those honored with Academy Award nominations
were hard at work on Stages 5 and 8, where, late in the
day, the main unit would rendezvous for a lineup and pre-
light on Scene 54, Interior Rebel Cruiser, Main Briefing
Room.

The telex relaying the Oscar nominations information did
not mention a Special Academy Award being given for an
innovative piece of design which had opened up the frontier
of special-effects photography even more. It was a device
that would remove the minimal jerkiness usually seen in
stop-motion photography in model filming. Attributed to a
thirty-two-year-old engineer from Fairfax, California, it was
being given to our very own Mr. Stuart Irwin Ziff—he of
the harassed look, vivid imagination, and weakness for telexes.

ATTN: PATTY
FROM: STUART
2/17

PLEASE TELL TONI THAT RANCOR'S BLOOD AND OOZING VIS-
CERA IS THE SAME COLOR, TRANSLUCENCY AND TEXTURE AS
KRAFT REAL MAYONNAISE. SO SAYS THE GOVERNOR.

SHOT CLOSE-UP OF ACKBAR. PLEASE INFORM EVAN IT WORKED
REAL GOOD. IT EVEN LOOKED GOOD.

LFLPROD SRFL
897932 STWARS G

By mid-March, Barbara Lakin and Kathy Wippert, in
the photo library of Lucasfilm at San Rafael, were sending
out scores of reference prints and reference slides with deep
and deliberate scratches across the faces of the pictures.
Reference prints are, as their name suggests, for reference
only; in order to make sure they will not be reproduced in
any form—or anywhere—the still department makes one
or two diagonal scratches across the prints. The list of people
who saw the reference prints was stringently regulated. Only
the special *Star Wars* team at Kenner Toys had access to
the pictures, and they all knew full well that if anything
slipped into print ahead of time, jobs would be on the line!
Pictures do not tell the whole story—size was important—
and the Freeborn/Tippett creature collection was being
measured and recorded.

ATTN: KATHY WIPPERT
FROM: PAT CARR
MARCH 17 1982

CHARACTER/CREATURE HEIGHTS AS REQUESTED:

WICKET	3'11"
CHIEF CHIRPA	4'1"
BIB FORTUNA	6'2"
EMPEROR	5'8"

YAK FACE	7'
SQUID HEAD	6'
HERMI ODLE	6'6"

LFLPROD SRFL
897932 STWARS G

Almost from the moment EMI opened for business on Monday, January 11, top executives from Kenner Toys, Fundimension, Parker Brothers, and the Bibb Company had been chomping at the bit to make the trip to EMI. Lead time is crucial in the toy and merchandising industry, and finally they were invited to come for a visit. The merchandisers were given a general briefing on *Jedi* by Howard Kazanjian; then those few who had been cleared to read the sanitized version of the screenplay did so at one sitting, locked together in Kazanjian's office. Following that, there was a limited, chaperoned tour of the shooting stages, and an opportunity to earmark Designer Norman Reynolds' models and blueprints for reproduction use much later on.

The Ewoks were being measured and the toy manufacturers were making plans for new toys; and while the filming of the scenes with Jabba were almost over on Stage Number 8, there was still the question of Huttese. Huttese is the language that Jabba and many of his creatures speak. C-3PO is pressed into service as an interpreter in the Throne Room. The question of Jabba's language was one small area that had always bothered Richard Marquand, but George Lucas was reassuring:

"The language for Jabba is the language we used in *Star Wars*. Greedo spoke it. So we'll deal with Jabba the same way. For *Star Wars*, they said you can't have subtitles in a children's film. But I said they have got to learn how to read sooner or later. And it's a good way to teach them. If the kid is too young to read, then it creates a bond between him and his parents; he relies on them to read things for him. So I did it. Same way this time—it's just more extreme. The truth of it is, the scenes are designed and written to be understood without knowing what is being said. You get only some of the humor that way. But a four-year-old, I think, could follow the Jabba scene without understanding the dialogue or being able to read it at all. People have taken kids younger than that and said they enjoyed it. It's hard to know where the line is."

Richard Marquand discusses Jabba: "Before we started shooting the Throne Room scene, Jabba's tongue and his arms and his eyes—one of the toughest problems that we had to deal with—were in place. We had to discuss—rediscuss—what the eyes should do: where they would go; how they would operate; the range of different emotions he would have to express during the course of the sequences, and how these would be done with his eyes. So the guys who were operating his eyes would go away and they would rehearse. Then they would show me and I would say, 'Yeah, now he's looking at me . . . now he's looking sly . . . now looking interested . . . now looking angry . . .'"

What exactly do the eyes do?

"The eyes open and close, the iris dilates, and the eyes move from side to side. The eyes are about the size of saucers. They are made of this very thin, opaque plastic that is used for airplanes. They open and catch the light. The irises are very, very carefully and cleverly constructed. We used a material that looks as if it represents the lines that you get in the musculature of the eyes."

What was directing Jabba the Hutt like?

"I was miked to the people inside, and the mike frequently broke down. They were miked back to the outside onto the P.A. system in the studio so people could hear them. In fact, one guy also actually spoke Jabba's dialogue so that the actors could hear their cues."

How did the actors react to Jabba?

"Jabba is so totally lifelike that you can act with him. I mean, he looks so grotesque and revolting that I think an actor can deliver his lines quite well. The problem is that you've got me yelling at him all the time—telling him what his reactions are, whether they are really coming across.

There were times when I would say, 'Turn the head, look down, look up, look more around, more around, look left, wave your arm, throw the mug.' If I hadn't, the people inside wouldn't really have been able to function properly.

"They had an annotated script, but the space inside Jabba is very constricted—just impossible. But that doesn't really work as well as telling them exactly when the cues come. The figure cannot operate as quickly as a human being. Human beings work on their time frame, their reactions, and their speech; Jabba is this lumbering, slow-moving thing."

How did Carrie Fisher feel about working with him?

"She loved Jabba. She just adored him. She was great. Her scenes with Jabba are terrific. That's a good example of there being a lot in Jabba that an actor can use, even if he's not getting a lot of immediate feedback. I was just worried for her because the chain that goes around her neck and that he holds is very tight. The guys inside couldn't pull the chain properly because they couldn't grasp with the three-fingered hand very well. So I told them 'Well, just hold the chain and try to keep it taut.' Carrie had to lean forward to keep the chain taut because they pulled her back. They didn't have any feeling, so they choked her. She said, 'Hey, pull the chain, pull the chain. I want to feel that I'm really being captured.' So she encouraged them to do that."

Stuart Freeborn has also been thinking about the finishing of these scenes. "Every time I finish a film, I get to thinking about creatures, about the public and how their minds work, about children growing up who are very much aware of going out into space, going to other planets, of possibly seeing alien creatures. Out there, there might be a completely different environment with gravitational pulls that have an effect on their shapes and sizes. They may not necessarily have the same five senses that we have. There might be creatures that are 100 feet tall or creatures that are on wavelengths that we could never tune in to. I would like to develop creatures in the future that won't be quite so tangible. I'm going into the field of opticals. So you see something on the screen and you say, 'My God, how the hell did this come about?'

"Moviemakers are going to demand more sophisticated images from my department, not just a case of making a solid mask and plonking it on somebody's head. It's got to go much further than that!"

Very little at Lucasfilm is ever discarded. Aside from any pure archival value, there are still six more episodes of the *Star Wars* series brewing. Phil Tippett recalls asking George Lucas what his ultimate goal was in making *Star Wars*, to which George responded, half seriously, "'To get rid of all the people and have only monsters and robots as the performers.' While we were working on *Jedi*, George said on a number of occasions, 'Hold on to these creatures or keep these designs. We'll save them for another movie that only has monsters.'" Phil says, "I told him that I was starting to take him quite seriously about saving sketches for other movies, and he replied, 'You should, because we're going to keep doing this until you get it right!'"

The filming in Jabba's Court was finished, and Mr. Ziff was just about done with all the creatures and would soon be able to report back to California in person. There was one more trip with a new friend named Nien Nunb who had an articulated head (with a costume attached).

ATTN: ROBIN/RENOWN
FROM: PAT CARR

STUART ZIFF WILL BE ARRIVING ON FLIGHT PA 124 SFO AT NOON TODAY AND WILL BE BRINGING THE FOLLOWING MIG:

TRUNK NO: 158

3 X MODIFIED HAIRDRYERS
1 X ELECTRIC KNIFE AND BLADES
ANOTHER 40 FEET OF VINYL HOSE
AND A DISNEY BOOK

PAT 934756 RENOWN G 897932 STWARS G

Robert Watts, meanwhile, was occupied with the Rancor. Soon, Luke Skywalker would fall into the Rancor Pit, and the beast would be destroyed.

ATTN: ROBERT WATTS
FROM: PATTY BLAU

THIS IS INFORMATION ABOUT THE RANCOR BLOOD MEANT TO BE INCLUDED IN CRATE WITH HAND.

MADE OF: + SUPER GOOP + AND WATER

— WATER SOLUBLE
— PRESENT VISCOSITY HAS BEEN TESTED AND ACHIEVED OPTIMUM PERFORMANCES
— WHEN MIXED, THE BLOOD EXPANDS WITH AIR BUBBLES. IF THE BLOOD HAS BEEN AGITATED DURING SHIPMENT, IT CAN BE LEFT OUT AND THE VOLUME WILL GO DOWN. IF THE BLOOD HAS SETTLED TOO MUCH, IT CAN BE MIXED AND THE VOLUME WILL INCREASE.

1) FILL BLADDER ABOVE INDEX FINGER WITH ENCLOSED IN-JECTION GUN.

CAUTION: VERY IMPORTANT: IF RUBBER CUTICLE IS PULLED OR STRETCHED TOO MUCH WHEN INJECTING, THE RUBBER FLAP LOSES ITS MEMORY AND A GAP WILL RESULT BETWEEN IT AND NAIL.

PLEASE EXERCISE CARE IN PLACING OF FINGERS AROUND AC-TOR, SO AS NOT TO AGGRAVATE THE BLADDER FINGER!

THANKS—
PATTY
LFL SRFL

But the Rancor was yet to come. That, too, would be a difficult scene to film. Now Richard Marquand was still remembering the filming of the band in Jabba's Court.

The trio. Were they difficult to film?

"We had the song. We had *a* song, which will probably be changed because it was a little bit too disco. But it was a terrific song. In fact, John Williams composed it, and his son, who wrote the lyrics, sang it for us. So we had a guide track—which, again, is all preplanning. I wanted that. And they had been rehearsing it for weeks."

Did it go smoothly? Snooty the singer is an incredibly complicated character.

"We had trouble with her wires. I mean, it's agonizing. Because you think you can't see them, and then you see the dailies and you *can* see them. That kind of thing. That was very difficult. Because your plane of focus is three-dimensional. When you film it, it becomes two-dimensional... just a single plane. So then you see stuff that you didn't see before. We did have to reshoot some of her. She's such a star and she's wonderful. When she's shown full-length, she's wired; she has wires to her hands and her back and her head."

Does Marquand think she's going to be a star?

"Oh, she's great. It's a measure of George's genius that when he saw her in the workshop he said, 'Oh, she's got to have some Mick Jagger lips'—which she didn't yet have. So now she has these amazing lips. The lips operate through her long snout, through the back of her head with a handgrip wire arrangement. I just treated her like a little nightclub singer—and was just very polite to her. On the whole, she took direction very well. I'd say, 'Jump up and down and look this way,' and she did. 'And scream and move your lips around toward the camera and do all of the usual things that you do and act them.' I think, frankly, that is the only way to deal with these creatures. They are actually real creatures. So you have to treat them the way you would any other actor."

Does he have a favorite creature?

"I like Jabba. I think Jabba is just fantastic. Whom else would I say? No, I like him a lot better than the Ewoks. Whom do I hate? There must be somebody I really hate.

"I hate R2-D2. But he's not really a creature. He's a droid. Whom do I hate? Actually, I don't really hate you, R2-D2, it's just that you are so hard to work with."

Months later, in his quiet office in the Lucasfilm San Rafael headquarters, Richard Marquand looked back on the months of filming and talked about the hardest scene in the movie to film. Jabba and his court won hands down.

"Oh, God. I think without any question the hardest scene in every way was the one in Jabba's Palace Throne Room. It was hard in many different kinds of ways. It's a very, very crowded set. It's full of characters, so you sort of find it difficult every now and then to pull back for a long shot to sort of tell the audience where they are at that point in the story.

"It was a completely built set—all of the walls were solid, the roof was solid, everything was constructed—so it was incredibly hot. Plus, you have all these people wearing rubber suits, which made it even hotter for them, and they couldn't move very easily. There were a lot of extras and a lot of crew, and nobody could sort of escape and be within call to come back quick enough. Plus, we had all the support people—to give the creatures cold air and resuscitation and food and God knows what. Everybody sort of somehow always ended up on that set. So between takes, the noise was infernal. I used to go crazy. David wasn't really able to control them. It was just agony.

"And telling the story was very, very difficult—because of that. I want great performances from the actors and, on the other hand, I want to get great performances from these ridiculous manic creatures. So that scene was by far the hardest."

But now, the most difficult creature scene was finished. Most of the remaining scenes, even if they involved a few creatures and some special effects, would be shot with actors—good actors are something the *Star Wars* movies have always had in strong supply.

CHAPTER 7

"All I care about is good acting. Star value is only an insurance policy for those who don't trust themselves making films." George Lucas is discussing a philosophy which led to casting relatively unknown actors and actresses in *American Graffiti* and in *Star Wars*.

"I always try to cast pictures as ensembles. Of course, you want good actors. But you want people who fit the roles—personalities that equate to the part. Plus the right look. I saw thousands of people, gave readings to selected groups of people, and did video tests on a smaller selection of people. I kept narrowing it down and reviewing it. Then I did a final screen test on those who remained. Ultimately, it's instinct again, once you get down to two or three people for each role. And finally you say: That's the one!

"Casting is a laborious job that goes on for ten hours a day. It's having a different person come into your office every ten minutes. You try to be pleasant and, at the same time, have your analytical eye attuned. It gets to be very difficult day in and day out, week after week. Brian De Palma was casting for *Carrie* at the same time I was casting for *Star Wars*. Since he was looking for the same sort of group I was, he asked to sit in on our sessions. It's great to have company, somebody to compare notes with and keep you alive so you don't become completely blotto toward the end of the day.

"Essentially, Luke is a young kid, a farm boy, and that was about it. We had two male characters—Luke and Han. I wanted the farm boy to be smaller than Han Solo. I did not want two guys who looked exactly alike. That's why we saw so many people. Actually, the person I had in the back of my mind was Mark. It's interesting. If you read the original description of Luke, it almost exactly fits Mark."

Lucas reflects on the casting that took place almost seven years ago.

"At the end there was Mark and one other actor—a guy who was a little older, more collegiate-looking. He wore glasses, seemed more studious, was a bit more of a thinker. He would have put Luke more in the twenty-five-year-old category. He was more of a college student's idea of a hero, more like Kurt in *American Graffiti*. Mark was younger, more idealistic, more naive, more hopeful, and a little more Disneyesque. The other boy was a mite more hip. I decided to go with the Disney type.

"For Han Solo, there were several different possibilities. I had decided, at one point, not to use anybody from the past—to try all new people. But subconsciously, Harrison always had an edge because I liked him a lot in *Graffiti*. Han Solo wasn't written for him, but I obviously had him somewhere in my mind when I was scripting. I had a black actor as one of the choices in the final pool, and another actor in his late thirties—more of a Paul Newman/Robert Redford type of actor. When I went younger with the actor for Luke, I decided to bring Han's age down too.

"Harrison worked well with Carrie and Mark. The test we did came out nicely, and the combination was so good I decided to use Harrison over the other actors.

"The Princess? It's always difficult to cast a princess. I had older princesses, more beautiful princesses, sexier princesses, and even one younger princess. The younger one was an actress who looked like a princess—very petite and pretty, but brittle, with a slight edge to her. Carrie is a very warm person, a fun-loving, kind of goofy kid who can also be a very hard, very sophisticated leader. The other girl was hard and sophisticated—she really was that way. There was no depth to her. She couldn't play a sweet goof, whereas with Carrie Fisher, if she played a toughie, you knew that she really had a warm heart. So I cast the part that way.

"I also tried very carefully to balance the British and American voices so that both the good guys and the bad guys sounded English and American. Alec Guinness and Peter Cushing had sort of mid-Atlantic accents, not strongly British. Tony Daniels had the most British accent of them all, so originally I said no to his playing C-3PO. I wanted to make C-3PO American because he is one of the lead characters. Threepio's voice should be slightly more car-dealerish, a little more oily. I had the idea of a con man, which is the way it was written, and not really a sort of fussy British robot butler. We went through 30 people whom I actually tested, but none of the voices were as good as Tony's because Tony WAS Threepio inside; he really got into the role, so I kept him."

Star Wars is filled with wonderful, descriptive names that, now, seem so perfect for the characters. Were they deliberate choices—or accidental?

"The name Princess Leia Organa just happened by accident. There was a planet called Organa Major in the film for a long time. There was also the planet Alderaan, which name I liked better. So the planet stayed Alderaan, and the name Organa stuck to her.

"The guy who did those *Star Reach* comic books thinks Han Solo was inspired by Cody Starbuck, although I hadn't even read Cody Starbuck. The first *Star Wars* script was written a year before that little issue came out. Chewbacca was just a compilation of words and thoughts. I came up with a whole bunch of Wookiee words, changed them around, and liked Chewbacca the best.

"R2-D2 cropped up when we were dubbing *American Graffiti*. We were working late one night and looking for Reel 2 Dialogue 2, and somebody yelled out R2-D2. Both Walter Murch, who was mixing the film, and I loved that name so much we decided to keep it. Darth Vader came to me out of thin air. It sort of bopped into my head one day.

I had lots of Darths this and Darths that, the Dark Lord of the Sith. I wanted a name that suggested dark Father and just came up with the blend Darth Vader.

"Ben Kenobi is another name that appeared from nowhere in particular. I picked Ben because it was a very easy name. Kenobi is the combination of a lot of words put together. Not old Ben from *Treasure Island*—nor did it come out of the Old Testament. I mean, you can draw any conclusion you want . . ."

The one concession to star value in the casting of *Star Wars* was Sir Alec Guinness as Ben Kenobi. As self-effacing in real life as he often is on the screen, Alec Guinness describes his stint in *Jedi* as "flitting across the screen" for his share of the "gold from outer space." Over lunch at the Guinness country home, it took all of George Lucas' evangelical skills to tempt him back just one more time—plus the promise of an ultradiscreet screen credit. "I don't mind doing it if it only takes one morning to film, but a big credit would be unfair. I'm gone in a cough and a spit. Suppose I have a fan somewhere who has paid money to see me?"

Mark Hamill, talking about Sir Alec Guinness in *Star Wars*, says, "I think all of us were extremely lucky and inspired by Sir Alec's appearance in the film. His reputation as an actor and the respect we all have for him work incredibly well for the storyline."

When *Star Wars* was being cast, however, Mark Hamill had no idea that someday he would be acting opposite one of his screen heroes.

LUKE SKYWALKER

In November of 1976, all Mark Hamill really wanted to do was get onto the set of *Star Wars* to watch the special effects. Instead, he ended up at the George Lucas and Brian De Palma double audition. "My agent told me there was going to be a meeting about it at Goldwyn Studios and that there was no script. The only thing she knew about the part was that the kid was from a farm. To show you how much

I knew about the story, I was practicing a Midwestern accent.

"It was what is known in the business as a 'cattle call.' Thousands of people sit on the floor, you wait two and a half hours, then you go in and talk. I spoke to Brian De Palma—George was the little guy who didn't say anything. 'Hi, I'm Mark Hamill. I have four sisters and two brothers. I grew up in Virginia, New York, and Japan.' They said, 'Thank you,' and I went away."

After seeing hundreds of possible Lukes, Lucas decided to tape a four-page dialogue test with Hamill and Ford.

"I was sitting out in the outer offices with Harrison. I was thinking, Gee, he seems real calm and everything. I asked him what he'd done and he told me about *Graffiti*. So he knew George Lucas a little bit. I don't believe George had ever seen anything I had done before. As far as he knew, I could have been just some guy who was working at Baskin-Robbins and had an agent. By the way, I *have* worked at Baskin-Robbins—and at Jack-in-the-Box and McDonald's and Associated Press—as a copy boy.

"The test was a scene that is no longer in the movie. Harrison and I are in the cockpit of the *Millennium Falcon*— I think we were saying that Alderaan had mysteriously disappeared. He says, "Okay fine, I'll just take the 15,000 and drop you off here.' I said something like, 'Gee, I've been meaning to talk to you about the money.' Harrison replies, 'You know, I think I'm beginning not to like you.' And that was the end. There was one other great line, though, the hardest piece of dialogue I have ever memorized. I got there about half an hour early for the test, and I went over and over the line: 'Fear is their greatest defense. I doubt if the actual security there is any greater than it was on Aguilar System. What there is, is most likely directed toward a large-scale assault.'

"Who talks like that? I don't; you don't. But you're selling it. I hadn't read the whole script. I really did not know what George was going for. The dialogue seemed so insurmountable—a real mouthful. I thought maybe it was a send-up. But, thank God, I didn't take it upon myself to interpret it that way. George said: 'Just do it.'"

Hamill still thanks his lucky stars that Lucas' casting is instinctive. "If George had had five more meetings with me, I wouldn't have gotten the part."

Mark Hamill has lost some of that wide-eyed, innocent look he had when he was in his mid-twenties and first played Luke Skywalker. Now he is thirty-one years old. His likable, youthful quality is still evident in his enthusiasm and in the sparkle in his eyes when he talks about *Star Wars*, but now there is a sense of adulthood having filtered and evaluated that enthusiasm.

"I'm the one who generally tries to say what is written on the page unless it is totally out of the question. Harrison has this great facility to be able to adapt his own meter and his own ideas to the dialogue. To me, it's more of a challenge."

Mark Hamill is not from anywhere. He was born in Oakland, California, and the places he remembers best are Virginia, New York, and Japan—those places he mentioned to Brian De Palma. One of seven children of a U.S. Navy Captain, he became an intercontinental traveler very early on. "As a little kid, I was always annoying people with my magic tricks and my puppets. My best act, however, was clearing the room of my six brothers and sisters in seven seconds flat. They would run out of the room yelling, 'Oh, NO. Not more magic.'

"I really loved fantasy movies—*King Kong, Jason and the Argonauts, Twenty Thousand Leagues Under the Sea.* It seems ironic that one of the reasons I really wanted to get into the movie business was to be able to ride one of those flying carpets. Now I'm aware of matte lines and special-effects techniques and all that. It's too bad in a way. I get a very strong enjoyment out of young people's reactions to our movies. To them, it's absolutely real—they don't want to hear about bluescreen techniques. To them, those are actual rocket bikes in an actual forest.

"*King Kong* was IT for me. I saw it at a very impressionable age—watched it five days in a row on the afternoon movies when we lived in Brooklyn. I thought, for some reason, that there was a chance of keeping *Kong* on the island and not taking him back to civilization. I think that *King Kong*, for me, was what *Gone With the Wind* was for a lot of girls I knew—leaving you in just a heap at the end: blobs of jelly.

"Reading *Famous Monsters*—some of those magazines—I first said to myself at the age of seven or eight: 'Wait a second. This is a job for some people. They go to work in the morning and do this for a living.' And that was it, boy. I didn't know how or where or when, but secretly, I always knew this—acting—was what I had to do."

First, however, he had to go to high school. He is the only known American film actor to graduate from Yokohama High.

In the shadows of Mount Fuji
Stands our school so dear.
Yokohama High forever
Sing we loud and clear.

"Our high-school song! We had a Japanese version that we learned too. It was an American-speaking school, but the students were mostly Japanese, black, and Korean. Living in Japan was my greatest filmgoing experience ever. The Navy gets all the movies free, and first-run—even ones that weren't released in theaters in the States—plus foreign movies. The programs changed every night."

Because of the nature of the story and the fine print on his contract, *Star Wars* was always a three-picture deal in Mark Hamill's thinking. "I assumed it would be easily as successful as *Planet of the Apes*, even if it did end up only showing at midnight in college towns. When I came to England to work for the first time, I decided: I'm prepared to have thoughts and opinions, but I am going to be the perfect soldier. Anyway, if George thinks you are wrong, there is no way you can convince him you are right."

When the film became an overnight phenomenon and bathed all the principals, Lucas included, in instant lime-light, many people thought it was Mark Hamill's first acting job. "Instead of being a real breakthrough in my career, the film only increased my struggle in a way. But, to be honest, you make your own obstacles. Hopefully, I'm investing well. I now look forward to a period where I can drop out and make those productive and learning years for me. I'm not in any hurry now to prove anything, which stems from a selfish wish to have fun again. *Jedi* is fun, but more fun for the editors, the sound people. It's what movies are all about."

What has he enjoyed about this movie?

"I've really had a good time on the speeder bikes. It reminds me of my Landspeeder on the first one. It's the only time I really felt I was flying. You can't do that in a cockpit—you can act, be intense—but in a Landspeeder you can't see the wheels. I had the costume, the robots, and the desert. If I looked away from the crew, I had just miles and miles of vast...nothing. I was imagining more Sergio Leone Spaghetti Western music when I was doing it. I was so pleased when I heard John Williams' score.

"What happened with the first film was that it was such a guaranteed good time—like a second ride on the Mat-terhorn at Disneyland—that there was a lot of repeat busi-ness from people who looked in the paper and said, 'Well, let's go and see *Star Wars* again.' *Empire* was a much bigger challenge to pull off and was not a repetition of *Star Wars* in any way. Round two went to Darth Vader, as it were, and the movie didn't have that same kind of triumphant, giddy, slap-happy feeling as *Star Wars*. It was a bitter pill to swallow, and I'm still amazed that it was so successful.

"*Empire* was more of a physical endurance contest for me—combined with the strain of my wife having our first child—and the hour trek each way to the studio started to take its toll. I finally began to think, Why don't I sleep in my dressing room? But, of course, I got through it fine.

"In a way, the first two films were an elaborate setup for *Jedi*. I think people really sense that this is the final chapter in the story—so far—and not a cliffhanger. It's the big finish—all stops out, all systems go. My costume reflects that. During *Star Wars* I was in a white, floppy, rag-doll-type outfit. For *Empire*, I was in a militaristic-looking khaki costume. Now I wear the black uniform of a trained Jedi Knight. But the question is: What kind of Jedi? A wizard, a religious figure, or just a glutton for punishment?

"In *Jedi*, it's a joy to reach the point with Sir Alec/Ben Kenobi where I can now express my admiration for him through my actions. Not so much in trying to copy his acting style—which, of course, I never could—but in the growth in Luke's character; now *he* is reflecting the strength I saw in Sir Alec's performance as a Jedi Knight in the original *Star Wars*, that amazing economy of both movement and gesture. I'm a strong believer that, in a film like *Jedi* where there is a huge menagerie of organisms involved—animal, vegetable, and mineral—you can't just grab the attention of the audience. You have to command it.

"*Jedi* has been a lot more work for me. I'm not complaining. But hanging upside down on a bluescreen wire and being battered around by stunt guys is not a lot of fun. I kept track of how much time Carrie and Harrison had off while we were in England—it was six weeks more than I had."

How does he feel about his two droid co-stars?

"I've a fair amount of practice with creatures, probably more than the other two actors. C-3PO was no problem. The minute I met Tony Daniels and did a little dialogue with him, I knew how Threepio would be. Artoo was more of a mystery—but actors have been called on to do a lot more pretending than that. Artoo is like your electric lawn mower—rusty, dirty—you haul him out when you need him, then throw him back in the garage.

"In the second film I had the majority of my scenes with Artoo and Yoda. I was really proud of the fact that, as far as I know, nowhere in the press did they ever say I was working with a puppet. It was really as if we were shooting a scene with two people.

"After Yoda, I thought there couldn't be anything more difficult dreamed up. But in this film there is Jabba the Hutt. He's wonderful on the set, operates very well, but it's difficult to hear what he's saying. It is like working in an Italian Western. You know when your cue is, because his mouth stops moving. I remember one of the notes I wrote in my *Jedi* script was: 'Any chance of speaking in an alien tongue here?' Han Solo spoke to Greedo in the Cantina, and there were subtitles. Now I speak to Jabba, and he'll be subtitled in Huttese. But just for the actors' benefit, they wrote out his lines in English. Sort of muffled and disembodied, coming from the floor, with smoke machines all around. So you really had to be alert.

"I also have an amazing encounter with this 30-foot creature, the Rancor, who wasn't there at all. It was all the old Ray Harryhausen school of acting—all bluescreen and tape measures for eyelines. It's great to have George around; he's like a walking textbook of the perimeters of his world. It comes up in the most unexpected ways—like how big a rock can I easily lift to smash down on the Rancor's toenail, because if it's too large, the scene might get an unintentional laugh.

"You also get into situations where the other actors can't be there physically because of the cramped space. Or you wind up doing a close-up that was soft in dailies, for a scene shot three weeks ago, and Harrison is out of the country. It takes every ounce of imagination you have, but the result looks so effortless cut together.

"The Sail Barge in Yuma is Jabba's pleasure palace. As a native of Tatooine, I guess I know about Sarlaccs—like Banthas or Tusken Raiders, they're just part of the terrain. Execution in the Sarlacc Pit would appeal to the sadistic side of Jabba's nature—to punish Solo and finish me off for killing his pet beast, the Rancor.

"Then there are the Ewoks, the new race of wonderful

little creatures. We're captured by them, tied to poles, and carried along in real jungle style. Rather than forcing the issue, I reason that these three-foot-tall creatures could be tremendous allies. 'Size has no meaning'—remember all those Yoda lessons. I'm a Jedi now, not a student, so I'm cool about the situation. There is a wonderful irony in the fact that all this massive technology built up by the Imperial army is rendered worthless by this very primitive race of small, furry creatures. It's David and Goliath. They form the last act in the movie, intercut with the Imperial walkers and my final confrontation with Darth Vader and the Emperor.

"*Empire* was left hanging in the air so much. People couldn't believe that the film was over and that they had to wait another two or three years to find out what really happened. I suggested that *Jedi* be retitled *The Other Shoe Drops* but was told there was no commercial potential whatsoever in that title.

"As in a three-act play, the *Star Wars* trilogy really pays off in the way a shorter film cannot. Everyone knows what to expect from the various characters and it's all the more satisfying. And *Star Wars* is unique—a three-part story that is meant to be a three-party story.

"It's taken me three films to adapt to the style and the pace. The last picture is going to be everything George Lucas would have liked to have done in the first place. But we weren't ready for it. We had to build—and we finally had to arrive at Jedi."

Mark Hamill is an almost missionary enthusiast for the *Star Wars* movies. Now, after three films, he is only just beginning to shed his young, squeaky-clean image. On *Star Wars*, in Tunisia, Associate Producer Robert Watts used to call out in restaurants to a younger Hamill, "Hey, you, get to bed." No one does that now!

Mark Hamill pauses and looks off into the distance for a few seconds, perhaps thinking back to that first casting call way back in 1976, when all he wanted to do was see the special effects. "There is never a dull moment in *Jedi*.

It should run a minute or so short of two hours. We trim all the fat and deliver it to your local delicatessen, summer of 1983. This movie is fun, with a capital *F*."

HAN SOLO

Harrison Ford was once asked to sit for several days strapped into a jiggling pilot's seat and bellow the word "asteroids" at the top of his lungs.

That he can cope with, part of the job. It's the movieland merry-go-round that unnerves him. "I'm a very ordinary person who lives in fear of being stuck for eternity at some Hollywood party." He is now at that critically successful yet, for him, awkward stage, where people in the picture business are starting to call him names: "a throwback to the old school of cinema heroes" or "a daredevil Clark Gable with a touch of Humphrey Bogart's fashionable asperity." His pal Steven Spielberg concurs: "Harrison is a very original leading man. There has not been anyone like him for 30 or 40 years. He is a remarkable combination of Errol Flynn in *The Adventures of Don Juan* and Bogart as Fred C. Dobbs in *The Treasure of Sierra Madre*."

If he showed his reactions to this praise, they would probably run something like this: a wince, a slowly raised eyebrow, and an even slower shake of the head—followed by that slightly lopsided, completely disarming, Harrison Ford grin.

Like Humphrey Bogart before him, Ford can stand stock-still and "say" more in a scene than most actors can say with several pages of dialogue.

He is protective of his privacy and his life. In the very early *Star Wars* days, when he was asked about his background, his answers were short and to the point. "Born July 13, 1942, in Chicago, Illinois. Parents: Dorothy and Christopher, both New Yorkers. He: Irish Catholic; she: Russian Jew. One brother: Terrence, younger." Later on, he loosened up a bit. "My father was actually in advertising in Chicago. He'd been a radio actor at one point in his career, and I have a grandfather who was a vaudevillian. I was studying English and philosophy at college and got thrown out for failing all the courses in my senior year."

He was educated at East Main Township High and at Ripon College in Wisconsin. "I didn't know what to do after I got thrown out of college. I was getting married that summer. I decided to be an actor—had no idea how to go about it. But I did know that you had to go either to New York or to Los Angeles. So that part was easy."

Why acting?

"I became an actor out of fear. I had performed in a couple of plays at college, and all it did was scare the bejesus out of me. It was the need to deal with that fear which compelled me to do it again. I don't have an anxiety about performing any more—just the normal amount of anxiety about doing a good job. I was very lucky. We got married and drove to California. Within six months I was employed as an actor for $150 a week."

His first visit to a movie studio, for an appointment with the Columbia casting director, was pure Hollywood. "I came into this huge paneled office, and there was this guy talking on two phones, and another guy behind him talking on another two phones. I sat in a straightback chair for about ten minutes while they talked big bucks, big names. They kept switching from one phone to another, covering one mouthpiece, then the other mouthpiece, shouting back and forth—just like in the movies."

Finally, after a cursory interview, Ford was on his way, with a quick detour to the rest room down the hall. "When I came out, his assistant was coming along the corridor, saying to me, 'Come back, he wants to talk to you.' If I'd reached the elevator, I would have been gone and no one would have bothered to chase me. When I went back in, the first thing the guy said was, 'How would you like to be on a contract?' I said, 'How much?' The guy said, 'Seven years for $150 a week.'" In hindsight, he was a reluctant contract player at both Columbia and Universal for several years. He did mostly television, with small parts in series like *Ironside*, *Gunsmoke*, or *The FBI*. "I was the bank-robbing brother or the business brother or the sensitive brother, any kind of brother. Or the guy who didn't do it— the guy they think, at the beginning, did it, but who really didn't!"

An occasional film followed. In one of the first, *Dead Heat on a Merry Go-Round*, he played a bellhop. "The Vice-President called me into his office. 'Sit down, kid,' he said—he always called me kid even though he was only six years older than I was—'I want to tell you a story. The first time Tony Curtis was ever in a movie, he delivered a bag of groceries. We took one look at him and knew he was a movie star. Now you, you ain't got it, kid. You just ain't got it. You ain't working hard enough. I want you to go back to class and study hard. Now get out of here.' That's when I knew I was right, because I knew how wrong he was. I knew that when a guy delivers groceries, you aren't supposed to think he's a movie star—you're supposed to think he's the guy delivering groceries.

"I didn't want to do episodic TV any more, because I was afraid I'd burn myself out before I got the chance to do any decent feature films. Besides, I was too young; I was twenty-four and looked nineteen. So for eight years I became a carpenter. I didn't know anything about it, but I got books out of the library, bought the tools, and just did it, making furniture and cabinets—remodeling. It was great. I taught myself acting the same way I taught myself carpentry—by submitting myself to the logic of the craft. My approach to both jobs is almost totally technical.

"In those eight years I did only four acting jobs, but three of them were good ones—*American Graffiti*, *The Conversation*, and *The Court Martial of Lieutenant Calley*. So after eight years nobody thought of me as a person who had been in anything but these good films.

"What I learned from carpentry, above all, was a work ethic. I used to be very lazy, but now I find it difficult to enjoy myself when I'm not working. It's allied to the problem of not being able to distract myself on a film set. Big pictures like *Star Wars*, *Raiders*, and *Jedi* are technically very complex, so actors often have to wait a long time between takes. I sit and stare at the walls or I walk around and bump into the walls of my trailer. Either I'm thinking about the next scene or I'm in a state of mental suspension—I can't read or concentrate on anything like that."

When the *American Graffiti* casting calls began, Harrison Ford was still "on the tools," so to speak. "I was out there kneeling in the hall, building this elaborate new doorway. Dreyfuss, the big movie star, came in to see George for a picture, and there I was, out in the hall, looking like the blue-collar worker."

Harrison Ford got the job on *American Graffiti*. Later, for *Star Wars*, he helped out with some of the casting tests. "I tested with girls and with guys—Luke Skywalkers and princesses. About a hundred other people for each part, as I remember it. Not many people who were good—which was amazing. First of all, the test scene was offered to the actors pretty much without explanation. Many times they asked me to explain what the story was about. George didn't want to talk about it.

"We'd read the scene. The dialogue is somewhat difficult, as you might imagine. In fact, to a certain extent it defies speaking. Lines like, 'It'll take a megasecond for the nava computer to calculate these coordinates,' are easy to mock but hard to deliver. That kind of testing only has limited validity, and I think George felt that way too.

"Some of the other dialogue in the movie is so on target that it helps immediately with the characterizations. 'Kid, I've flown from one side of this galaxy to the other. I've seen a lot of strange stuff, but I've never seen anything to make me believe there's one all powerful Force controlling everything.' It's real easy the way George has set it up.

"I wasn't at all sure how the first film in the series would do. I thought either it would reach a big audience who saw it as a fun, space-age Western or it would be so silly that my two kids would have been embarrassed for me even to leave the house."

Was he ever afraid it would fail?

"No, of course I didn't think it was going to be a failure. I was in *American Graffiti* and knew George made good films. I just didn't know about success and the orders of success."

Many Solo fans were deeply disturbed when he was left carbon-frozen, fate unknown, at the end of *Empire*.

"Naturally, there are questions in the second act which will have to be answered in the third act. I guess it depends on what you go to a movie for. I figure that there was at least $11 worth of entertainment in *Empire*. So if you paid four bucks and didn't get an ending, you are still seven bucks ahead of the game."

But in the spring of 1982, it was back to Han Solo and his further galactic adventures. "For that, I intentionally keep my interpretation simple. Han is no longer the only stamp in my passport, but somehow he has become a part of me. All the characters have progressed, not to mention the fact that all the actors are at least six years older now.

"I desperately wanted to die in *Jedi*. I thought it would give the myth some body, that Han Solo, in fact, really had no place to go—he's got no Momma, he's got no Poppa. He's got no story. He would have best served the situation by giving it the weight of sacrifice, but that was the one thing I was unable to convince George of. George has a predisposition to happy endings. There's no less enthusiasm on my part because my idea didn't pan out—I just say that to illustrate the fact that I feel I am finished with the story."

Star Wars has a reputation for technical surprises, and the *Jedi* variety is mechanical, optical, and sometimes very noisy. But after three pictures, Harrison Ford finds it puts little strain on his continuity of performance. "It's the same job, all the time. Really no different in *Star Wars* than it is in *Macbeth*. You still have the actors' problems of bringing the language to life, or remembering where you are. There are certain things that you have to do on a particular day, under the circumstances that prevail. You have to accept the fact that acting is a very haphazard business, and that most things are accomplished to the highest degree of efficiency possible by effective compromise. So, you compromise!"

To the observer, Ford plays the long waiting game between takes extremely well, being more involved than most with what comes next. He is not reticent about putting forward his opinions. "I hope I usually have opinions after I have the answers—which is half of the process. I try to sense what the writer wants from the scene we are about to do. I think, 'Does this line help us here?' or, 'Is this line killing us here?' Everybody works differently—there are many scenes where I just walk in and say my lines as written."

He is a serious actor who resolutely refuses to take himself too seriously. "I keep saying I want to do contemporary comedy, and they do send me good stuff but they always give me the straight-man role. If I'm going to do it, I want to play the Marsha Mason part!"

What is next?

"My job is to invent behavior. I would like to do what I'm doing for as long as I can make a living at it and not go entirely bats—that's my ambition. My father spent 25 years in the advertising business, but now he does voice-overs—he's seventy-six and he does voice-overs! There are lots of actors working who are in their seventies and eighties. I like to work more than almost anything. I like to work. What else to do?"

With the next Indiana Jones movie firmly on the horizon and set to start production possibly as early as the spring of 1983, Harrison should not have to worry about staying hard at work.

PRINCESS LEIA ORGANA

"During my very first day on the set, someone described the next scene I was in as: 'The girl crosses the room and exits stage left. The camera operator will have to pan to keep her in the frame.' I asked whether I was to be the 'girl' or the 'camera operator.' They got the message!"

For the daughter of Eddie Fisher and Debbie Reynolds,

a career in show business was always in the cards for Carrie. "Everyone around our house assumed that I would do it, so I kind of went along with that assumption."

Her mother, who sang and danced her way through many of MGM's movies in the 1940s and 1950s, still spends an average of four months a year on the road. "A lot of youngsters don't know my name," Debbie Reynolds says. "But they are hooked on *Star Wars*. I sign their autographs *Princess Leia's mother*, and they love it." Carrie Fisher recalls one of her early impressions: "For a long time, when I was young, I thought of my mother as a movie star and not as a person. I thought she only sang in the movies. It shocked me one day when I heard her singing in the car. I thought singing was something she did for other people, for a living—not for me just because she happened to be feeling good."

Carrie was brought up in Beverly Hills and on the MGM backlot. "I remember Mother falling down in the mud, getting hosed down, being sent home in a limousine, and being paid for doing it. Occasionally, she would have to talk to someone while they filmed the scene. I thought—that's the life for me.

"I was riveted by Laurel and Hardy and the Marx Brothers movies. They destroyed me—*Way Out West*, *A Night at the Opera*. We used to watch *A Night at the Opera* all the time. We got a print of the movie once, got a projector, and ran it about six times. Once we ran it backward for the scene where all the people go into the tiny stateroom on board ship, and then the door opens and they all come pouring out.

"Then I started to like the *real* movies. We used to go out to Westwood and hop from one theater to the other. We would look for the date when a movie was coming out—that's what people mostly talked about; *Ryan's Daughter* was coming out on Wednesday and then on Friday...*Ryan's Daughter* was the first real romantic movie I ever saw. I was only 13 or 14. That scene in the woods was luscious.

"When I was 16, my mother did a horror movie titled *What's the Matter With Helen?*, and she died in it. In the last shot of the movie she had blood running out of her mouth. I'm glad she didn't do that one when I was younger. It would have been a real shock for me. When I was really young, about four, in *How the West Was Won* she got dressed up to look about fifty years old. It was amazing. Magic.

"I wanted to be an actress because you get to wear costumes and make-up. When I was a child, that was neat. We used to dress up constantly, more than the average person, because my mother had all these clown outfits and things. Halloween was ridiculous at our house. And it seemed just as if you got an endless Halloween when you were an actress."

At fifteen, Carrie was rejected by the Royal Academy of Dramatic Art in London. After that, she played a year with the chorus of the Broadway musical revival of *Irene* (starring Debbie Reynolds), gave a telling performance as the tennis-playing teenager in the movie *Shampoo*, and spent two years a couple of miles up the road from RADA at the Central School of Speech and Drama.

"I loved the period at Central. It wasn't my second childhood—it was my first! I was catching up with life. I had the feeling of belonging to a family. In a group of 30 students, there were only two other Americans." Her sense of humor comes bubbling to the surface: "The training helped a bit with lines like, 'I have placed information vital to the survival of the Rebellion in the memory system of this R-2 unit.' That line is actually more difficult to deliver than all that iambic pentameter stuff. In drama school, the printed word was absolutely gold. Not so in films."

She was only 19 when she was chosen to play Princess Leia Organa. "The original *Star Wars* was the only film I have tested for. I understand George Lucas interviewed about 400 other girls and tested about 50—everybody from sixteen to twenty who could still look sixteen. Apparently there was another set of actors in reserve in case we three didn't work out. We didn't get along right off the bat. We carefully psyched one another out."

Like Mark Hamill, she was worried it might all be taken away. "When I worked at Elstree for the first time, I was so agreeable because I kept thinking they were bound to realize their mistake in hiring me." But then the whimsical side of Carrie Fisher takes over. "One of the first things I said was I wanted to have lunch with the monsters from the scene at the Mos Eisley spaceport. I could just see everyone going to lunch like that. I wanted to have real conversations with people with bubbles on their heads. You know— Nietzsche and stuff. Just be very serious and blasé about someone from the Ugly Agency sitting across from me at the table.

"We'd go to lunch at the local Chinese restaurant. I'd have my hairy earphones on. Peter Mayhew is 7 feet 2 inches tall, and I'm as close to being a dwarf as you can be. They'd have to serve us as if we were regular customers. They didn't react at all. That's the best thing. They wouldn't look at us twice, and we were in Borehamwood, which is the English version of Crazy Lady, Wyoming. I also used to go out all the time in my entire outfit to get cigarettes and magazines. Nothing. No reaction. That's what I like about people.

"In *Star Wars*, I don't think George had the characters that well defined. The first day we met, he said I could change any dialogue I felt uncomfortable with. He gave me a lot of responsibility and freedom. The only thing you couldn't tell from the script was the style.

"When there was chaos, George was the best one around, because he was immune to it. I wasn't. In terms of directing, he'd say, 'Now act more like a princess. Stand up straight'— things like that. Very black and white direction. Faster, more intense. We made fun of 'faster and more intense.' It was very specific. Faster you can do. More intense you can do. That worked fine with me. I was glad I wasn't getting directions like, 'There's an amused hysteria about her in this scene, a kind of aggravated lonely.' He'd also refer to other scenes: 'Do you remember how you were with Peter Cushing? Now just do that.' I learned when he didn't say anything, I was okay. I was relieved after that. Before, I thought I was being ignored, and they would go up to the principal's office and say, 'I think she's really going to have to do detention and extra homework. We might even have to suspend her.'"

How did she prepare?

"My preparation for the day was a Coca-Cola first thing in the morning. In the beginning, I used to sit in the bathtub the night before and go over my lines. Like the line in the hallway when I would say, 'This is some rescue. When you came in here, did you have any plan for getting us out?' I rehearsed a reading for it. When I went in the next day to do the scene, the entire hallway was blowing up, so there was no other way to do it than: 'THIS IS SOME RESCUE. WHEN YOU CAME IN HERE. . . .'

"After that, I would memorize my lines and wait to see if we were being blown up—which we were a lot. Being blown up is being blown up. So I would just react very realistically. I liked Peter Cushing so much I had to substitute someone else in my mind to get the hatred for him I was supposed to feel. I had to say, 'I recognize your foul stench.' The man smelled like linen and lavender."

For *The Empire Strikes Back*, Carrie Fisher asked to play the role a little less straight. "Not exactly helpless or victimized, but the sort of girl who might lose her passport—or the spacecraft." In *Jedi* she is even more mature, and more human. "*Jedi* is going to be a spectacle. It will transport you. This time they found a way for Leia to be very nice, but still strong and committed. She even dresses like a woman—no longer the warrior—and she's not always telling Han Solo what to do."

Carrie still feels a little uneasy about all the Princess Leia products: dolls, comic books, wallpaper, puzzles. "And an eraser; don't forget I'm an eraser. I go into airport shops sometimes when I have to wait for a plane, to look for me. There was a time when I used to say, 'There's a lot more dolls of Wookiees,' but there's no reality to it any more. My excuse is that I was nineteen when I started. I grew up, sort of, on these films. I'm still slightly shocked, though, to be an eraser."

The future?

"I have no idea what I am going to do when *Star Wars* ends. Just act, I guess. I like doing films. Although Peter Robb King, the make-up man, might need an assistant. And I can type!"

CHAPTER 8

Jedi has now been in production for a month. During the coming weeks the production will shoot on the large set of the Rebel Main Briefing Room, in Yoda's tiny house in the Dagobah swamp, and in the Emperor's Throne Room. There are also a couple of small scenes set in the basement of Jabba's Palace. The various scenes involve all of the principal actors and the usual amount of behind-the-scenes planning, rehearsal, and preparation in order to keep the movie on schedule. Following is a day-to-day diary of two separate week of filming.

Friday, February 12, 1982
INT. HEADQUARTERS—MAIN BRIEFING ROOM
Stage 5
Scene 54

Today is the shooting of the big scene in the Rebels' Main Briefing Room, where they watch a hologram that gives them information about the force field around the new Death Star and the Green Moon of Endor. The hologram image will be generated by a computer at the Sprockets division of Lucasfilm and will be added later by ILM to the film shot today. The Rebels also plan their attack on the Imperial Forces in this scene.

The scene includes all the principals plus Admiral Ackbar, Mon Mothma, and General Madine. The call sheet also lists many additional players:

8 Calamari Men
4 Star Fish
1 Nien Nunb
3 Prune Face
4 Dignitaries
11 Rebel Technicians
8 Pilots—Orange
7 Pilots—Green
7 Rebel Generals
4 Pilots—Dark Red
11 Camouflaged Rebel Forest Troops
5 Pilots—Grey

It is certainly going to be a crowd.

Several months ago, Richard Marquand had a different concept of how this set should look.

"I was excited about this sequence and about the fact that the Rebels get together to plan their final attack on the Imperial Forces. My concept of the Rebel Briefing Room was a rather beaten-up sort of run-down kind of meeting place. You know, the kind you think of guerrillas having. You don't think of them as having a lot of money, and they have just managed to get a few guns from somewhere, a few planes . . . tied together with string, that was the kind of vision I had. So I was working with Norman Reynolds on sketches and sets, and he thought it was terrific too.

"Then we showed them to George and he told us, 'No, no, no. You've got it completely wrong. That isn't what I intended at all. Your concept of how the Rebels win is not the way they win. The Rebels,' he said, 'win because they've got the best equipment. They've got these terrific, modified spaceships.' It's like the kid on the block who doesn't have the fanciest bike, but his bike is the best bike because he's improved it himself. The Rebels certainly don't have the best or the newest bike on the block, but they have improved it and made it the best."

When Kazanjian arrived on the set this morning—this

set takes up about half of the sound stage—it was still covered with great sheets of plastic. He always thought that the plastic was to protect the set from the construction dust from the other part of the stage. Wrong. It turns out that several families of pigeons have taken up residence in the rafters of Stage 5, and the EMI management, despite repeated attempts, have been unable to get rid of them. This, of course, only adds to the woes of Stage 5. To complicate matters further, the walls and roof of the building are covered with tin and the building is not soundproofed, so when it rains it is impossibly noisy inside—and it is usually cold.

The first shot of the day was a hand-held camera shot following the people entering the Briefing Room through one of the two corridors that lead up to it. The Vista Vision camera was used for the special-effects shots of the hologram image; the actual image itself will be done and added later at ILM.

There was a rumor that someone—Marquand or perhaps David Tomblin—was bombarded by a pigeon today, but no one will confirm the rumor.

(NOTE: November, 1982, San Rafael. Mon Mothma, General Madine, and Admiral Ackbar all have fairly lengthy speeches in this important scene, and it has just been discovered that all their speeches will have to be re-recorded because there are, very definitely, pigeon noises discernible in the background of the sound track!)

Monday February 15, 1982
INT. HEADQUARTERS—MAIN BRIEFING ROOM
Stage 5
Scene 54

The call sheet for today looks exactly like the call sheet for Friday, since today is a continuation of the same scene. The slowest part of the shooting is the work with General Ackbar. In the long shots he is a man in a Mon Calamari head and a costume; but in close-ups and for the dialogue, the head is a hand puppet with a puppeteer underneath. Getting the shots right is a slow process because, besides the puppeteer, there are also hand controls to be operated by other people.

The extras hired to play Rebel pilots and to wear some of the masks were all extremely well behaved. These are mostly people whom David Tomblin has gotten to know and come to rely on for work as extras. Some of these people have already been established as Rebels, so they can be seen in the background; others, who have already been seen as Imperials, can wear the masks of a Star Fish or a Prune Face, for example.

Marquand has some insights into positioning the people for the scene and shooting it: "The hardest thing was actually putting everyone and the extras in the right places. It was sort of difficult to get them to look casual. What we were striving for was reality, and you just want to make them look as if they were a bunch of people in a World War II movie. Just sitting there for the briefing. You want them slightly relaxed, holding their helmets, talking amongst themselves, reacting, and looking up. It does take a while to get that, and you also want it to happen at the right moment. So your actors are having to put up with the fact that during rehearsal you are yelling at the crowd to react, to talk, to look amongst themselves, to laugh...big, big, big moment here...meanwhile, the poor actors are out there reading their speeches with all of that going on behind them. But if you can get some juice going, then the crowd will do very well."

How many cameras are used to film the scenes?

"I had two cameras. One camera that was picking out crowd reaction shots while the other one was really doing the master shot of the actors plus the group of people that they were talking to. I didn't go in and pick out any specific crowd reactions because this wild camera was doing that quite nicely."

All in all, the shooting of Scene Number 54 went well. By now, everyone knows that *Jedi* is hard work, and everyone is trying to be as professional and as hard-working as possible.

Joe Johnston arrived in London today from San Rafael. He will be here for a week to meet with Lucas and others in order to keep the coordination perking between the London departments and the California departments. One of the things he will do is look over the sets—the Docking Bay and others—so that when ILM begins doing matte shots and adding the effects, everything will match. Richard Edlund arrived on Friday, and he will be doing essentially the same preplanning coordination.

Ian McDiarmid was in today to see the optician and have his Emperor contact lenses fitted again. The lenses do not seem to give him any trouble, and he should have no problem wearing them for his scenes. His lenses are the same size as normal contact, unlike Bib Fortuna's, whose are larger and make his eyes look larger and oranger than eyes should look.

Howard Kazanjian notes, with a certain irony, that it is Washington's Birthday in the United States and wishes that he had the day off, but he takes the time to talk about some aspects of the production.

Does he meet with Richard Marquand every day?

"No. We will talk sometimes in the morning before dailies, sometimes after dailies, sometimes during the day. There is no set pattern. There are times when we don't have to sit down and talk at all. A lot of it is just a group effort— George, Richard, and myself—in getting it done and knowing what the next guy wants or the direction we are going in or the attitude. Or how long we were going to take on a shot; or if it didn't work, how we are going to move over and make it a little different so it will work—without spending a great deal of time on it.

"Sometimes we talk at lunchtime. We just about have lunch together every day. So it is like a family. Lunch is usually George, Richard, myself, Robert, off and on, Norman Reynolds."

Does George Lucas make a lot of suggestions?

"He makes many suggestions. George understands the characters as no other person does. He is a good filmmaker, a fast filmmaker. He is like an assistant director, or a production manager, where he can suggest ways of doing things quicker or organizing something or say, 'After this shot start moving the dolly track over to the next shot,' or, 'Start pulling that wall out, because in two more shots we're going to be there.' And he does a lot of the things normally I would do or Robert Watts would do or the assistant director would do. He just . . . it's not that he says it first, it's . . . yeah, he says it first. He's just always thinking as a good director should think. And there are very few directors who are assistant directors as well. So that is what a good assistant director does. Not only moves the camera, not only moves the company, not only has everybody in place at the right minute, but also knows from conversations with the director or from practical experience that the next shot is going to be in a certain direction and starts getting things ready. And that the next shot after that is going to be a wall exploding, so he starts getting ready for that shot. And remembers the whole time that you are two minutes away from shooting, so he knows to bring the smoke and effects up."

How does he preplan the sets?

"It starts with blueprints, and after the blueprints are okayed, then it is built in miniature. Sometimes the miniature and the blueprints would come in simultaneously. Then we would look at the model and know that the actors are going to go down this corridor and that we would shoot in one direction and later shoot back in the other direction in order to make it look like another corridor. Occasionally George would look at a model and say, 'Well, we don't need this corridor.' And that just saved us $70,000. And usually he made every set smaller and smaller and smaller. But when you see the movie, you'll see that the sets are all gigantic.

"The models are usually carried to my office—the office that George and I shared.

"Sometimes Richard and George would discuss shooting angles and sets, and George would say, 'Well, you know, this is just too expensive. Let's not build this entire wing, but instead, put in a bluescreen and let ILM paint it in.'

"A lot of the sets weren't even finished being designed when we started rolling the cameras. We knew approximately what they would look like. I really didn't know what the Landing Platform would look like until we were halfway through production—shooting production. That was one of the last sets. And it was one of the few sets that George said wasn't big enough or built well enough. So we went back and added to it even after it was nearly completed. Fortunately, we had enough time to change it."

What does Kazanjian think it is that makes George so conscious of everything?

"George keeps the story in mind at all times. A lot of times filmmakers will shoot something because it looks beautiful or looks gorgeous, but it has nothing to do with the story. Also, George loves big sets, exciting sets. But he throws them away. He doesn't dwell on them. He doesn't show them unless they're a part of the story. Often, we can give a sense that there's a big set there without really building it and that's all the better."

Tuesday, February, 16, 1982
INT. REBEL STAR CRUISER BRIDGE
Stage 5
Scenes 85, 101, 101A, 113, 113A, 121

Today the shooting is concentrating on the Bridge, the balcony that runs across part of the Main Briefing Room set. These are the scenes that take place during the attack on the Death Star. The call sheet listed Ackbar, Madine, and an Officer/Aide, and called for seven Calamari Men and a few spare technicians to be background extras.

Richard Marquand is working quickly—as he usually does—and today's shooting was a workman-like day on the set. The production is two days behind schedule, at this point, although Kazanjian is confident that they will make up the time and be back on schedule soon.

Elsewhere in the studio, Harrison Ford and Peter Mayhew both arrived at 10:30 this morning for a session of still photography. (After all those 7:00 A.M. pickups, it's nice to let them sleep late once in a while.) Mark Hamill is also here for an interview for the documentary that is being made about the filming of *Jedi* and Hamill must also rehearse with Peter Diamond for his upcoming lightsaber battle with Darth Vader.

Maureen Garrett, the director of the *Star Wars* fan club, arrived in London today from Lucasfilm headquarters in California. Started after the release of *Star Wars*, the fan club has grown over the years into an international organization of over 100,000 members. Here to gather information to be used exclusively for the newsletter quarterly, *Bantha Tracks*, she will talk to people involved with the production and visit the stages at EMI in order to offer the members some behind-the-scenes glimpses of the production in the coming months.

Howard Kazanjian took his usual walk of the sets and departments today and reports that everything is moving along. Frank Oz was in for about half an hour this afternoon to hold his first meeting with Stuart Freeborn and Howard Kazanjian about Yoda. They talked about the controls built into the Yoda puppet and about the script. The new Yoda is not yet finished, although Freeborn swears that the Jedi Master will be ready by the second week in March, when the production moves to the Dagobah swamp.

Wednesday, February 17, 1982
INT. REBEL STAR CRUISER BRIDGE
Stage 5

This morning's work is back on the Star Cruiser Bridge. Yesterday they concentrated more on the wide shots and this morning they worked on the close-ups. The call sheet for this morning looked exactly as it did for yesterday's shooting, except everyone is hoping to finish up here and move to Stage 7 this afternoon.

INT. DUNGEON CELL CORRIDOR
Stage 7
Scenes 9, 12

In the afternoon, the production was able to move on. The bottom of today's call sheet asked Peter Mayhew, Tony Daniels, and Kenny Baker to stand by at home until 1 P.M., and it is a good thing that they did. One unusual notation was listed under props. The line reads: "PROPS: Weapons, Dustbin Droid, Animals (4 rats to S/BY)." This is the subterranean dungeon in Jabba the Hutt's Palace, and how could Jabba be a self-respecting bad guy and not have a few unusual-looking Tatooine rats in the basement?

George Lucas decided to stay on Stage 5 and work on second unit shots of the battle. He is working with the VistaVision camera because he is really the only one who knows what is happening out in space—what is going on outside the Bridge window—explosions that would cause a blast of light inside, ships crossing, possibly crashing, and so on. All this is in Lucas' head, so it is easiest and most efficient for him to function as a second unit director for these scenes. One has a hunch that he also enjoys the work because it is technical, without all the directorial pressures and responsibilities of keeping the entire movie on track. He will probably spend the next two or three days finishing up the shoot on the Bridge on Stage 5.

Chewbacca is marched down the corridor by two Gamorrean Guards—remember he has been sold to Jabba the Hutt by the mysterious bounty hunter Boussh—and thrown into a dark, creepy cell. It is a very short scene which takes up about three inches of space in the script and will occupy about 20 seconds on screen. It only took 3 hours and 40 minutes to shoot.

But there was, nevertheless, another small element of preplanning that had to go into the scene. Kazanjian explains one consideration that was thought of weeks ago: "We had to make sure that the Pig Guard hand that pushed Chewie into the cell was strong enough to do the pushing. The hands on the guards are extended. There is no real feeling in the end of the hand for articulation and movement. If the guard is going to lean up against someone or grab him or push him, there has to be strength in the hand. So wherever strength is needed, we have to shoot it in such a way that the actor's hand, inside the suit, is actually down in the section of the Pig Guard's hand. Then we have to shoot it in close-up, or in such a way that the camera will not reveal that a shorter arm is on the guard."

They were able to complete the scene this afternoon.

It was Carrie Fisher's turn to come to the studio today for a stills session. She was here from 9:30 until 6:00.

Thursday, February 18, 1982
INT. DUNGEON CELL CORRIDOR
Stage 7
Scenes 9pt, 12pt, 14, 10

Everyone is back in the dungeon corridor today.

The corridor was planned a long time ago in order to accommodate R2-D2. The floor was textured but was made smooth enough that the droid could roll down it without any trouble. There is also a sewer trough that runs down the center of the corridor (this probably will not show up on screen) in order to give the passageway a true feeling of a dank, dark corridor.

The other preplanning for this corridor involved whether it should be wide enough for two Gamorrean Guards, who are quite broad in the beam, to walk side by side down the corridor. Two guards will be used in Scene 12, when Chewie is marched down the corridor. It was decided that one could walk in front and one behind.

In this scene a hand reaches out from one of the cell openings and a tentacle tugs at poor Threepio and scares him. It is a fairly simple scene, and the shooting went well. Even the four S/BY rats performed admirably.

Mark Hamill was in at 11 A.M. to continue rehearsing his sword fight sequences with Stunt Arranger Peter Diamond and Darth Vader's sword fight stand-in, Bob Anderson.

Wardrobe is preparing for the big scene at the Imperial Docking Bay, and 30 male extras were in today for costume fittings/auditions. The 30 people are divided like this: 12 men for Emperor's Dignitaries, 6 for Royal Guards, and 12 for Imperial Officers (Black and Green).

Ian McDiarmid paid another visit to the eye doctor for his contact lens fitting.

A small amount of work was also done today on Scene 10, which is the scene set in the droid torture room.

Friday, February 19, 1982
INT. DUNGEON CELL CORRIDOR
Stage 7
Scene 10pt

The call sheet asks the art department for the Dustbin Droid and EV-9D9 and asks the special effects department to prepare smoke, steam, and tentacles. Tony Daniels and Kenny Baker are required, and so are two Pig Guards. In the screenplay, the scene takes up about a page and a half and should run about 90 seconds on screen.

Howard Kazanjian talked about the scene: "The scene is all droids—8D8 and EV-9D9 and Dustbin Droid and another robot that we never gave a name to, a little baby one on the torture rack. The hardest part was getting the droids to work. EV-9D9 is a very thin droid—its legs are almost like the bones of a human. How does he stand; how does he walk; how does he move his arms and legs; and so on? Some of them are held up by wires—and it's a question of hiding the wires and making the droid really look like a human being.

"The special effects department in London built the droids for these scenes. There was a little person in the Dustbin Droid moving the feet as he is rotated and tortured. The Dustbin Droid was self-contained. The droid that was on levers torturing him was standing there on his own. His hands were attached to the levers and his head was moved by wires. EV-9D9, our chief droid, was operated by wires and rods, and sometimes you could see a rod coming out the back of an arm or an elbow. He also had a control panel there that he was operating. It was real puppetry.

"Of course, Tony Daniels was inside the C-3PO suit and Kenny Baker was inside R2-D2. It wasn't very difficult. At one time EV-9D9 was going to walk; special effects said it could be done, and George said it couldn't be done. And they said, yeah, we'll show you. He said, I want you to show me three days before the shoot. No problem, they answered. We walked in three days before the shoot and there was this elaborate rig overhead and wires and all kinds of stuff. And they tried it and it didn't work. And they said, oh, we'll make it work. George said, no, he won't walk in the scene. And George was right. Special effects would still be working on it and saying, oh, we'll have it ready tomorrow.

"Richard Marquand was reading EV-9D9's lines. There was big equipment moving in certain shots and there was a lot of noise, and it turns out that, most likely, we will use Richard's dialogue—filtered—for EV-9D9's voice."

The shooting is rolling along now. This is a small scene, and though there are some effects to consider and the droids can, at times, be temperamental, the call sheet lists the afternoon schedule as a move to: Interior Death Star Corridor, Scene 47 and Scene 70.

They were able to move to the Death Star corridor this afternoon and to complete both scenes there. Scene 47 looks like this in the screenplay:

47   INT. DEATH STAR—CORRIDOR TO
     DOCKING BAY
     Lord Vader strides down the hallway
     accompanied by a phalanx of Imperial
     brass, including a very nervous Death Star
     Commander.

Scene 70 is the corridor to the Emperor's tower and the Elevator and is three lines of dialogue long. An officer tells Vader that he cannot enter. Vader chokes him and convinces him that Vader should, indeed, see the Emperor.

Next, the production is scheduled to spend two weeks filming in the Imperial Docking Bay and in the Emperor's Throne Room, and then it is on to the Dagobah swamp.

Joe Johnston has been hard at work all week, and today he sent a telex home to brace his department for even longer hours at the drawing board.

ATTN. PATTY BLAU
FROM: JOE JOHNSTON
2/19

8 PAGES OF NOTES. 120 BOARDS. 20 NEWSHOTS.
100 REDOS. LOUSY ODDS. SEVERAL OMITS.

MODEL LIST IS FATTENED SLIGHTLY.

SEE YOU TUESDAY

JOE

(NOTE: November 1982, San Rafael. According to
Howard Kazanjian, Scene 70 has now been cut from the
picture, partly because of the running time and partly because it doesn't move the action along. The scenes of Vader
choking people are now almost classics, but Kazanjian says
that there are lots of other scenes to make up for this one.)

Monday, March 8, 1982
INT. YODA'S HOUSE
Stage 1
Scene 50

Scene 50 is a long scene. It is just a shade over two and
a half pages long and is all between Yoda and his pupil,
Luke Skywalker. Set inside Yoda's house, it is a very moving scene between the old Jedi Master, who is weak and
weary, and the young Jedi Knight, who is begging for more
instruction, for a glimmer, for more enlightenment.

As Howard Kazanjian says: "This is a very special day.
Yoda is a very important person to all of us. His house was
one of the first sets we moved out of the warehouse and
onto the stage, and we are all very excited about Frank Oz
as Yoda."

There are, however, a couple of problems. Stuart Freeborn finished the new Yoda late the night before, and the

Richard Marquand, wearing booties so he wouldn't leave scuff marks on the black floor of the Imperial Docking Bay, goes over a scene with the Emperor.

A full-size head of Bib Fortuna was built, using a small model as a guide.

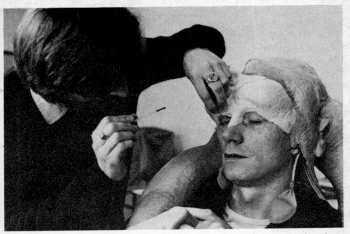

Actor Mike Carter undergoing part of the lengthy make-up session that transformed him into Bib Fortuna.

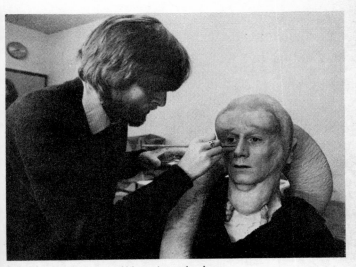

Bib Fortuna with most of his make-up in place.

Sy Snootles was operated from below by a series of tension wires, and from above like a marionette.

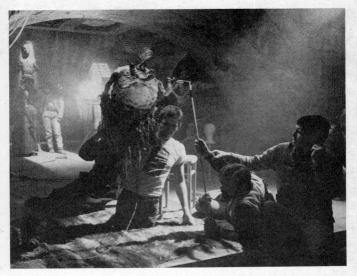

(Top) For close-ups, Sy Snootles' head was operated like a hand puppet.

(Bottom) An ILM technician makes an early model of a Gamorrean Guard.

Jabba the Hutt gets a quick touch-up between scenes.

Jabba the Hutt and his creature retinue pose with Phil Tippett and Stuart Freeborn.

A few members of Jabba's creature menagerie.

(Left) Richard Marquand confers with R2-D2.

(Opposite) Richard Marquand and C-3PO check a line in the script.

(Below) Richard Marquand explains to Salacious Crumb exactly how he wants him to play the scene.

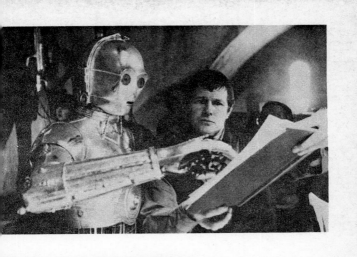

Anthony Daniels and his golden alter ego, C-3PO.

(Opposite, top) Richard Marquand explains a scene to Mark Hamill, with George Lucas on the right.

(Opposite, bottom) Carrie Fisher, her slave girl costume covered by a warm robe, chats with George Lucas.

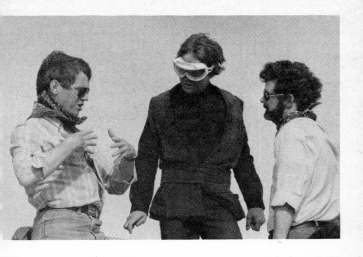

Phil Tippett prepares an Ewok for shooting on the ILM stage.

(Right) An Ewok warrior is fitted with a leather helmet.

(Bottom) The finished Ewok heads, carefully wrapped in plastic, in their storage room at EMI.

The little people, out of costume, pose for a group shot in Crescent City.

Chewbacca and the Ewoks on location in the redwood forest.

The Ewok Village set under construction on Stage 3 at EMI.

An Ewok warrior holds the clapper board for a second unit shot in Crescent City.

The finished village, populated with Ewoks.

Kazanjian, Lucas, Marquand, and Reynolds discuss the Tatooine desert model which was built at ILM.

On location in Arizona. Two I-beams held the skiff above the Sarlacc Pit.

Shooting a close-up of the actors on the skiff.

(Opposite, bottom) The full-size Sail Barge on location near Yuma, Arizona. The back and space underneath were used as storage areas and meeting rooms.

Shooting a scene on the stationary skiff that was only about eight feet off the ground. Note the thick foam rubber pads piled around the skiff.

Mark Hamill is lifted into place for the filming of a special effects stunt on the stationary skiff.

Preparing for the scene where Han Solo rescues Lando Calrissian from the Sarlacc.

The desert had to be kept well tended.

(Left) A technician checks the mouth of the Sarlacc Pit.

(Opposite) Stuntmen and crew prepare for filming above the Sarlacc Pit. The skiff was specially built to rock onto its side.

The Dagobah Swamp trees slowly took shape on Stage 2 at EMI. Luke Skywalker's X-wing was already in place.

Sir Alec Guinness (Ben Kenobi) and Mark Hamill (Luke Skywalker) meet again in the Dagobah swamp.

Frank Oz and Yoda inside Yoda's tiny hut on Dagobah.

The Emperor's Throne Room under construction at EMI.

George Lucas, Howard Kazanjian, Norman Reynolds, and Richard Marquand on Jabba's throne room set.

George Lucas and Richard Marquand look on as Luke Skywalker confronts the Emperor.

Darth Vader gets a quick adjustment from a technician right before the cameras are ready to roll.

Co-producers Jim Bloom, Robert Watts, and Producer Howard Kazar jian, watch from the balcony as David Tomblin, loud speaker in hand readies the actors for a scene inside the Rebel Main Briefing Room.

Phil Tippett administers a cooling breeze to the actor inside Admiral Ackbar's costume.

Lando Calrissian (Billy Dee Williams) and Han Solo (Harrison Ford) during the filming of a scene in the Rebel Main Briefing Room.

The Imperial shuttle under construction.

Sound stage number 2 at EMI-Elstree studios in England where the Tatooine desert sandstorm scene was filmed. One half of the full-scale Millennium Falcon was reassembled for the scene.

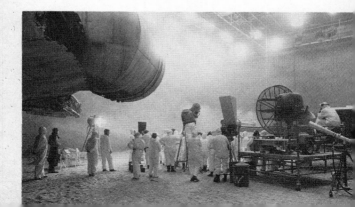

On location in Crescent City, California, which doubled as the green Moon of Endor, Chewie and two crewmen perch atop an AT-ST walker in order to get a shot.

(Opposite, bottom) Shooting the sandstorm scene. The crew members all wore suits and goggles to protect them from the flying sand. (The scene was later dropped from the final cut of the movie.)

The Industrial Light and Magic team pose with some of their creature creations at Lucasfilm headquarters.

(Opposite, top) Two ILM team members work on the intricately detailed model of the new Death Star.

(Opposite, center) A model AT-ST walker and model redwood trees are prepared for filming at ILM.

(Opposite, bottom) Howard Kazanjian holds one of the precisely detailed scale models of an Imperial trooper on his speeder bike.

Carrie Fisher's stunt double about to be launched into the mid-air somersault that happens when Princess Leia is thrown from her speeder bike.

Han Solo (Harrison Ford) and Princess Leia (Carrie Fisher) try to break into the Imperial bunker.

puppet is too new-looking and too green. The solution to this problem was to have make-up age him down a bit. The other problem is with the controls in the puppet, especially the controls that operate his eyes. They are not working properly, and one of his eyes has a tendency to wander over to one side.

Frank Oz and his helpers spent the weekend rehearsing in order to be ready for this morning's scene. There are three other people besides Frank Oz who are necessary to make Yoda work. Oz has a video screen that is showing him exactly the same picture the movie camera is shooting, so by looking at his monitor, which is under the floor with him, Oz can see what Yoda looks like and how he is doing.

Though complicated, it is a small scene in terms of crew members, actors, and special effects people, and it gives the production a chance to take a deep breath for the big scenes that are yet to come.

George Lucas is again acting as a second unit director and is on Stage 9 with the bluescreen, doing X-Wing Fighter pilot shots. According to the call sheet, he will be working with the Rebel pilot, Wedge, and with three other X-Wing pilots.

The order of shooting is:
1. Through cockpit onto pilot.
2. Profile X-Wing.
3. Over shoulder pilot.

Lucas will spend most of the week doing these shots. The reason, again, is that he is the one who knows the most about how the shots of the raid on the Death Star will fit into the final film. He knows, for example, where the pilots should look, how the ships will rock, where the flash of light from outside the ship will come from, and how the planes will veer off in either direction. All of these very short shots will then be cut dramatically into the final sequences, and it is most expedient to have Lucas do the shooting now because he will be working on the final editing too.

Tuesday, March 9, 1982
INT. YODA'S HOUSE
Stage 1
Scene 50

Everyone is back, crouched inside Yoda's house. The interior is so small there is barely room enough for Yoda, Hamill, Marquand, Alan Hume, and one other technician. Everyone spends the day hunched over inside.

Thinking that this scene might go faster than the two days allotted to it, the production people asked Sir Alec Guinness the night before to stand by until noon today. But they realized this morning that it would take the rest of the day to finish the scene, so Sir Alec was called and asked to come tomorrow.

Richard Marquand remembers the shooting inside the hut as exciting but exhausting: "Yoda's house is so tiny. It's as if we were crouched under an office desk for two days— with a camera crew and Mark and this little green thing for two days.

"Frank Oz is under the floor... with all of his TV monitors and equipment. So he is seeing roughly what's going on. Problems? We had problems with Yoda's eyes. They used to stick, and suddenly they would stick on one side or the other. And because Yoda is very old—because he is not feeling well—you feel his eyes can go slightly off center. But it was annoying at the time because you just wanted everything to be really perfect. Frank worked out some great moves for Yoda. You see his little legs and you see him get up and sit at the edge of his bed. And he gets into the bed and he pulls the blankets over him. It's magic stuff. But, boy, it took some doing—take after take after take to get these actions. We broke the actions down into about seven or eight blocks of action—beyond which Frank just could not go. Either because there is a major rearrangement of hands and things or because by now his arms are dead and he just literally has to stop.

"The ends of some of the takes are hilarious—where Yoda is lying in bed and we get to the point where I'm going to say cut, so I say cut, and sometimes the camera doesn't cut immediately and you see Yoda just disappear through his bed— and he's gone. It's very funny. But Yoda's lovely.

"Luckily there were a couple of shots we were able to do from outside where we actually sawed the wall off and set the camera in. Then we could stand up and walk around a bit. But the main shooting was done squatting inside his house."

Wednesday, March 10, 1982
EXT. DAGOBAH SWAMP—X-WING
Stage 1
Scene 5

Luke wanders back to where his ship is parked. Artoo beeps a greeting, but is ignored by his depressed Master. Luke sits dejectedly on a log and puts his head in his hands.

LUKE
(TO HIMSELF)

I can't do it. I can't go on alone.

BEN
(O.S.)

Yoda and I will be with you always.

Luke looks up to see the shimmering image of Ben Kenobi.

Howard Kazanjian explains the shimmering image. "The shimmering image, sort of glowing aura that surrounds Ben Kenobi, will be added in post-production as a special effect. We promised Sir Alec that in *Jedi* he could act with real people against a real set. In *Empire* his scenes were shot of him alone against a black velvet background. The aura was then added to his image, and this film was composited together with the film of Mark. But it's awfully hard to get into the scene and deliver your lines to another actor who isn't even there.

"In order to have Sir Alec and Mark in the same scene and still be able to add the shimmer to Ben Kenobi's image — remember, he isn't actually 'alive' in these scenes — we had to do certain shots with the VistaVision camera. The VistaVision film will give us a rock-steady image to work with later. Shooting this scene as one normally does, also meant that Sir Alec couldn't touch Mark or cross in front of him, because we don't want the shimmer, when it's added to overlap onto Mark. It's more difficult to add the shimmer in the lab, but we think that the performances will more than make up for the extra trouble."

Unfortunately, when Sir Alec arrived this morning, he had the flu and was not feeling well. Normally, an actor of his stature would be used first in the shooting, but Richard Marquand decided that the best thing to do would be to work with Mark Hamill first and give Sir Alec a chance to get a bit better acclimated and work on his dialogue. Hopefully, he would begin to feel better as the day went on. This strategy worked to everyone's advantage.

Thursday, March 11, 1982
EXT. DAGOBAH SWAMP
Stage 1
Scene 51

A continuation of yesterday's shooting this morning, and then it is on to the Emperor's Throne Room. Sir Alec was feeling better today, so they were able to go right into his scene. The morning went smoothly, and Richard Marquand moved on to the Throne Room while the second unit continued to work with Sir Alec and Yoda. They are doing a shot of just the two of them standing up against a black velvet screen. This shot of them will be used at the very end of the movie.

(NOTE: November 1982, San Rafael. Ben Kenobi's voice is slightly hoarse in the scenes on Dagobah, and it also now appears that a couple of lines of dialogue need some tinkering. When Howard Kazanjian and part of the production team are in London in January to score the movie with the London Symphony Orchestra, they will redo some of Ben Kenobi's lines with Sir Alec Guinness. This is called automatic dialogue replacement, or looping.)

Friday, March 12, 1982
INT. DEATH STAR—EMPEROR'S THRONE ROOM
Stage 4
Scenes 118pt, 122pt

Luke has come back to the Death Star from Endor to force a confrontation with his father. This is the big scene. Richard Marquand describes a George Lucas insight into this scene: "There was a feeling I had that I would like the fight to be bigger than the fight in *Empire*. And then George said that it doesn't have to be bigger, because basically it can't be. George is very blunt. He said, 'It's just a couple of guys banging sticks against each other. Don't worry about that. It is bigger because of what is going on in their heads. That is what makes it bigger.' That was nice, because then I saw exactly what he meant and I think up to that point I had missed a trick." This conversation took place in January, when George arrived.

"Luke goes through sort of three changes during the fight. One is just straightforward anger. The next is not wanting to fight and withdrawing. And then the next one is, you son of a bitch, okay, I'm going to kill you. So it's three different fights.

"Plus the whole thing with the Force going on there—if he gives in to the dark side he will become like his father, and if he doesn't give in he will probably be killed...it is this conflict that will make the scene very exciting, indeed."

The fight sequence is carefully choreographed and has been thought out precisely by Peter Diamond. There are stand-ins and stunt doubles for Mark Hamill and David Prowse at the ready. With the Emperor's throne at one end of the set and with the Imperial set of steps leading up to it, the fight sequence should have a grand, almost old-fashioned movie-duel feel to it, with Luke and Vader fighting up and down the steps and all around the Throne Room.

Once again, a great deal of preplanning has gone into today's shooting. Special effects is involved because, at one point in the fight, they will have to fly Luke, and then Darth Vader, across the set. In the duel, Vader cuts through the gantry with his sword. The questions of where he is going to cut it and how it is going to fall had to be answered and planned. One consideration for Peter Diamond in choreographing the duel is the amount of gymnasticlike moves involved and the sheer physical limitations of Mark Hamill and Bob Anderson, Vader's sword-fighting and stunt double. The other difficulty is with the color. Luke is dressed in black; Darth Vader and the Emperor are dressed in black, and the set is black. The entire set and sequence had to be very carefully lighted in order to make them photograph properly. In terms of time, most of the scene will have to be shot in VistaVision because the star background outside the windows will have to be added later by ILM.

The movie has been in production for almost two months now, and even with the short respite from the big scenes which was afforded by the filming on Dagobah, the production is back into a major, complex scene. Even though only three actors are involved, this is a major piece of work.

The day goes slowly, as expected, and everyone will report back to Stage 4 on Monday for more work on these scenes.

CHAPTER 9

LANDO CALRISSIAN

"I wasn't going to pass up the opportunity of playing Lando Calrissian. I fell in love with the name. If you're an actor—the kind of actor I am—I like to have fun. I want to do everything I can conceivably do before I'm dead. I'm in these films, the comic books, and now the radio serial. It's Toy City!!! I'm living out all my fantasies. How do you not do a *Star Wars*?

"I may look very relaxed, but I'm like my father—he was a character. My whole family is sort of eccentric, really . . . I think we all have a device to keep us from going crazy, to keep the balance. Probably what you see in me is that device, because underneath, there are a lot of eruptions going on."

Billy Dee Williams is from Harlem, where he had what he calls "an interesting childhood." His grandmother was a British West Indian lady who never gave up her nationality or her passport and used to stride around the family house singing "Land of Hope and Glory." "My mother had always wanted to be an opera singer, and my uncle was a professional musician who used to sing all the German *lieder* songs—though he wasn't very successful at it. And my sister and I started painting at an early age. I think part of my make-up came from the fact that I saw so much latent talent in my own family. They are nice people, but not nearly as ambitious as I was, so that created more drive in me."

Williams played with Lotte Lenya in a Kurt Weill musical on Broadway at the age of seven. "I was just a cute-looking kid." When he was a little older, he spent two years on full scholarship studying painting at the National Academy of Fine Arts and Design. He was also a pupil of Sidney Poitier at the Actors' Workshop until the movie *The Blackboard Jungle* snatched Poitier, who had become his mentor, away to bigger and better things.

For a long time it was a toss-up between acting and the art world in terms of a career for Williams. "I was one of the top students at the National Academy, and when my instructor found out I wanted to be an actor, he got very upset. He rang my mother up: 'Please, he's a painter, don't let him be an actor,' he pleaded." But the heavy cost of paints and canvases forced the young artist to moonlight as an extra on live television shows. "I didn't really choose my career—it chose me. It's slapped me around a bit, but it's been good to me too.

"I was doing pretty well in New York for a black actor—working more than almost anybody. But acting is a curious way of life. Your life is sporadic—you work and then you don't work. If you're a minority actor, most of the time the roles are just not there. Then I went through a bad time. It became hard. The lucky streak was over. My reaction was to become hostile—something I was not brought up to be. I locked myself away in a room on East 9th Street in New York City for a year. It was like going into the desert.

"When I emerged, my work became better. I began to see differently, to understand things. I began to look at life as a whole rather than as just a series of fragments. Opportunities came, but when they didn't, I didn't panic—that was the most important thing."

Then it was on to Hollywood. "Luxury for me is moving around. Everything's not New York, not L.A.—or big cities. I do like London enough to live there a few months of the year, because I find English people interesting, naturally funny. That's why so many great comedians come out of England.

"I had some reservations about doing *The Empire Strikes Back*. I thought that perhaps Lando was just another romantic character. But Irvin Kershner came over to my house, and we sat and talked. Ultimately, I made the movie for a lot of reasons: Kershner, and the opportunity to work with George Lucas. He is part of the new breed of filmmaker, and I wanted to be part of that."

What was it like joining a phenomenon?

"It was difficult coming in cold because the others understood the rhythm of the whole piece. They were very helpful, all of them, and I picked up an awful lot. Although the movie is serious, there are three levels: philosophical, real, and cartoon. I don't have the problem of being typecast as a *Star Wars* person. I've been in the business long enough that people know me—I've presented myself in so many different ways, done so many kinds of roles. Lando is all the things I look for: leading man, hero, and a character. It all works for me because I'm like Lando—he's always in transition. He has to be—that's where the fun is."

What does Williams like about *Jedi*?

"I love the *Jedi* creatures. I think they are funny and an extension of something very real. George has a perverse way of looking at things. Here's this little, quiet guy with all these 'things' going on in his head—and they have lots of humor. He's like Picasso, in a way. I liken George to Picasso only because I think that, in his own way, he's also created something quite monumental."

Does he like working with movie directors?

"I trust the director. On this movie everything moves so quickly. We'll spend two weeks on location in Yuma, and all you'll see is a few minutes on the screen. These movies—the Yuma section is all about action, and I know everybody is going to come out looking super-great.

"Often I feel as if I'm walking through a dream. You see all the things that surround being a movie star, and yet you realize you are just another person who is born, lives, and dies. In *Brian's Song* I played Gale Sayers. There is one scene where I tell my teammates that Brian Piccolo, played by James Caan, is dying of cancer. I realized how well the scene was working when the real football players used in the scene started to cry on each take. After the first showing on television, a man came up to me and said he taped it because whenever he wanted to release his emotions, he showed it to himself."

What about acting?

"I'm acting only when I'm acting. Most of the time I'm just like everybody else—trying to figure out what's going on. I hate to get stuck with a so-called 'black role,' because when you start talking in terms of black or white roles, you're talking about limitations. That's my frustration. I keep thinking, Why are people so afraid? I know that when you hold on to something for centuries and you think it is going to be taken away . . . that's understandable, it's human nature. But a guy like me, I'm not interested in taking anything from anybody. I just want to introduce ideas— that's what excites me. It's hard, really hard, being a brown-skinned guy.

"I don't think of Lando as a black person. I don't think of myself as a black person, or white, or green, or yellow, or blue. Lando Calrissian becomes a good guy because he always was a good guy. He may be a bit of a chameleon— but that is part of survival too."

As to the future?

"I don't want to make a career out of *Star Wars*. I decided to do two pictures and that's fine. A great experience. I hope that George and I will work together again. He really wants the same people—technicians, crew, actors—around in order to keep a kind of repertory feeling going. I would love nothing better. You have to align yourself with people who are looking to the future if you want to get things done.

"I once heard a guy say: 'It's not so much about winning, but that you don't want to lose. It's good to stay in the ball game.' As long as I am still in the ball game, I can make the moves. But when I finally go, I hope the thing they say about me is: He tried."

CHEWBACCA

At the peak of *Star Wars*'s release, Peter Mayhew and

Chewie received from 2,000 to 3,000 fan letters a week. That was a rather startling turn of events for a man who was a medical worker for 15 years, most recently as Deputy Head Porter at Kings College Teaching Hospital in London.

His life first altered after an audition for the biggest-feet section of the *Guinness Book of World Records*. Peter Mayhew's feet—United Kingdom size 16—didn't win; but at a well-proportioned 7 feet 2 inches tall, he cuts an impressive figure. Then Charles H. Schneer cast him as a minotaur in the movie *Sinbad and the Eye of the Tiger*, and the film's make-up artist reported to Gary Kurtz and George Lucas that he was good, raw material.

"I realized before I got into this business that I would almost certainly be limited either to heavies or to large costume characters, and I accepted that fact. For *Star Wars*, I had a call from the production office saying they were looking for someone very big. I went down, met George and Gary. They were not my idea of film producers at all. I'd seen the Ralph McQuarrie paintings on the wall, and the original Chewbacca had apparently been very short. I think it was the fact that I stood up very slowly as George came into the room. He was amazed. He looked as if he thought: This is the guy we need.

"There were two ways of playing Chewbacca, either big, gruesome, and terrible, or sort of intelligent, knowing, and still strong and effective. I think—I hope—that the latter is the way it has turned out.

"There was never any thought of his having a human voice. He's got every other human feeling, but he can't talk. There is, however, a definite language in those barks and growls—aggressive, inquisitive, or passionate—well, 'passionate' is probably not the right word.

"The success of *Star Wars* came as a total surprise to me. We hadn't seen any of the special effects, we'd just been shooting the movie, totally out of sequence, and it wasn't until I saw the first box office receipts ... I had been in Malta working on *Sinbad* when *Jaws* broke. I saw the headlines and what the figures were—millions and millions and millions. I thought, Hmmm, it would be nice to get into something like that. It never occurred to me when we were shooting *Star Wars* that it would be that big.

"Once the character was established in my own mind, Chewie changes very little. He wasn't really developed fully until *Empire*. In *Star Wars* he was just background material. In *Empire* he got his own little niche among the heroes; hopefully, in this one, it gets even better.

"Under studio conditions, the maximum that I can keep the head on is about a half to three-quarters of an hour. It's a face cast inside, which is far more comfortable than any of the monster masks, and the beauty of it is, it fits around my eyes, so I can see everything that's going on.

"So many things happened—like when I was set on fire. We were doing bluescreen. Carrie and I were in the *Falcon* cockpit. They had baby spotlights placed between my legs. Next, there was smoke coming out. Carrie turned and said, 'Oh, Peter, you are on fire.' I was totally oblivious to what was happening. It was a confined space, my head was on, and I thought, Come on, let's just get on with it. If Carrie hadn't said something, there would have been a burned Wookiee."

Playing a two-hundred-year-old creature in a knitted suit made of yak and mohair is physically punishing. Particularly in temperatures ranging from Finse's 26 degrees below zero on *Empire* to 100 degrees above in Yuma. "In Yuma the air was drier, and the lack of humidity made it, surprisingly, very easy to work. There was a lot of wind, so if I turned into it, I cooled off. With less humidity, I didn't sweat so much. It was worse up in Crescent City, among the trees.

"Socially, the part hasn't made that much difference to me—nightclubs and discos are not really my scene. I've been able to buy things I've wanted for a long time—I just go out and say, I'll have that, and that. Every job has its bad days, but all the traveling, meeting people, and going new places make up for it."

As one of the principal "undercover" stars of the series,

Peter Mayhew delights in being able to slip into a movie without people recognizing him. "They think: Big guy— basketball player! Obviously, I came to terms with my height years ago—I can usually get a drink at the bar pretty quickly. But I'm still just coming to terms with being a personality."

What does the future hold?

"I don't really know what I am going to do next; that is a big question mark. But I'm sure new channels will open."

Does he enjoy acting?

"You realize it is just another job and you are getting extremely well paid for doing it. You look forward to the release date on each picture—that sort of thing. That is when it is going to hit you.

"If George goes forward in the trilogies, it's all right, because I am still alive and kicking at the end of the movie. Even if he goes backward, I'm old enough to be around. It would be nice.

"Several times on *Jedi* people said, 'We know when your double is in the costume; we can tell.' It's the same with C-3PO. You spend time; you build up a good character like that. It is rather sad when it all comes to an end."

C-3PO

Behind every successful robot there usually lurks a very good actor. But at first Anthony Daniels' parents wanted him to be a lawyer, and he spent several years practicing law. Finally, with a legacy from an aunt, he put himself through drama school and, in his final year, won a BBC radio award. After appearing in a couple of plays outside London, he was asked to join the Young Vic Company. He was with the company for almost two years and traveled the world "doing rather zany Shakespeare." He was appearing in a production of *Rosenkrantz and Guildenstern Are Dead* in London's West End when he asked to audition for *Star Wars* and won the role of C-3PO.

What started off for him as an attitude of "So, okay, it's only eleven weeks out of my life" has become seven years of considerable dedication to the *Star Wars* cause. "C-3PO is extremely lovable, which is one reason I stuck with him. He is also very neurotic.

"He has the manners and qualities of a well-bred, well-paid, high-class English butler. He is very much at home in any social gathering where cocktails are being served and people are behaving politely to one another. He doesn't like loudmouths, although he is sometimes aggressive himself.

"He thinks he's really rather clever. He's a protocol droid with a great store of knowledge, but he doesn't always take the direct route, which R2-D2, of course, does. But then, he is prettier than Artoo. They have a typical relationship. Threepio's just terribly fond of Artoo in that strange buddy way, rather like *The Odd Couple*. One of the things that bugs him about Artoo is that the little fellow is very pushy. Artoo is essentially a plumber, and Threepio hates for him to forget that. They are basically designed to look after their masters, but they take care of each other too. Humans can go so far, but they have their limitations. Threepio helps round off those edges for them. The other thing that Threepio was invented for was to translate all those odd languages they encounter in their quest about the galaxy."

Daniels remembers how *Star Wars* first entered his life. "Eighteen months after I started acting, my agent telephoned to say, 'A man called George Lucas is making this film and he'd like to see you.' I've never really been a great cinema buff, but I had seen *American Graffiti*. I was thrilled that my agent had actually persuaded anyone to see me. Then she went into the details—it was a science-fiction film; there was no money, apart from the sets, special effects, and costumes. More damning than anything—this was in the tone of her voice—and she said it quickly: 'He wants to see you for the part of a robot.'

"I remember being a little insulted at the time. I was doing quite well as a human being. And science fiction was just above cowboy movies in my ratings. Fortunately, that was pure ignorance. I had nothing to lose, so I went. Somebody had warned my agent that George was extremely shy.

I walked in and we shook hands—and this was about as far as we were going to get unless one of us made an effort. There was a strong possibility we were going to have a really great silence together, which would be a waste of my bus fare to Twentieth Century-Fox.

"The walls were plastered with Ralph McQuarrie's impressions of the film. In a fit of abandon, as if we were taking tea on a sunny afternoon outside, I asked, 'What are these?' George casually began to explain how the film would look. He became extremely talkative and enthusiastic. Enthusiasm in anyone is attractive. I liked his quietness, his un-American lack of aggression. We went along the wall looking at these pictures, and then we came to one of C-3PO. The eventual costume turned out to be similar to the one in the painting. Here was a tin figure, a sort of gaunt, metal man; the overwhelming quality of the picture was one of sadness. He was the sort of creature you could feel for. C-3PO was standing with this little box nearby and nothing but rocks and moons in the distance.

"When the *Star Wars* script arrived, I became very confused. It was an early draft, and I could not make head or tail of it. It was like no play I had ever done—it certainly wasn't Stoppard or Shakespeare. So I read it again—I thought I at least owed that to the man. I actually read it five times. It sounds like hindsight, but the reason I took the job was because Threepio, even in that early draft, was the most perfectly formed character.

"C-3PO depends an awful lot on human beings' reactions to him. It's the human reaction the audience loves to see. Working with his droid sidekick is awfully difficult because, even with Kenny Baker inside, Artoo is little more than a large tin can. As an actor, you rely on the others knowing their lines and giving you clues as to what yours are. The first time I heard Artoo beeping was when I was dubbing the film—they had already done his track. Then it was wonderful, but on the set this was a bit of a problem."

How was his experience on *Jedi*?

"In the true tradition of filmmaking, the last scene for

Jedi was shot very near the beginning of the schedule. Here we were, at the climax of three pictures, and we were only in the first week of shooting. It was strange knowing that we were all together, perhaps for the last time. Who knows? Some characters may go on; some may go into cold storage, carbon freeze, whatever. There was an air of nostalgia on the Ewok studio set when we posed for the final frame.

"I think George Lucas likes to use Threepio as a butt. The basic idea is that you can't knock around humans like Luke Skywalker or Han Solo because they wound easily. I know how easily Threepio wounds, but nobody else does. The other point is that Threepio has not one ounce of humor in his whole make-up, so anything that happens to him is a disaster. The reason he gets pushed around so much is because, juxtaposed against his personality, the result becomes quite funny.

"In *Jedi*, for the first time, he doesn't really have it so bad. After *Empire*, I think George sorted out his problems with Threepio. In *Star Wars* I just lost an arm, the second time I lost everything, but fortunately, they put me back together again. This time I lose an eye under rather sinister circumstances.

"After *Empire*, I plucked up courage to have a meeting with George. He isn't one of those people to whom you can say, 'May I have a word with you?' You actually have to ring up his secretary and say, 'I would like to talk to George Lucas.' We had a very long discussion—about the future, not the past. I explained that I felt C-3PO was a little this and that in the second film, which was slightly beyond my control. I said this character is really created for a function, like a car is to drive, or a refrigerator is to keep things cool. And C-3PO's functions have never been explored.

"We also talked about the problems of writing a script in which four or five main characters each have to have their own bit of action and yet all arrive at the end of the story at the same time. I went away very glad I didn't have to write it. When I received the screenplay, I saw that

George had taken notice of everything I had said. He doesn't always appear to hear you. But he came up with something really terrific for C-3PO. Now, that I take as a compliment, George's way of saying, 'Okay, you're speaking sense.'"

How did he like Jabba the Hutt?

"Interestingly enough, working with Jabba, who is a totally plastic, rubber, and mechanical figure, was pretty easy. He was quite well behaved, because he can't disappear to the hairdresser for half an hour and keep you waiting.

"I think George makes up for selling me into slavery to Jabba because I get to be a deity later on. The Ewoks, little creatures obviously with superb taste, regard me as the greatest thing since fur. They also abuse the other actors, which I liked.

"Sometimes the character almost takes over. When I was sitting on the Ewok throne, I was feeling very much the center of attention because I was playing a king at the time. I found that Threepio—that is, I—kept saying: 'Excuse me, but could we...and what if we did this...and what chance is there...' Very bossy, very movie-star-like. It was like the story where the puppet takes over. I got a pen and wrote, 'DON'T,' on the inside of my hand. Every time I wanted to say something stupid to David Tomblin or Richard Marquand or George, I just looked at my hand, thought, Uh-uh, and shut up. For once, Threepio really seemed to be getting into my brain.

"I think one of the things that makes C-3PO popular is that he's a machine with a range of emotions—most of which are fear and terror! He was never conditioned to be big and brave like human beings. There's no guile about him, and you want to protect him. In an extraordinary way, he is the common man.

"People keep asking how long this is going on. I just wonder at what age I would find it beneath my dignity—which is a great deal lower than Threepio's—to dress up like this. I would be over forty when the next lot comes around.

"I have a beautiful house, mostly because of Star Wars,

and I don't worry about having the central heating on. And it's certainly made it easier for me to be out of work than for most of my friends. I'm not the sort of actor whom people come running up to demanding that I star in this or that movie in 1983 or 1984. I sit at home and wait like everyone else. My career has its highs and lows, but they kind of even out in the middle. Overall, the experience has been quite good.

"For a person who originally almost refused to meet George Lucas because in those days I wouldn't have dreamed of playing a robot, it's all very odd—the footprints outside the Chinese Theater, Oscars on various people's mantel-pieces—that will never die. It's an extraordinary feeling to be part of film history. Even a small, golden part of it!"

R2-D2

At 3 feet 8 inches tall in his stocking feet, Kenny Baker is one of Britain's busier and certainly shortest actors. He is a 32-year show-business veteran who joined Burton Lester's Midgets, a vaudeville touring act, at the age of 16.

For the last two decades, with his diminutive partner, Jack Purvis, Kenny Baker has had a successful nightclub act called The Minitones. They have performed all over Britain, Europe, North Africa, and, recently, the United States. They do stand-up comedy, written by Purvis, with Baker playing vibraphone and harmoinca; Purvis doubles on the trumpet.

"I've had two steppingstones in my career—no, three, with *Star Wars*. I was in show business since 1950, working the music halls in every big city and small town you can imagine in England, Scotland, Wales. Then I did a few shows of comedy on ice. Through the other skaters I got wind of the ice show of *Snow White and the Seven Dwarfs*. They had the rights to use the original score, lyrics, and names from Walt Disney. I played Dopey and met Jack Purvis, who was playing Bashful. We were in it for five years, even touring South Africa.

"I was fairly good on the blades . . . probably lost a lot

of it now ... getting older. I wasn't great at spinning, but I could ice-dance and jump about a bit—the way you start and stop, that's the main thing.

"When I teamed up with Jack, we named ourselves The Minitones and traveled around to clubs and pubs, went to Europe, and did a lot of work for the American air bases in Germany. It was my principal source of income for about six years. It is a patter act interspersed with musical numbers. We sing, do some instrumentals, and do a three-minute mime routine. It gives us a chance to dress up and clown around. It's about a 45-minute floor show, and we generally do two or three a night."

Although he now seems the obvious choice for Artoo, Kenny Baker only heard about the *Star Wars* project on the London club grapevine. "At one time, I more or less lived in the West End of London. I'd run around to all the clubs, either working or socializing, so everyone knew me. When the word went out that someone needed little people, I was the first guy they thought of. I made myself available— you can't just stand and wait, you have to get out there and hustle. I went up to Fox to see Gary Kurtz and George. I was quite impressed. I said, well, as long as I'm making the same money, I'll do it. Jack and I were doing something like 12 shows a week in cabaret. They said they could use him as well, as a Jawa.

"They wanted me because of my height and because of my strong legs. My arms aren't so strong, but the legs are good. They wanted a contrasting height between C-3PO and the rest of the characters to give them a bit of scale, because Carrie's not very tall, nor is Mark.

"I'd have done it for nothing, and a minute percentage! Expenses only—had I known. But who knew? I suppose Alec Guinness must have had a hint!

"It's usually me in there when Artoo is reacting to the dialogue, but I can't always make it move fast enough for some of the action scenes. I can sort of go, 'Yes,' or turn the head to say, 'No.' I can stay in for quite a long time, with an occasional breather between takes. You just lift the head off, which lets the air out. At first I used to operate the lights from inside and I had a hard time hearing what was going on. I only had this opaque window, which made everything seem farther away than it was. And the inside of the head was full of screws and nuts and bolts. I was all cuts and bruises for the first film because I kept banging my head around on the roof. Eventually they cut them all off or covered them with foam, and cleaned up all the wires connecting the lights and wrapped them in a tube.

"In *Empire*, Jack was an Ugnaught. One of the highlights of *Empire* was going to Washington, D.C., for the premiere. It was held at the Kennedy Center. We were introduced by Mrs. Shriver, President Kennedy's sister. We went out on stage with a little girl named Amy. I said, 'Are you Amy Kennedy?' She said, 'No, Amy Carter.' That was a right clanger. I felt such a fool afterward.

"*Star Wars* does give me an 'in.' I can say I was R2-D2. It opens doors. Then I can also say that I was in *Elephant Man* and *Time Bandits*. I really enjoyed *Time Bandits* because it gave little people a chance to show what they can do as actors—not that I'm any great shakes. It did give me a chance to act without being wrapped up in a robot suit or an Ewok skin. The director was Terry Gillam, one of the Monty Python team. He's a real live wire, a whiz kid. I played the part of Fidget. They were going to black out my teeth to make me look a little more wicked and horrible. I said, 'I don't fancy that. I'll just take my false teeth out and do it with no teeth at all.' It gave me a really different character.

"The three *Star Wars* films have been magic, truly. You're paid to hang around a lot, but at other times it's very exciting."

He sounds very happy. Is he?

"I've got everything I need now, a nice house, a pool in the garden, a made-to-measure kitchen, a new Mercedes—which I always wanted. All I've got to pay for now is my insurance policies, and keep the kids educated. They are eight and eleven years old, with a bedroom just full of *Star*

Wars stuff. One goes to a boarding school in Hertfordshire where the other kids are oil people's kids, diplomatic corps kids, from all over the world—a real mixture. They're always sitting around saying, 'My dad has a Rolls Corniche,' or, 'Mine has a Merc.' My little boy says, 'My daddy is R2-D2, shoots them all down in flames!'

"For *Jedi*, they said there was another part for me. I play an Ewok. Nice little character, but it's a very uncomfortable costume. We let the other little people playing Ewoks know what they were letting themselves in for—it was hot, hard work. The tighter you wear your mask, the better it is, because the air flow is more direct. You breathe in through the nose and out through the mouth, otherwise your own air circulates inside the head.

"I think little people are more accepted than they used to be. They used to think: little guy, little money, and no respect. Although there don't seem to be very many jobs for little people in America.

"When I talked to little people in America, the only thing they mentioned was the movie *Under the Rainbow*. I don't know what else they've been doing. Jack and I have an agent in Los Angeles working for us for our double act. I said to him, 'Surely we've got opposition?' He didn't think there was one midget double act in the whole country. Yet they can pick up the phone and find 300 little people for a movie.

"There are still, unfortunately, a lot of wrong impressions about little people. I can be walking around a supermarket with my wife, and a four- or five-year-old will say, 'Hey, look, Mum, there's a little man.' And the mother whacks the child on the ear, saying, '*Shhh*, come away.' That's the wrong attitude completely. All the mother has to say is: God made him small, like the lady who's fat or the man who's 6 feet 6 inches tall. It's as simple as that. But to whack him . . . it's embarrassing to us, and the poor kid— every time he sees a little man after that, he will be frightened.

"If I had to get out of the business, the only thing I can

think to do is to be a chauffeur. I've been driving since 1962—all over Europe. I might get bored, but at least it's a job I know I can do. I wouldn't particularly like it after being connected with the cabaret business. And, well, I can't stand all those early mornings!"

CHAPTER 10

George Lucas has the answer to the question Why Yuma, Arizona? "There was nothing emotional in the decision to come home. No, it wasn't based on the fact that the actors weren't real enthusiastic about going back to Tunisia. I wasn't enthusiastic about going back either. Truth of it is, Tunisia didn't have very many sand dunes. Which means we'd have to go into Algeria, or some other place. The best dunes for shooting are in Yuma. It's close to hotels, it's got beautiful, incredible dunes. In Algeria the dunes are 1,200 miles from the nearest civilization." Yuma is only 183 miles from Phoenix, 176 due east of San Diego, and just 269 from downtown Los Angeles.

Louis Friedman, Associate to the Producer, weighed in with more figures on Yuma that made it seem like no-contest.

FROM: LUCASFILM YUMA
ATTN: HOWARD KAZANJIAN

BASED ON THE PAST 5 YEARS WORTH OF CLIMATOLOGICAL DATA FOR APRIL TEMPERATURES IN YUMA:

AVERAGE DAYTIME HIGH: 85 DEGREES
AVERAGE NIGHTTIME LOWS: 57 DEGREES

THAT SEEMS FAIRLY ACCURATE FOR THIS YEAR. PRESENT TEMP, AVERAGE RANGE IS:

77–85 DAYTIME
52–58 NIGHTTIME

AS INDICATED EARLIER, ADD AT LEAST 10 DEGREES FOR BUT-
TERCUP VALLEY DAYTIME TEMPS. AND 10 DEGREES LESS FOR
NIGHTTIME LOSS.

PLEASE NOTE THAT CURRENTLY MY MIDNIGHT OIL IS BURN-
ING ONLY TO 11:30 PM (MOUNTAIN STANDARD TIME).

LOUIS FRIEDMAN

Yuma straddles the Colorado River. It is a city of 34,000
inhabitants and 48 species of snake—only 12 of which are
dangerous. Even the official state tourist guide admits that
Yuma is Arizona's best-kept secret, which was fine by the
Lucasfilm folk, who like to keep themselves to themselves.
Yuma is the sunniest spot in the nation, guaranteeing 300
cloudless days a year and only 2.67 inches of rain to those
who want to come and visit.

But more important to Director Richard Marquand and
his 125-man team was the fact that approximately 18 miles
due west of the town, on Interstate 8, past Sidewinder Road,
past the Sleepy Hollow Dump Depot, past a highway sign
saying, "Mexico Next Right," and about a mile past the
freeway comfort station turnoff, was Buttercup Valley. Buttercup Valley's proudest feature is the sharply inclined Competition Hill, with some of the biggest and best-looking sand
dunes in the world.

The details of shipping lists, flight plans, visas, and prop
consignments meant lengthy messages snaking from the
EMI telex machines to the San Rafael telex machine.

The number of British technicians required to make the
trip had escalated sharply, causing Robert Watts and Jim
Bloom to confront their contacts in both countries almost
daily with new names and inarguable reasons why these
particular people were indispensable. In the face of such a
barrage, bureaucracy, as bureaucracies will, finally capit-
ulated. Jim Bloom borrowed the Emma Lazarus sonnet carved
on the base of the Statue of Liberty for one of his telexes:

ATTN:
HOWARD KAZANJIAN, GEORGE LUCAS AND ROBERT WATTS
FROM: JIM BLOOM

GIVE ME YOUR TIRED, YOUR POOR,
YOUR HUDDLED MASSES YEARNING TO BREATHE FREE
THE WRETCHED REFUSE OF YOUR TEEMING SHORE.
SEND THESE, THE HOMELESS, TEMPEST-TOST TO ME.
I LIFT MY LAMP BESIDE THE GOLDEN DOOR.

THE US DEPT. OF IMMIGRATION AND NATURALIZATION AC-
CEPTED OUR PETITION FOR THE STAR WARS TROUPE. CON-
GRATULATIONS.

The party that would head west over the next few days
was composed of nearly all seasoned travelers. Nonetheless,
mounting an expedition of this size and speed was hardly
like preparing a picnic. So Pat Carr produced an eight-page
survival kit for the British team, detailing almost every facet
of future life in the United States over the next couple of
months. It contained such items as: Yuma is eight hours
behind London time. There will be a daily laundry allowance
of $4. Don't forget weatherproof boots and sunglasses. Any
non-smokers in the group are encouraged to pick up a carton
of Silk Cut in the Duty Free Shop in London. Some of their
British colleagues already on location were gasping for English cigarettes.

The care-package memo prepared by our man in Yuma,
Louis Friedman, bade the new arrivals: "Welcome to the
Land of Milk, Honey, Sand, and Sun, and sun and sun and
sun . . ." It also offered advice on where to find the best
steak, order flowers, develop those color photographs secretly to sell to the magazines, whack a racquet ball, or
have your spine cracked. There was also a paragraph on
sidewinder snakes that lurk under "wood, steel, tarpaulins,
and Sarlacc Pits;" with the encouraging final advice—"But
if bitten, please remain calm."

Robert Watts was pragmatic. "On *Star Wars* we had a
good experience in Tunisia. On *Raiders*, a less good one.

Part of the problem was going in at the hottest time of year, which isn't a good idea in the Sahara Desert. It was very difficult to estimate what it would cost to shoot *Jedi* in Tunisia and put a finger on substantial enough savings to create a two-country situation, because whatever else, the redwoods in Crescent City were a status quo."

Buttercup Valley is generally quiet during the week, but on weekends and holidays it becomes the Dune Buggy Capital of the World. During the Memorial Day weekend in 1981, it drew 22,000 buggy enthusiasts.

Keeping *Jedi* Arizona's Best-Kept *Other* Secret was proving to be something of a trial, and gave birth to what became known as "The Blue Harvest Affair."

A journalist for a local newspaper tried to ferret out a story on the film company, but was only partially successful. Dunbar Norton of the Yuma Chamber of Commerce told him, "There was a flurry of excitement before Christmas when the news of the film first hit the newspaper. But once the people found out there were no actors around, the excitement dried up. It's not thrilling to have a guy out there hammering nails. What's exciting is to have some glamorous actor walk in and make a fool out of himself in a local bar."

Lucas, Kazanjian, and Marketing Vice-President Sidney Ganis decided that a small white lie was in order. *Jedi*'s code name at Lucasfilm over the past few months had been *Blue Harvest*. So a guarded statement was prepared for use with future inquiries, and copies were sent to Jim Bloom, Louis Friedman, and U.S. Art Director Jim Schoppe. The statement said, in effect, that *Blue Harvest* was to be the official name of the movie production while it was in Arizona and in Crescent City. Described as a horror movie —the *Blue Harvest* subtitle was "Horror Beyond Imagination"— it would operate on a closed-set policy with round-the-clock security. *Blue Harvest* would be shooting in tandem with, but on the other side of the Atlantic from, Lucasfilm's other current project, *Return of the Jedi*. This statement only stretched the truth a little, since *Jedi* had already finished shooting in England. *Blue Harvest* would be produced by Jim Bloom and directed by David Tomblin. The film's release was scheduled for Halloween 1983—that was the one outright inexactitude.

This new information galvanized the local paper, the *Yuma Daily Sun*, into print once more, and it reviewed the activities in and around town. Writer Dan Smith was bothered by blueprints lying about labeled *Return of the Jedi* and models of what appeared to be spaceships. His contact at the Motion Picture Development Office in Arizona reasoned, "Hell, they can tell me anything they want. I don't really care what movie they're doing as long as they spend money in Arizona."

Howard Kazanjian, however, reacted sharply!

ATTN: LOUIS FRIEDMAN
FROM: HOWARD KAZANJIAN

WE WILL BEGIN TO MARK ALL BLUE PRINTS "BLUE HARVEST"—TRY TO CHANGE YOUR PRINTS OR CUT OFF THE CORNERS—SHRED ALL OLD BLUE PRINTS OR LOCK THEM IN YOUR OFFICE. THEN FIND OUT WHO IS "CLOSE TO THE SOURCE" AND TALKING.

WHO KNOWS ABOUT THE MODEL—"ITS INTRICATE STRUCTURE" ETC. KEEP IT COVERED WITH BLACK PLASTIC.

I'LL TALK WITH YOU ABOUT 7:00 A.M. TODAY.

Within hours, an in-depth defense was set up at the Yuma location, and Louis Friedman sent back the following telex:

ATTN: HOWARD KAZANJIAN—JIM BLOOM
FROM: LOUIS FRIEDMAN

GENTLEMEN, AS OF TODAY PLEASE REST ASSURED THE FOLLOWING MEASURES AND PRECAUTIONS HAVE BEEN TAKEN TO ADD ADDITIONAL SECURITY TO OUR PRESENCE HERE:

1) ALL "JEDI" MARKINGS ON PLANS, SKETCHES, RENDERINGS . . . HAVE BEEN ELIMINATED, BLACKED-OUT/CUT-OUT

2) BLACK DUVITIN NOW COVERS OUR ON-SITE MODEL

3) INSTITUTION OF DAILY GUARD ON SITE DURING WORK HOURS

4) GATE TO COMPLEX GUARDED AND/OR LOCKED AT ALL TIMES

5) SECURITY BADGE I.D.'S AND ENTRY LIST NOW IN EFFECT FOR COMPOUND ADMITTANCE

6) HIGH BEAM LIGHTS, MOUNTED HIGH ON BARGE STRUC-TURE, CAPABLE OF ILLUMINATING COMPLEX 360 DEGREES

ALSO, PLEASE NOTE CLOSER INVESTIGATION HAS REVEALED AT LEAST TWO "LEAK SOURCES" WHICH HAVE NOW BEEN CAPPED, TRAPPED, ELIMINATED.

LOUIS
RESIDENT KOMMANDANT
STALAG BLUE HARVEST

As the date for the complete crew to arrive drew nearer, there was a final word on security from Howard Kazanjian:

ATTN: LOUIS FRIEDMAN
C.C.: JIM BLOOM

FROM: HOWARD KAZANJIAN

BEGINNING IMMEDIATELY, THERE SHOULD BE NO JEDI SCRIPTS IN YUMA. WE PLAN TO ISSUE BARGE SEQUENCE PAGES ONLY TO CAST AND THOSE CREW WHO NEED THEM. RICHARD, GEORGE AND I MIGHT LEAVE OURS BEHIND IN SAN RAFAEL. I DO NOT WANT SCRIPTS IN HOTEL ROOM, ON THE SET OR IN THE OFFICE.

HOWARD
GEORGE

Sidney Ganis, on his return from London, made a day trip to Yuma to coordinate the small amount of publicity that would be released during the film company's stay. In essence, this was an offer to the *Yuma Daily Sun* that it could not refuse. In return for its holding its peace during the actual Buttercup Valley shooting, *Blue Harvest/Jedi* would offer an open house to Dan Smith and his managing editor toward the end of the shoot, enabling them to publish a comprehensive 20-page Sunday Supplement issue once the film had safely moved on to Crescent City. It was a considerable promise and, in real terms, a world exclusive.

Meanwhile, the location setup was progressing well under Jim Bloom's supervision. "When we first saw the valley, it was during February of 1981. Then we went back to scout more extensively in June and July of 1981. There was no sign of dune-buggy people at that time because it was too hot. Actually, the whole Sail Barge sequence didn't develop until George, Howard, Richard, and Larry Kasdan sat down to talk about the script and to storyboard. When it got to storyboard, it went *woooooosssssssshh*—it blew up like a balloon! It became a major, major construction.

"The timber was all shipped in—what could not be found there, that is. The bulk of the work force was there and the bulk of the hard machinery was there, but we did bring a lot of skilled labor down from Los Angeles. The biggest worry I had going into the Yuma set—other than the size and the logistical problems—was about the sails to be put on the barge. I had nightmarish visions of a surprise wind coming up, catching the boat, and the entire thing falling apart—about the scope of what happened to the set on *The Day of the Locust*!

"The other big thing was, we were two miles off the road and the area had to be maintained daily, seven days a week, to allow access. We originally thought we could just water the road to get the heavy equipment in and, once that was done, use four-wheel-drive vehicles. That would also limit access to private cars to the valley. But we found out we needed a water truck the whole time.

"When we were due to start shooting, over that Easter weekend, there must have been 2,000 vehicles in that valley. We increased the patrols, and over the Easter weekend I do remember increasing the camp guards from four to ten and having the fire department there on a 24-hour basis. I couldn't see that set burning down—not at those prices."

George Lucas had also been worrying aloud about the possibility of the Jabba Sail Barge set on the desert floor being overrun by dune buggies; he even had visions of the structure being carried off piecemeal by souvenir hunters.

Howard Kazanjian was the calm member of the production team concerning the location filming in Yuma and was always 100 percent confident that everything would work according to plan. And in order to make it work, he insisted that Louis Friedman be in constant touch with him about any problems or potential problems, and brought in Lucasfilm's own security head to set up a coordinated security effort. With help from the local sheriff's department and highway patrolmen, a network of walkie-talkies, and posted signs declaring the area a film location site, the company managed to insulate themselves safely and get the isolation and the shots of Tatooine that they needed.

Production Designer Norman Reynolds had been allocated a million-dollar budget to clear the valley floor of vegetation and construct a four-acre shooting area behind a chain-link fence. The set was a 30,000-square-foot platform topped by a 60-foot-high, fully rigged, anti-gravity Sail Barge designed to skim across the sea of sand. Reynolds will never forget the reaction of his construction crew when they first heard the news. "Building what?" "Where, Norm?" "Oh, there!" It became, in the opinion of Assistant Art Director Chris Campbell, "one of the biggest single sets ever. You see streets and whole towns that are really huge, but for a single set, this is probably it."

Tuesday, April 6

The main party of British travelers were in Minneapolis today. Someone had discovered that they could save a small fortune on tickets by pausing there overnight. Pat Carr remembered a nice incident from that stopover.

"I traveled with Stuart Freeborn. When you carry anything, you have to show a pro forma invoice at immigration. We had described them as monster masks. Of course, when we opened the boxes and got out the Chewbacca heads, we had the officials eating out of our hands. The Minneapolis customs man said, 'So you're the guys who make me spend all my money on *Star Wars* toys for my son!'"

Those at the production office, safe in San Rafael, were, however, chortling. Against all weather predictions, there was snow in Crescent City and there was rain in Yuma!

Thursday, April 8

The crew arrive and check in at the Stardust Motor Resort Motel in Yuma.

The Stardust is on 4th Avenue, which is off Main Street. Main Street is traffic lights, fish fry restaurants, shopping malls, thrift shops, and the Palomino Pony Cocktail Lounge. The largest movie house in town opens only when the proprietor feels like it, and the last time he felt like it was for *The Empire Strikes Back*.

A faded newspaper clipping on the wall of the film unit office offered some further advice on snake handling, specifically about the 11 species of rattler found in the area and the venomous Arizona Coral snake. The writer advised that "the best and most direct method of controlling snakes is a shovel or club, preferably one with a very long handle!"

A box of studio footage, replaceable, but priceless on the black market, was lost on the London/San Francisco trip. Someone makes a joke about seeing a *Jedi* script for sale for $300 on Hollywood Boulevard and another about buying back the missing film from the videotape pirates. The jokes are not well received.

Friday, April 9

George Lucas arrives with his family and the shooting schedule.

In all, nearly 125 out-of-towners have now moved into the Stardust Motel and a couple of satellite motels. (Before *Jedi* left Yuma, the production would have paid for slightly over 4,000 man-nights in the local motels. That's enough paid motel bills for one person to spend 11 years in a motel in Yuma!) Sunnaire's Metrolines 18-seater aircrafts are learning to cope with the flood of commuters on their Los Angeles/El Centro/Yuma leg. The commuters are an interesting crowd that ranges in size from 7' 2" Peter Mayhew to 3' 8" Kenny Baker.

A team of local Boy Scouts has been hired to help clean up the weekend litter from the desert floor for Monday's start of filming.

Saturday, April 10

George Lucas, Howard Kazanjian, and Richard Marquand are in the lead vehicle of a four-car convoy that goes out to inspect Jabba's Sail Barge and the Sarlacc Pit. The Sarlacc color scheme has its detractors, but most of the day is spent discussing the camera angles for the almost nonstop action scenes that happen in this sequence.

Script Supervisor Pamela Mann and Cinematographer Alan Hume take seats in the shade. Hume resolves to remain relaxed. "There are so many people deciding the setups in advance that I tend to stay back and try to make up my own mind on the actual day."

Norman Reynolds still shakes his head in wonder—a

total of $2.5 million for a 2.5-minute screen-time sequence.

Toby Lofthouse, C-3PO's custodian, is an anxious man because the droid's number one suit is missing somewhere in San Rafael. The suggestion that he fell in love with an ILM computer is scotched when, thankfully, the suit shows up on the early evening truck from the offices.

Two stuntmen are injured before a camera has even turned. Colin Skeaping, Mark Hamill's double, sprained his ankle, and Frank Henson has a suspected fracture from a double practice fall they were rehearsing. Testing new rigs and new landing areas is always a tricky business.

Characteristically, Mark Hamill is the first of the actors to arrive in town. He is sporting a limp to match Stuntman Skeaping's. Hamill received his sprain on the hectic last day's filming at EMI Elstree.

Sunday, April 11

Billy Dee Williams, Carrie Fisher, and Harrison Ford arrive from Los Angeles.

Louis Friedman and several others anxiously scan the horizon for rain clouds as the sun goes down.

The Yuma newspaper's temperature chart was not that encouraging either. Although a high of 85 degrees is normal for this time of year, there have been extremes of 101 degrees in 1936 and 42 degrees in 1927. Sunrise is, however, more or less guaranteed for 6:13 A.M.

Monday, April 12

Zero Hour in Yuma, Arizona.

The hotel's Pueblo coffee shop serves its first fix of caffeine at 5 A.M., and shortly afterward, in the parking lot surrounding the Stardust, a predawn chorus of trucks begins revving up.

At precisely 7 A.M., the cavalcade rolls away from the Stardust. It goes 23 blocks north to the Colorado River, then turns west on Interstate 8 and rolls on into California toward Buttercup Valley.

Work on the Sarlacc Pit is still in progress as the crew arrives. The newest recruits to the company are intrigued by a wardrobe box which was left standing out in the early morning sun. It is labeled: "2 pairs Weequay hands, 1 pair untrimmed Wooof hands." The veterans yawn and go right by it.

The space underneath the Sail Barge has been built to serve as offices and storage areas for the production. Parts of the space are an Aladdin's cave of technical hardware— a tentacle-repair shop, assorted ILM secrets, camera trucks, and also a 150-seat commissary. All of this is scattered among the forest of 27-foot-high wooden posts that hold the barge up. Each post has been set four feet into the ground. The production office, medical center, and carpenters shops, however, are out in the open and are disguised as sand dunes.

Kenny Baker, almost submerged in an unexpected sand eddy, cheerfully greets old friends on the crew.

The first morning of shooting has its problems. The wind is playing games at 40 m.p.h., and at 10:30 a decision is made to move "downstairs" to the Sarlacc Pit level.

The barge's sails are furled for the day. Otherwise the whole edifice might have moved on—on its own power— into the next galaxy.

The wind also caused a couple of problems during the construction of the set. Reynolds' labor gang spent a fair amount of time and energy carrying sand to the top of the Sail Barge platform in order to hide the understructure. The wind then blew for 13 hours straight and stripped it back to its bare boards again.

Back in town, Jim Bloom is organizing a room in which to show the rushes. The finished film will be processed overnight in Los Angeles and sent back to Yuma posthaste in order to check the content the following evening.

Late in the evening, the hotel's outdoor heated mineral pool becomes overcrowded as the crew members ease the aches and pains of their first 12-hour-plus day. Word filters back that the last Sunnaire plane out developed a technical problem and the first day's film almost didn't make it to the processor in L.A. The problem was fixed and the film took off.

Five months later, Marquand had a chance to sit down and talk about Yuma. There was a general impression that the location filming had been a hard, gritty, and sometimes unpleasant experience. So the question "What was Yuma like?" seemed a good place to start.

"It was a great surprise for me. I'd been down to Yuma a lot—obviously—and I had had this horrific experience the second time of finding that all the sand dunes had moved. So, now, it was nice to know that we were going to build the set right and we were, in fact, going to spend the money. I had an open mind about the value of going to Tunisia, which would have been cheaper, or going to Yuma, which was more comfortable. I didn't really care, as long as I got the shots on camera that I needed. Once we had made the third trip down and had decided precisely where the Sarlacc Pit was going to be built, and where the dunes were going to be built, and, therefore, where the barge was going to be situated—then, really, it just became a huge logistical problem for the art department and the construction people as to whether they could get the set built in time. That was a colossal job. Huge.

"The first day of shooting I immediately did the Vista-Vision camera shots of the arrival of the skiff and the barge at the Sarlacc Pit. And the secne where Mark is prodded out onto the plank of the skiff and he makes his last speech to Jabba. He says, in essence 'Hey, you are in deep trouble now, Jabba.'"

Was it frightening having Mark Hamill out on the end of the plank?

"The whole set was terrifying. It was a very, very frightening set—although we did get used to it in the end. But the first few days it was hilarious to see these hefty, macho guys all pussyfooting around with harnesses on as they carefully hung themselves over the edge of the Sarlacc Pit. The skiff was right on the edge of the pit. And it dangled and wobbled and trembled when you stood on it. It was very frightening. I was on the skiff or off it or just on the side or on a platform—depending. The best decision we made was to build a second skiff. There are, in fact, two skiffs in the sequence, and we used the second skiff for much of the close-up work. It was about four to five feet off the ground, and we were able to do all the close-up stuff on zip-up platforms around it. That wasn't nearly as dangerous."

Did the actors do most of their own stunts on the skiff?

"One thing that I wouldn't allow Mark to do was go to the end of that plank on the skiff—that was just too dangerous. The other thing I wouldn't let him do was in the Emperor's Throne Room, during the fight on the balcony. It collapses. And Luke falls off and goes skidding way down. I wouldn't let Mark do that one either. But apart from those two, he does everything—his own fights—everything.

"On the skiff at Jabba's Sail Barge—there's a scene of Lando about to slip into the Sarlacc Pit. That's really Billy Dee Williams. The only thing that Billy didn't do is the fall off the skiff. I couldn't let him do that. But when Harrison Ford is hanging over the side of the skiff, the actual fall is done by a stuntman; but once the fall is completed and the character is hanging, then it's Harrison again. He is attached by a very, very thin cable tied around his waist."

Tuesday, April 13

At 9:30 this morning, on the set, an exploding steam boiler engulfs Special Effects Technician John Chapot, causing first- and second-degree burns to his chest, body, and legs. He was immediately attended by the on-location nurse.

Anthony Daniels has rustled up English afternoon tea in real china cups, delivered on the set to expatriates Richard Marquand, Alan Hume, and Script Supervisor Pam Mann, who cannot leave their posts.

The barge's main deck sail rig is skippered by Commodore Warwick Tompkins, who was hired to help mount and watch over the sail rigging. "Commodore" is only a nickname from when he was five weeks old, but it serves him well. He has been in and around boats all his life, but this is the first time he has sailed on a boat which is 150 miles from the nearest ocean. Norman Reynolds needed a full head of sail in 38 days in order to build the barge. It is a job that would take at least four months under normal circumstances. So, with the help of an engineer, a seamstress, and three full-time *Jedi* carpenters, they adapted a production drawing to give the Sail Barge the menacing look of an old square-rigger with modern baton features.

The actual sail making was done by a seamstress in a Sausalito loft. She fashioned the immense sails from 4,000 square feet of new 6.8-ounce polyester material. It was sewn with triple stitching and strengthened by nine-ounce corner panels.

At one point, the Commodore had to clear the deck of other workmen in order to attach the thousands of feet of wire and rope before the red sails were mounted in place. His staccato instructions, issued on the walkie-talkie, were littered with seagoing phrases like "topsail," "aft bilge," and "starboard sheets." His sailing crew of 12, including three carpenter apprentices, were learning a whole new range of disciplines. "I wouldn't mind sailing with them," was the skipper's verdict after two weeks of training. It was quite an accolade from an Americas Cup man.

At the end of the working day, the heat is still strong enough to throw road-surface mirages behind the crew's transport as it heads home to the motel.

Wednesday, April 14

The core production group was up at 6:00 this morning in order to watch the dailies in the motel's Apache room. They also watched dailies well into last night—four cameras' worth, then the VistaVision coverage that is enough to exhaust everyone but the very hard-core members.

Gusting winds cause the sails to split. The shooting schedule, because of prevailing winds, runs something like this: "Continuation of the day (before the day) before yesterday."

Thursday, April 15

Mark Hamill sits in the sun for a short break and explains his morning—so far: "First I was wired for sound in a shot. Then it became a stunt, so the wiretap went. Finally, I wasn't in it at all." That is assuredly the way of the movie business.

A salvage man invited to place a bid for the removal of the set came to look over the barge today. His impression is that perhaps it would be better to burn or blast the Sail Barge down. Louis Friedman was now negotiating to tear down the very set he had so stoutly defended. "I had about 30 parties that were interested in it," he remembers. "The city of Yuma was very excited about making something like a coffee shop out of it. I offered it as a donation to the fire department, to burn down, but they couldn't afford to use it for practice. In the end, we settled on a group of local businessmen. I think most of the timber would be sold as salvage, probably in Mexico. A very strict contract was written up between them and Lucasfilm, stating that it would not be used for any souvenir purposes whatsoever. We also had an obligation that the land be returned to at least equal condition, as it was when we found it. Considering we took away a lot of the vegetation—which is growing back, by the way—it will be even cleaner."

Friday, April 16

The morning storyboard conference held by Richard Marquand, David Tomblin, and George Lucas has become a regular feature of life at the Pueblo coffee shop counter, and they were huddled there this morning, carefully going over the boards.

The *Yuma Sun*'s two newspapermen dropped by again today, "just checking." Sidney Ganis is in town, so they get their money's worth of Lucasfilm background briefing.

After a slow Friday of special-effects stutters and nagging shadow problems, George Lucas gets the best-quote award: "Today there have been better weeks."

Saturday, April 17—Punish the Innocent

Enough word on *Jedi* has leaked out so that fans have begun to show up in Yuma and at the location. Some of the faithful fans at the gate have traveled 300 miles round trip just on the strength of a rumor. One girl wears a T-shirt which reads, "R2-D2 is a Four Letter Word." Another fan has seen *Star Wars* 80 times. His friends don't rate him that unusual for seeing the movie that many times. The *Star Wars* grapevine is astonishing. They knew about Luke and Darth Vader's father-son relationship well before *Empire* came out. "It's a hobby. It's like a party. We all get together," one explains. They attend conventions, read Japanese magazines, and screen British trailers. They know the screen credits by heart. Associate Producer Robert Watts, who claims he's never had a decent picture published, was recognized immediately by some of the people gathered there.

Since he felt they didn't know him, Richard Marquand stepped aside politely to reveal Boba Fett when a few fans waved at them from a distance. "No, no, *you!*" they cried in unison to Marquand.

The sand gets everywhere. Almost half a pound was vacuumed out of the high-tech film magazines in the cameras. Even light is not supposed to penetrate that far inside the camera. No one is quite sure how the sand works its way inside. Director Richard Marquand, in protective goggles with a handkerchief tied around his face, is a dead ringer for a World War II desert general.

Inside the Sarlacc Pit, Mechanical Effects Supervisor Kit West and Special Effects Supervisor Roy Arborgast have convinced themselves that simple is best. After one grain of sand choked the whole hydraulic system, the tentacles are now operated from beneath by six men with poles and wires.

Director Marquand does not remember the Sarlacc Pit fondly. "Oh, I hated it. God. Well, it's a very ugly sort of creature, which is terrific. I mean, it looks exactly the way you want it to look—absolutely disgusting. It's the mouth and tentacles, with all these horrid razor-sharp teeth all around. But the damn thing kept on getting covered in sand all the time because it's at the bottom of the pit. That was inevitable. So we had to build a little sort of rim above the lips of the Sarlacc where a guy could get out with a high-powered air blower and keep blowing the sand off it.

"Then the Sarlacc's got these big flaps, sort of like a three-section valve, which is its huge mouth. These flaps are supposed to pulsate. So each time anybody falls in, of course, he knocks them apart and the flaps get torn and they flap around. And then they have to be fixed. It was very tedious, but the effect looks wonderful in the movie."

Most things boil down to money. Although it is hard to

guess, George Lucas is a man with about $32 million on his mind as he leans nonchalantly over the retaining rail of the 60-foot-high Sail Barge poop deck. Far below him, it will probably cost $1,000 in additional costs for one stunt-man to hang harnessed over the pit in order to get the shot that the film needs.

Taking lunch at 2:00 is also a complicated matter, because an early start on the day means the meal break occurs after a certain number of hours, and each union shop has its own protocol for breaks and lunch. Production Manager Bob Brown, Jim Bloom, and Robert Watts will later check time sheets from the Los Angeles Local, the San Francisco Local, the United Kingdom contingent, the ILM delegation, and the Teamster imports from Phoenix and Tucson to make sure everything is billed properly.

The day ends in hoots of laughter when a technician is summoned by two-way radio to the gate where a lady is waiting with a baby in her arms. Has anyone been here that long?

Sunday, April 18

And on the seventh day they rested. At cookouts, on the golf course, or by the pool. Several set off for Havasu Lake, where the man who bought London Bridge has rebuilt it stone by stone. Producer Howard Kazanjian crossed the border and did Mexico in 12 minutes flat.

Richard Marquand answers the question: Have you done a lot of this kind of action work?

"Quite a bit. Because a lot of television relies on it. I enjoy it, it's good fun to do. It's very time-consuming—getting it right. Because you just dare not endanger anybody. We had one terrible accident on the skiff, in fact. It's the scene where bombs are going off and the whole skiff is being blasted. Suddenly Chewie burst into flames. Luckily, somebody spotted it. I didn't. Suddenly you see that he is ablaze. It was a piece of spark, because it is so dry out there. Luckily, we got the fire out and he wasn't hurt."

Did you have most of the Tatooine scenes storyboarded?

"It was all storyboarded, and everything went very much according to our design. It had to. You cannot do it any other way, because it's such a complicated sequence. Luke is fighting his way through two skiffs and up onto the deck of the barge to rescue Leia. Lando is fighting a skiff guard, and he falls off and is about to slip into the Sarlacc Pit. Boba Fett lands on the skiff, and Han, completely by accident, happens to hit his backpack, which explodes. Boba Fett sails off into the wild blue yonder and then plummets into the Sarlacc Pit. Han pulls himself together, manages to realize where Lando is, and hangs over the edge to pull Lando up from the pit. During all this, Chewie is wounded, and he is sort of groveling around and making a terrible fuss. Then Luke and Leia come back from Jabba's barge— the whole scene is all incredibly complicated. So if you don't follow the storyboards, you just wouldn't get anywhere—you'd just be sunk.

"It's one of the most expensive sequences for its length in the history of motion pictures."

Monday, April 19

A group of visitors arrived from Marin County. Financial Controller Ron Hein, Merchandising Vice-President Maggie Young, and George Lucas' Executive Assistant Jane Bay get their first chance to see what all the fuss is about. *Jedi* has been occupying their minds for the past two years, and continues to do so for the next three years. They have journeyed to the desert to see the barge.

The breezes from the south are gusting up to 45 mph, according to the wind-speed device that is located in the

Sail Barge aft bilge. The wind causes the horizons to disappear and reappear. Even with the telegraph pole foundations that are driven eight to ten feet down into the sand for support, the barge still shudders occasionally.

Remarkably, since the first construction worker set foot on the site on December 13, there have been no serious accidents. Even during the construction phase of the barge, when the workers were dangling from a 60-foot crane and grappling with sheets of wind-whipped plywood, the crew remained safe.

The shooting crew is working on the ground level today. They are filming extreme close-ups of Mark Hamill walking the plank and of the assorted somersaults that his stuntman, Colin Skeaping, executes on the end of the plank.

Howard Kazanjian manages a bleak smile as he watches a lot of expensive hardware and manpower sitting idle. "It's my responsibility the wind is blowing today," he says. "It's been blowing like this for thousands of years. But today, it's my fault."

An ancient Ford tractor chugs out of the gloom with an Ernest Hemingway look-alike in the driver's seat. "Should blow out in a week. It's worse in the next valley," he says, after he comes to a halt. His name is W. A. (Bill) Pender, and he has been out in the dunes since 1926. In the early days, movie crews from Paramount, Fox, and RKO were regulars in the dunes. Bill Pender supplied them with trees, burros, chickens, or whatever else he could scare up for them. Mules were used to drag in the equipment for the first pictures shot here. Big films have dried up a bit recently, he observed; now it is the turn of the three-day television commercials. Of the 95 movies he has worked on, he remembers the three versions of *Beau Geste*. Bob Hope, Bing Crosby, and Dorothy Lamour also took this road to both Zanzibar and Morocco. Pender has learned how to deal with reporters—and he has quite enjoyed keeping up the *Blue Harvest* smoke screen.

It was a good day for the two visitors/reporters from the *Yuma Daily Sun* who accompanied the caravan to the location today. The severe winds brought the company to a standstill for three and a half hours, one of which the newspapermen spent in conversation with George Lucas. He explained his side of the *Blue Harvest* affair to them. "The whole reason for doing it under another name is just not to make it that important. It's very easy to draw people, a lot of people, say 3,000 or 4,000 out there. We really want to get on with our work and get the job done.

"Again, part of the secrecy comes from wanting the audience to have a little bit of surprise. We kept Yoda a secret for a long time. So when people went to see *Empire*, it was a surprise to them, he sort of came out of nowhere, and it was a big thrill. If you printed the end of an Agatha Christie novel in *The New York Times* and said, 'This is who did it,' everybody would resent it."

Both Carrie Fisher and Mark Hamill also had time to reflect on their last appearances as Princess Leia and Luke Skywalker. Carrie said, "The film being the star—I'm used to that. Being sort of not guilty by association—but famous by association. If the film wasn't the star, then no one would know who the hell we were!" Mark Hamill was equally frank: "I'm an old kid, but too young to be a grown-up. It's really kind of an odd situation. If the audience cheers when I do this or that, it's really for Luke, not for me. On stage I know it's for me."

Thursday, April 22

The high winds are replaced by a collective sigh of relief because it is calmer today. The dummy sand dune over the production office collapsed, and the set's main platform was stripped bare of its sand cover. So, once more, sand was hauled back up to cover it. An ironic note was sounded when, at the same time, a bill for $2,800 worth of sand which was used on the Stage 2 desert set arrived at the studio in Borehamwood.

Billy Dee Williams has been out on the location since the start of the day, "standing by to stand by," as he wryly puts it.

Friday, April 23

The rumor in the coffee shop is that the production will push for a finish by tomorrow evening. With three cameras on every shot and six on some of the shots, Sean Barton will have his work cut out for him back at the San Rafael editing facilities.

As the Jabba the Hutt Sail Barge sequence nears port, a full set of sails is aloft all day. R2-D2 malfunctions when he is asked to fire his master's lightsaber to him. Patience and more takes get it right.

Luke Skywalker has a few spare moments, and he causes quite a flurry outside the fence when he wanders over to sign a few autographs.

Finally, the last shot is finished. Everyone tumbles into the cars and buses and trucks and heads back to the haven of the Stardust Motor Resort Motel.

Saturday, April 24

Call sheet Number 71. A second unit group will stay on for three days to redo a couple of the stunts. Mark Hamill now helpfully offers to take the late, late plane out so that Still Photographer Ralph Nelson can finish a setup shot with the skiff guard on the top deck of the Sail Barge.

A private charter stands by to whisk part of the team to Burbank, San Francisco, and points north while the production trucks begin a 24-hour drive to Crescent City. The rest of the company shakes the sand out of its shoes and begins to pack. At 4 A.M., however, the hot tub is still very busy.

Richard Marquand answers the question: How was it being British and being in small-town America? "Our guys loved it. Because all film people talk the same language and all crews are pretty outrageous, pretty extroverted kinds of characters. You know, they ride in like cowboys—whether they are cockneys or Americans.

"I didn't see much of it. I used to get back from the dailies about 10 P.M., have a sandwich, and fall asleep. And then I'd be up at 5:00 in the morning, have breakfast, and go right out to the location."

Marquand didn't socialize much, but he remembers a few good moments. "The best thing was seeing Chewbacca, Peter, out with Artoo, Kenny, walking across the road. That caused a little disturbance. That was when people began to say, 'You're not shooting *Blue Harvest*. Come on, you're shooting *Star Wars*.' And then one night some kids kept asking Carrie Fisher where Carrie Fisher was. And Carrie replied, 'What do you mean? A lot of people take me for Carrie Fisher. Why do they do that? Who is she?'

"She pulled it off wonderfully. Carrie has a terrific English accent, so she stopped me as I was walking past with my wife and she asked, 'Do you know who Carrie Fisher is?' And I said, 'No, why?' And she said, 'Well, I don't know. But these girls here keep asking for Carrie Fisher. Somebody's making a film here . . . do you know about it?' And I said, 'No, I don't know anything about that.'"

After receiving clearance to fly over Edwards Air Force Base—the shuttle landing site—and skimming an offshore lighthouse, the fully loaded plane came to an abrupt halt on the Crescent City airstrip.

The next location, for two more weeks of shooting, is the giant redwood forest near Crescent City, California.

CHAPTER 11

Bringing your own hanging vines from England to the largest forest of redwood trees in America—in the world—is a close cousin to that old idea of sending refrigerators to the Eskimos. But the set for the Green Moon of Endor needed vines, and Norman Reynolds, Set Dresser Michael Ford, and Prop Master Peter Hancock had to provide them. They also probably had a sentimental attachment to the vines, which are called "old man's beard," since the plants had already appeared in both *Empire* and *Raiders*.

Pat Carr sent off a telex to Lata Ryan in San Rafael about the vines:

897932 STWARS G

TO: LATA
FROM: PAT

12/11

RE THE PLANTS PROPS ARE PACKING INTO THE NEXT SEA CONTAINER: THE ANSWERS YOU SHOULD FILL IN ON U.S. DEPT OF AGRICULTURE FORM NO 587 ARE AS FOLLOWS:

COUNTRY OF ORIGIN: ENGLAND

QUANTITY AND DESCRIPTION OF PLANTS: 400 x 30 FT. LENGTHS OF (BOTANICAL NAME) 'TILLANDSIA'—PART OF THE CLEMATIS FAMILY. KNOWN COMMONLY IN ENGLAND AS 'OLD MAN'S BEARD.'

NOTE: THESE ARE CUTTINGS WITH NO ROOTS OR SOIL.

THEY WILL BE COMING BY SEA FREIGHT AND THE U.S. PORT OF ARRIVAL WILL BE OAKLAND.

THIS SHOULD ANSWER ALL QUESTIONS.

REGARDS

PAT

The second telex between Lata and Pat concerned the fully grown principal Ewok, Wicket:

897932 STWARS G
ATTN: LATA
FROM: PAT

WICKET'S MEASUREMENTS:

NECK TO CROTCH	21 INCHES
COLLAR BACK TO FLOOR	33 INCHES
HIP TO FLOOR	20 INCHES
KNEE TO FLOOR	11 INCHES
HEIGHT	3 FOOT 8 INCHES
CHEST	31 INCHES
HIPS	32 INCHES
INSIDE LEG	13 AND A HALF INCHES
TONGUE	ONE AND A HALF INCHES

Had the good folks of Smith River and Crescent City, California (two small towns perched on the very corner of Northern California), seen either of these routine *Jedi* telexes, they could not have known what was about to invade their quiet corner of the world. But magic or chaos—depending on which way you look at it—in the form of 71 movie crew members, 40 little people, actors, actresses, directors, producers, and all the paraphernalia that accompany a movie on location, was about to descend on them. Pacific Express BAC 1, Charter Flight Number 11, was due to arrive on April 25 in Crescent City. Co-Producer Jim Bloom, waiting with a convoy of cars at the edge of the landing field, remembers the arrival.

"They told us beforehand that a plane of this size had never landed at the field before. The film crew of 71 people was due at about 10 or 11 o'clock. It was Sunday morning and a bit foggy. If you looked up into the sun, you could just see, through the high fog, the outline of this jet coming in to check out the airport. It flew over once. Then five minutes later it passed over again. The local pilot we were using to shuttle our film back and forth to Los Angeles came out and said, 'They're landing on the wrong runway.' I asked him what he meant. 'Well, we have two runways. The right one is the long one and the left one is the short one. I don't know how he's going to stop the plane in time.'

"I thought, I've got a whole crew on that plane—God forbid there will be an accident. Down comes this big jet, and I have never in my life seen one screech to a halt the way that plane did. When the people got off, they said cheerfully, 'Oh, the flight was great, but gee, the landing . . .'"

George Lucas had been fairly certain all along that somewhere in Northern California he could find the Green Moon of Endor. "We could have done the big trees in England, but they would have been different. The giant redwoods are up here, so I figured I could get the biggest trees up here. From a production point of view, it worked out to be the most sensible thing to do."

Unit Supervisor Miki Herman, a four-year veteran of the *Star Wars* team, spent the first few months of 1981 searching for Endor. "I did realize right off that the redwood location was going to be a big research project. Jim Bloom said to me, 'This is yours. Go out and look for a forest. We are looking for private property, a forest where they'll let us build a set and let us stage a small battle. Have a good time!'

"I had some Ralph McQuarrie paintings, but there was no script. I started out in February. I finally found the location in March.

"I did a lot of research on the phone first, because it was like looking for a needle in a haystack. I would get a lead on a forest, then I would fly in, rent a car, and drive or have a local contact drive me to the site. The ride was invariably along bumpy roads in old rickety jeeps on logging trails that seemed to stretch on for miles and miles."

For almost the entire search, it was Miki Herman on the road alone, but occasionally she had company. "Robert Watts would whistle the *Raiders* theme as we hiked along or fought our way through dense undergrowth or walked across log bridges. His second favorite theme was the Monty Python number, 'I'm a Lumberjack.' Robert and Norman Reynolds have this wonderful saying when they find a location they like: 'I can smell the bacon and egg sandwiches.'" No self-respecting film company in the western world would miss its morning bacon and egg sandwich—preferably toasted and 90 percent of the time eaten on the run.

Miki Herman was scouting very hard, and Jim Bloom knew it. "I used to say to people, 'You could go out with Miki in a helicopter, fly from the southernmost end of Marin County up to the Oregon border—probably a 250-mile stretch of coastal redwoods—and she could tell you who owned exactly which piece of property you were looking down at. George Lucas, Richard Marquand, and Norman Reynolds would much rather have photographed Endor in a nature reserve or a national park, but I knew from the very beginning that that was impossible," Bloom says. "We were going in to shoot a battle sequence, with large explosions, troops running about, and Imperial walkers crashing through.

"So we went to the lumber companies. They don't want to know from cameras: 'I don't have the land.' 'Very sorry, but we don't have the time.' 'Maybe you should talk to the public relations man up north.' I guess we were lucky. We eventually ran across an individual in Smith River, California, who was willing to talk to us."

Miki Herman had been up that way before, "but I couldn't get in the front door until I learned about a local guy named Lenny Fike. I called him up at Saxton's Tackle Shop, which is behind the Ship Ashore Resort Motel. He said, 'Oh, yes, I'm just looking out the window now at old growth timber.' Old growth means the big ones that have been there since primeval times. I said, 'I'll be there tomorrow.'

The Lenny Fike connection was a godsend. Jim Bloom also went up to look at the forest. "That first day at the Miller-Rellim Lumber Company, rather than having to go through the introductory letters and telephone calls, we just pulled up at the main gate with Lenny in the car. The guard said, 'Hi, Lenny...' In we went and that was it!"

They had spotted a possible location earlier from the helicopter. "It didn't look anything the way it did once it was manicured, but it was a true forest with ferns growing six feet tall. We clawed our way through the underbrush and finally got to a high spot. In front of us was about a 40-acre ground area that was relatively flat. The disadvantage was that it was a bit thin. There was a clear cut to the east and the Pacific Ocean to the west, but you got a lot of good fog coming into the area, and it was carte blanche in terms of the shooting. Plus, it was 15 minutes from Crescent City, ten minutes from Smith River, and I could house the entire crew without having to get on a logging road and drive for an hour and a half.

"Back in Richard Marquand's office, we got out the scouting pictures, and George, being George, said, 'You're right. Let's do it.' And that's what we did."

The search for the Green Moon of Endor was over. Norman Reynolds supplies a possible reason for using the redwood forest. "I think George Lucas wanted to shoot in the redwoods a long time ago. It may even have been going through his mind on *Empire*. He'd spoken at one point about a Wookiee planet, and I suppose a natural choice for that would be redwoods.

"We decided that Ewoks live high up in the trees. I've approximated them to other primitive people, like the aborigines or early man. They make all their weapons from natural materials—wood and stone. We avoided anything that might suggest otherwise. Yet in some ways they're rather like normal families with children, parents, and so on. The huts, hopefully, reflect the lifestyle.

"Because of the nature of redwoods—long and thin—they do not lend themselves readily to cinema screen proportions. We have had to do matte shots, looking up and down, adding the extreme tops and bottoms of the trees. That will be locked off VistaVision footage. My whole thinking, as far as the interior set at EMI and the Imperial bunker and other Ewok exteriors were concerned, is based on what early man would do, with all his limitations."

The city of Smith River, California, is 14 miles north of Crescent City and is almost in Oregon. The Ship Ashore Resort Motel housed the film production offices and many members of the cast and crew.

The classic redwood tree (*Sequoia sempervirens*) is often ten stories tall and is often older than Christianity. These trees usually grow within 30 miles of the Pacific Ocean. They have, for decades, provided one of the major industries of the Pacific Northwest.

There are dangers, however, to working in a redwood forest, whether you are a lumberjack or a movie person. In windy weather one has to watch out for "Widowmakers"—dead branches which are often balanced hundreds of feet up in the trees. Dislodged, they can penetrate the soft earth below like a javelin.

Into this land of redwoods came *Jedi*. Norman Reynolds summed it up best: "Moving from Yuma, Arizona, to Crescent City—the southern and northern ends of California—is like working in London and Athens—like two different countries, really."

Once again Lucasfilm was temporarily in the road-building business. They had to widen existing trails and clear new roads to the locations scattered throughout the redwood forest. The locations were renamed Bunker Hill, the Heart Shaped Tree, the Spaghetti Stump, and Norman's Log.

Twenty-six greensmen, nicknamed the Fern Brothers, were employed full-time, stripping away and replacing the tangled undergrowth, for nearly eight weeks prior to the start of filming. Meanwhile, bulldozers and earth-moving equipment rearranged the terrain to the shape that the moviemakers wanted. San Francisco Set Dresser Douglas Von Koss played big brother to the *Jedi* landscapers—a crew of local men who sometimes numbered as many as two dozen. "By the time we got the sets built and the land cleared, there was nothing green around except the trees. Suddenly, I had four locations to keep green. My greenhouse is about four square miles. We were constantly out in the valleys finding ferns, sallow, and wild huckleberries."

In the northern reaches of California, *Jedi* was still very much *Blue Harvest*. Shooting on private property hidden behind the tree line was pure bliss after Buttercup Valley. The turnoff for the road to the location didn't even hint at what was going on up in the hills. The mailbox merely read, "JL RT2," and security consisted of a narrow wooden bridge checkpoint over a local stream. The checkpoint was staffed by a recycled San Francisco flower child complete with psychedelic camper van.

The local newspapers showed only guarded interest. *The Curry County Pilot* reported "an aura of mystery surrounding Smith River" with "dwarfs" in the cast and local residents who were employed on the film staying "for the most part mum," although "a number of small persons had been observed dining in restaurants and enjoying the Curry County beaches."

Monday, April 26

One thousand and seventy-six land miles from Yuma, Arizona. It is a complete change of climate. Morning mists. Temperatures in the 60-degree range. Yellow weatherproof suits are standard issue.

Four miles away from the Miller-Rellim location, on a

country back road, is the warehouse—a series of garages where Construction Manager Roger Irvin and Prop Master Peter Hancock supervise a small production line of artificial redwood trunks and logs. But pride of place goes to a 25-foot-high, gun-metal-colored Imperial walker. It stands at ease against the fence, its front shielded from the farming traffic by a large piece of black plastic. But it does appear to be a source of constant and wide-eyed wonder to the herd of Jersey cows in the next field over.

Out in the woods, the constantly changing light is a recurring problem for Alan Hume and his work gang of electricians. The shifting shade and shafts of sunlight cause hot spots—spots of bright, overexposed areas—on the film which Hume and his crew work very hard at eliminating.

The dailies are viewed at night in the Ship Ashore Redwood Room. It is a small room now crammed with projection equipment—and bodies.

Accommodations at the hotel are at a premium. Room Number Four, the Production office, houses two publicity people, one producer, his executive assistant, one supervising accountant, one still photographer, and, for the graveyard shift, four assistant directors. (The room, at times, resembles the room in Carrie Fisher's favorite scene from *A Night at the Opera*!) When Howard Kazanjian needs a confidential chat with his money man Arthur Carroll, they or the others have to step outside and feed the sea gulls on the dock.

In total contrast, the little people's hotel across the Oregon border is spacious and has an indoor swimming pool and sauna—which they manage to mention every second sentence around the set.

The decision to board the Ewoks across the state line had been a conscious one for Jim Bloom and Miki Herman. Jim Bloom said quite simply, "I put the little people up in Brookings because I wanted to keep them separate from the crew. I was afraid of an *Under the Rainbow* syndrome—stories that had come out of another production, of these little people getting together and having the wildest parties.

I could just see the entire town being disrupted. But everybody loved them—it was wonderful. They were very well received. If I had to go back and do it all over again, I'd put everybody in the same place."

Tuesday, April 27

The restaurant critics on the production team are already fanning out. They have given a couple of coastal inn restaurants the thumbs-down gesture, but Jim's, a restaurant in Crescent City with a home-style atmosphere, receives a thumbs-up review. Harrison Ford is so enthusiastic about the restaurant that he plans to go back most nights. "I don't need treats any more," he says, "just good food." The Sunday in the middle of the two-week shoot will now be the only day off, but someone is already trying to line up a white-water adventure trip upriver.

Wednesday, April 28

The company is now on a 7 A.M. to 7 P.M. day. Minimum. By the third morning in the woods, all the suntans acquired in Yuma are beginning to fade. The Pacific Express flight into the Crescent City airport has been dubbed the "White Knuckle Run."

The Imperial walker arrives from its storage space near the warehouse. It is still in several pieces and is assembled near the bunker location.

Anthony Daniels, dismissed early on in the day, takes off for a quick spin through Oregon. Suddenly they need him again, so a local logger is hastily recruited to play C-3PO for a couple of pickup shots. He will certainly have a tale to tell his grandchildren. On his return, Tony Daniels is clearly not amused. R2-D2, having shaken the desert sand from his system, is in far better form and finds the gentle forest paths more to his liking.

Thursday, April 29

George Lucas and Richard Marquand are full of fire as the end of the shooting schedule approaches. There is still, however, a tall stack of storyboards left to shoot. The story boards are all color-coded and the scenes are complicated. The two weeks allowed for the second unit to finish up do not appear, at this point, to be enough time.

The cost of stunts appears to be keeping up with inflation. Certain stunts cost $800. If a retake is necessary, the stunt will cost another $250—each time it is done. Other stunts, a bit more risky, cost $600 the first time and $600 the second time.

Saturday, May 1

Business as usual in the redwoods. "Roll, speed, action, cut!" Set up, rehearse, shoot, print. Only those actually taking part in the moviemaking are really aware of the slow rhythm of the operation. Sound Mixer Randy Thom likens moviemaking to riding shotgun on a stagecoach—"long stretches of intense boredom punctuated by short periods of extreme terror!"

In one of the shots, Harrison Ford falls accidentally.

"Drunk again," Mark Hamill stage-whispers to the crew. "What about my dignity, George?" Ford shrieks in mock anguish from his prone position on the ground.

The most picturesque of the redwood locations, well

away from the battlefield bunker set, is called Norman's Log. It is a part natural, part man-made bridge across a ravine. This is where the tiny Ewok warriors will carry their trussed prisoners—Chewbacca, Luke, and Han Solo—bringing them back to their treetop Village. Their new god, C-3PO, will be splendidly borne along on a hastily constructed throne.

Mark Hamill, an avid collector of games, draws a crowd with a new batch of magazines on the subject. The favorite game is a spot-the-car competition. The players must identify the cars in the pictures from a few square inches of chrome fittings.

It is *American Graffiti* revisited. George Lucas, who might well have been a motor mechanic in another life, wins the game easily. He had no trouble at all recognizing a 1950 Oldsmobile series 88, a 1952 Mercury Custom, and a 1957 Chevrolet BelAire station wagon.

For two days now, there has been talk of a visit to the volunteer firemen's benefit dance in Brookings. Just talk.

Sunday, May 2

The hardier types leave at 7 A.M. for the white-water river trip.

Harrison Ford has the best idea. He hires a boat to cruise the Smith River lazily all day.

At sundown there is a fish fry in Cameraman Jim Glennon's trailer, which is parked in the Ship Ashore parking lot. Someone suggests that the trailer is more spacious than some of the star suites across the way! In fact, it might be, since the rooms at the motel are rather small.

Monday, May 3

The Ewoks are having their final costume fittings and have been getting in shape with movement rehearsals in the dance hall of a local roadhouse. The big battle scenes are only three days away, and George Lucas is taking a very paternal interest in getting the warriors into proper condition.

"My head, I need my head," one Ewok cries while dressing. "Anyone over there with a spare left foot?" Kenny Baker, Mike Edmonds, and Jack Purvis, old hands at the Ewok game, have learned to pace themselves throughout a day's filming in the stifling furry suits, and they pass on the tricks of the trade to the newer performers.

The sun is cramping Alan Hume's shooting style. He must have more lights, so general arc lamps are dragged off a truck bound for Los Angeles as it begins to roll down the hill. This is a typical emergency that causes sweating Chief Electrician Mike Pantages to chant the movie technicians' constant lament: "Never time to do it properly. But always time to do it over."

Tuesday, May 4

"May the Fourth Be with You." Five days to go, and the jokes are getting tired too. It is a very up-and-down day. First, a widowmaker 70 feet overhead forces the company to another location while a woodsman climbs up to dislodge it. Then our heroes spend the last part of the afternoon being hauled in and out of an Ewok net trap. They are suspended six feet in the air, with C-3PO in a spread-eagled position on the very bottom of the pile.

Thursday, May 6

The Battle of the Bunker. Five principal cameras are being used, and a 16mm documentary crew is also at work.

There are a total of 325 mouths to feed today, and the local caterer has been replaced, by popular demand, by Michaelson's, the movie catering company that also did the catering down in Buttercup Valley.

The number of people necessary for the scene in front of the bunker, and the quantity of vehicles and equipment needed, are almost frightening. There are 130 Imperial guards in uniform, 40 Ewoks, and a cast and crew of 150.

Howard Kazanjian double-checks the lines of heavily armed and armored stormtroopers. They are being put into place in front of the bunker. He tells visitors rather tartly, "They don't exactly drive themselves to work dressed like this, you know!"

It is 11:45 before the first shot is ready. Director Richard Marquand, keeping an eye on the leading actors, neglects to shout the last cue for the scene of "Ewok Three." An attacking wave of little people is supposed to appear over a massive fallen log with bows and arrows aimed, like archers at Agincourt, when they hear the cue. Since it wasn't announced, they didn't appear.

Take 2 is a vast improvement, but it needs to be done again. Assistant Director David Tomblin primes the assembly for a third and last take. "Just the same, only better," he instructs everyone.

Kenny Baker ignores his own advice and almost faints from the heat inside his Ewok suit, but he is soon all right again. Between takes, Jack Purvis clears the space around himself by smoking a big cigar. He is watched anxiously by several of the production assistants, because earlier, sparks from a special-effects laser had ignited some moss on a tree and leaped several feet up the trunk before they were extinguished.

It was a big day for *Jedi*. If all turns out well on film, it will be $100,000 well spent. There are three hours of rushes to come, and dinner tonight will be finger-lickin' chicken from the Colonel.

Friday, May 7

Exterior Forest. The Battle Continues.
All the principals and:

  6 Stand ins
15 Stormtroopers
  5 Speeder bike troops
10 Controllers
  4 Officers
12 Rebel troops
35 Ewoks

The feeling on the set is one of "let's get finished." It has been a long production, and now—close to the end of the four-month shooting schedule—everyone is ready for some time off.

Carrie Fisher is squibbed today. A small explosive charge is fitted inside her tunic. There is a small blast plate behind the charge in order to simulate a gunshot wound. But she had to endure a running comedy gag from the camera crew about this nice Irish girl they knew who had her head blown off accidentally in her very first film. Everything goes according to plan, and the explosive performs perfectly.

Saturday, May 8

The Battle concludes. Same cast and crew as yesterday.
There is a 5 P.M. deadline for Harrison Ford to finish
today. A Warner Communications Executive jet is standing
by to whisk him to San Diego this evening for a sneak
preview of his new movie *Blade Runner*.

Sunday, May 9

Next stop ILM. It is back to the Lucasfilm headquarters
in San Rafael to do several days of bluescreen work for the
speeder bike chase.

David Tomblin, promoted in the field to Second Unit
Director, will stay on in Crescent City with a substantial
second unit crew and many of the Ewoks to complete the
forest scenes. These are almost all Ewok scenes and do not
involve any of the principal actors.

The Pacific Express charter plane is back at the airport.
This time it is on the long runway, so hopefully, the takeoff
will not be as exciting as the first landing.

Marketing Chief Sid Ganis, who conducts most of his
business on the telephone, cannot break the habit. Even at
8:30 on a Sunday morning, he finds someone to call from
the airport lounge telephone.

The Crescent City/Ewok forest shoot had its ups and
downs. Certainly it was more comfortable working in Northern California than it was working in the heat and sand of
Arizona. Nearing the end of principal photography also acts
as a spur to get it done. The director, rested and sitting in
his office several months later, talked about the two weeks
in Crescent City.

"Only the principal Ewoks came from England and worked here, and some of them were stunt people. There were a lot of stunts. They had their own costumes made to measure in England.

"The American Ewoks had just as much spirit and just as much energy. They also had been through a training program for two or three weeks. They used to go on walks and rambles and hikes and runs and do physical exercises to get up to strength. But the very nature of shooting—not 20 feet up in the air, but shooting in the forest—meant that it was much harder to have crowd control. I would say, 'Run, disappear, hide.' And then I'd find that they were lost. We didn't know where they'd gone, and it was difficult to get them to come back again. So someone would yell, *Come out! WHERE ARE YOU?*"

What about the battle scenes—what was staging them like?

"We had a very, very tight schedule for principal photography. The forest battle and everything were all very carefully storyboarded. Then I went back up for two days and I did some extra shooting with Threepio and Artoo. In fact, I asked Harrison to come up and do another extra little piece that I needed in the blowing up of the bunker. Han is in the foreground; he comes running out of the bunker, and it all blows up in one shot."

What was working with the chicken walker like?

"We had the static chicken walker, which just stands in front of the bunker. We had decided to put it on one side— the rest would be painted in on a matte painting. This one would move its head, and a man could be in it. That has a very definite function in the end sequence in particular. Then we had a chicken-walker head which we put on a tractor for a sequence where Chewie hijacks the chicken walker and gets inside. And that was just a head. Sort of moving along—the same where Chewie is inside and pops out."

Did Marquand ever stop and ask himself what he was doing in this redwood forest with Ewoks and Chewbacca and all of those characters?

"Oh, yes. Oh, it was insane. You could see it when we all got together—there are all these weird-looking people sitting around in the middle of the woods. Having lunch. The stormtroopers, actually out-of-work lumberjacks, wondered who these people were in the movie. Some of them hadn't even seen *Star Wars*—and so they thought the whole thing was pretty crazy, but they were all hard workers. The stormtrooper helmet is extremely uncomfortable. You can't see very much and the hat wobbles around as you run—and I kept telling them to run because they had a lot of action to do. Some of them were very brave, falling over all the time, tripping on logs and stumps and stuff.

"The costume is very hard to move in. I always try on all of the costumes that I can. I always do that so I can appreciate all the problems people will have. I can't try on an Ewok's costume, but I did put on an Ewok head—and I could see NOTHING. I've worn Chewbacca's head as well, and Darth Vader's helmet. Dave Prowse would say endlessly to me, 'But I can't see, I can't hear.' And I would say endlessly to him, 'I know.'"

Was Crescent City difficult?

"Just the terrain was difficult. We were always going up and down hills and we were all, as I say, very spread out. It's not easy to keep a hold on an open location. If you've got sequences in woods or fields or hills, everything sort of flows off the edges of the camera range. And you're always asking people to come back together, to move back to the center.

"Looking back, no, it was hard, but it wasn't that dificult."

For two weeks the redwood forest slopes of Northern California were the scene of the Endor battleground as the Rebel Alliance raiding party, led by Han Solo, Princess Leia, and Luke Skywalker—plus Chewbacca, C-3PO, and R2-D2, and bolstered by the Ewok shock troops—took on the Imperial squads of Darth Vader. Miki Herman, who stayed on to tie the loose ends together, recalls: "Suddenly one day everybody was gone. The locals were in shell shock.

It really was strange, out on location, that what took six weeks to build was disassembled in two hours. We didn't have to replant the vegetation—just make the area safe. We cleaned up some and filled in the main bunker hole so that nobody would fall in. We were so lucky. It's hard to believe that from the day the unit arrived, it never rained again for the whole stay. Heaven-sent. Before that, Crescent City had 22 days of straight rain, sleet, and snow."

CHAPTER 12

Monday, May 10, 1982

Today is the last day with the full cast at the Industrial Light and Magic sound stage in Marin County.

The skiffs from Yuma are also making a final appearance today. They are balanced high in the air and are silhouetted against the bluescreen that dominates one end of the new ILM stage. (Yuma is still around. Even after two weeks in Crescent City, members of the crew have sand left in their shoes, and some of the backup R2-D2s have to be vacuumed regularly.)

Closed set, says the call sheet. No husbands, wives, children, or friends. The call sheet for *Jedi*, once the production began location filming and now that they are at ILM, looks different from the call sheets that were used in London. The *Blue Harvest* logo is at the top of the sheet, and now the sheets are forms that have to be filled in every day. They seem more businesslike and more formal than the sometimes chatty call sheets that were issued at EMI. Today's call sheet looks like this:

The action is for "Skiff 1 to move past the camera revealing all the characters with the principals in close-up." Later, Skiff 2 will "come toward the camera with the monsters firing." Since the lighting is so critical for this scene, the skiffs stand still and the camera crane does the moving.

BLUE HARVEST

1ST UNIT **CALL SHEET**   ay of Shooting R4

H.L.L.

BLUE HARVEST	Shooting Call 8:30A	Producer H Kazanjian	Date Monday, May 10, 1982
Leave Corte Madera 7A – Report to ILM 7:15A			Director R Marquand

SC No:	SET DESCRIPTION	D/N	PAGES	LOCATION
22pt.24pt	Ext. Skiff #1	D		ILM
	(cast: 1,3,4,6)			(Blue Screen)
	moving toward & past camera,			
	Revealing characters - closeups on floor			
33pt	Ext. Skiff #2	D		↓
	comes in firing			

ADVANCE

DAY/DATE	Scenes		pages	location
Tues., Wed., Thur.	67pt, 91pt	Ext. Endor Forest (D)		ILM
May 11,12,13	93pt, 115pt	Biker chases		

NOTE: The entire company-cast and crew alike-should be aware that the SET IS CLOSED. No visitors! No husbands,wives,children or friends will be allowed to visit the set.

Conditions: Cover Set: lv. report

Cast and Bits	Part Of	Lv. Hotel	Makeup	On Set	NO.	Crew	hotel	to ILM
1. Martin		7:30A	8A	8:30A	1	Director		7:15A
2. Caroline		hold			1	Unit Spvsr	7A	
3. Harry		7:15A	8A	8:30A	1	Cameraman	7A	
4. William		6:45A	7:30A	8:30A	1	Cameraman ILM		7:15A
5. Anthony		9:45A	10A	looping	1	1st Asst. Dir.		7:15A
6. Peter		7:45A	8A	8:30A				
Peter Diamond-Stunt	Arranger		8A	8:30A	1	Production Des.		7:15A
Frank Henson	Stuntman	7:45A	8A	8:30A	1	2nd Asst. Dir.	7A	
					1	Script Sup.	7A	
					2	Prod. Asst.		7:15
					1	Cam. Op ILM		7:15A
					1	Cam Asst ILM		7:15A
					1	Mixer	7A	
					2	Sound Crew	7A	
					2	Makeup	7A	

No.	Extras		Report To ILM	On Set		Creature MU		7:15A
4	Stand-ins		7:15A	7:15A	3	Creature MU		7:15A
8	Extras		7:30A	8:30A	1	Hairdresser	7A	
					5	Costumers	2@ 7A	2&1 @7:15
					1	Gaffers	7A	
					1	Grips	7A	
					6	Stagehands (ILM)		7:15A
					2	Prop Crew	7A	
					4	Special FX (ILM)	3@7	1@7:15
					1	Painter	7A	
					3	Construction	7A	

TRANSPORTATION
All calls per Cptn unless otherwise noted

Dest. SPECIAL INSTRUCTIONS:
ALL DEPTS: The viewing of dailies is restricted. Please check with the Production office before attending a screening.

* THIS FILM IS STRICTLY CONFIDENTIAL !
DO NOT DISCUSS YOUR WORK WITH OUTSIDERS.

Kit West begins to wonder if his journey from England was really necessary. Temporarily, he says jokingly, he has become the "most expensive fan operator and wire puller in captivity." After the usual delays, the actors are lifted onto the skiff to test the wind speed and movements. Mark Hamill says to Richard Marquand, "It's like riding on a subway." Harrison Ford hoots derisively, "He's never been on a subway."

Han Solo's "eyeline" to Jabba the Hutt, aboard his Sail Barge, is simulated by a stagehand holding a 15-foot stick up in the air. The swaying stick is moved according to Ford's instructions: "A foot to your left, sir." Ford calls all the new technicians "sir." For many of the ILM technicians here, it is the first time they have been on a shooting set with live actors. There is a constant stream of visitors—disregarding the call sheet's closed-set command—from the ILM and Sprockets back rooms. The average boredom threshold seems to be about ten minutes.

Finally, Mark Hamill and Harrison Ford complete their last shot together. It is the end of an era. The final chore of the day for both is to autograph yet another pile of photographs. Even out of costume they seem to echo their screen characters. The Luke Skywalker message is, "Follow the Force"; Han Solo signs off with, "Force Yourself!"

Tuesday, May 11

Today begins the speeder bike bluescreen work. This segment has been very carefully planned. Back in January, George Lucas hand-carried a videomatic of the chase to London with him. Howard Kazanjian explained videomatics recently: "It is a form of video, or film, that uses animation, or models, or props, or sometimes stand-ins, to show the details of the scene to be shot. The detail is not polished, but it gives us an idea of what a scene is going to look like.

"In order to get a fairly accurate feeling for a scene like the speeder-bike chase scene, George guided Joe Johnston in drawing a set of storyboards based on the scene as it was written in the screenplay. Next, Dennis Muren and the ILM technicians made a videomatic of the scene based on the storyboards. Then, sound effects are added, and the video is transferred to film. (It is transferred to film so that it can be intercut into the work print.) From viewing these scenes on videomatics, the timing of the scene can be adjusted, the camera angles can be changed, and all the minor changes can be made and planned out before the "real" scene is shot for the movie. The videomatic is also a template or guide for pre-production planning."

For the videomatic of the speeder bike chase, ILM has constructed a miniature forest set with tree trunks, bushes, and forest trails. The miniature forest rests on a large table and has been lit to give a sense of forest light. The model speeder bikes are about eight inches long, and the models of Luke, Leia, and the stormtroopers are about five inches tall. Each bike has a wire attached to the back which curves up and out of the frame of the picture. Each bike is manipulated by an ILM technician who holds the wire and guides the bike through the forest. For the shooting of the videomatic, a cameraman operates the videotape camera much as a cinematographer shoots a movie.

The viewer gets a real sense of speed, of the flickering lights of the forest, and of the shadows of the bikers as they rush along the forest trails. The video has been cut together in a way that approximates how the final film of the chase will be cut together. There are close-ups of the front forks of the bikes with the forest floor rushing by underneath, a swooping shot of a stormtrooper as he rushes in from the upper left-hand corner of the frame, and close-ups of Luke and Leia. At one point, Luke's bike is sideswiped by a stormtrooper's bike, and the viewer sees the bikes as they knock into each other; then, in close-up, there is a shot of the two forks on the front of the bikes as they clash and almost lock together.

One of the stormtrooper's bikes crashes into a tree, and ILM has rigged up a miniature explosion. Another exciting bit of business happens when a stormtrooper zooms his speeder bike into the end of a hollow log. There is a *whoosh* of dust and an explosive exhaust as he enters the log completely and disappears from view.

The models of Luke and Leia are not finely detailed and look more like dolls than miniatures. The speeder bikes are not carefully crafted because, for this videomatic, it is the action and the overall feel of the sequence that are important. The videomatic is only a blueprint for how the chase scene will be filmed and put together.

There will be three separate sets of film that must be spliced together in order to get the chase for the movie. First, there is the real footage shot among the redwood trees in Northern California for the Green Moon of Endor location; second, there will be the speeder bike film shot against the bluescreen at ILM; and third, there will be the carefully crafted model work and miniatures shot, again, by ILM in the studio. In the final composited film, lasers will be animated into the scene, and some of the explosions will be enhanced as well.

To the question of why the videomatic was done way back in January, Kazanjian has the following answer: "You need to begin preparation months and months in advance to help give you a sense of what the final scene will look like. All kinds of questions have to be answered: How high off the ground is the speeder bike? Does a certain character bank to the left or the right for a specific turn? What shot do we film with the life-size speeder bike on a sled in the forest, and what shot do we film against the bluescreen? When will we need a miniature? What special effects, like crashes and explosions, do we need—and where?

"First we have to plan every element months in advance; then we do extensive storyboards of the whole scene and break them down into First Unit work, Second Unit work, and bluescreen work. We wanted all these details planned for as soon as possible, even though we wouldn't be on location or at ILM for about six months."

Is the speeder bike chase going to be one of the exciting chase scenes in the movie, then?

"The chase is about two and a half, three minutes long, and it's a great chase. It's with our heroes—who are usually up in ships flying through the air. This time it's down on a level you can relate to—down on the ground in the forest, where we have all been before. And they are zooming through these giant trees at 200 miles per hour, careening around the trees, hitting them, and having a ball!"

The actions for the speeder bike bluescreen work have been broken down into minute detail, typed on *Blue Harvest* stationery, and circulated to everyone who is involved with the scene. The memo looks like this:

ILM BLUE SCREEN SCHEDULE

DAY	SC #	SKETCH #'S	DESCRIPTION	CAST
DAY 1	22, 24, pt. 33 pt.	3,4,5,82	Skiff # 1 Moving past camera Skiff # 2 Moving in, firing	Luke, Han, Lando, Chewie
DAY 2–4	67–	12,15	Luke & Leia on bike	Leia, Luke
	67–	23	Luke leaps onto Biker	Leia, Luke, Biker #2
	67–	24	Luke lands on Biker #2	Luke, Biker #2
	67–	31a	Luke slams on brakes	Luke
	67–	41,52	Leia pursues Biker #1	Leia

67–	70,76	Luke & Biker bang together	Luke, Biker
67–	78 (78 alternate)	Luke leaps off bike	Luke, Biker
67–	9	Luke & Leia chase Bike #2	Luke, Leia
67–	16	Luke & Leia pull alongside bike #2	Luke, Leia, Biker #2
67–	18	Luke looks at Biker #2 while Leia keeps driving	Luke, Leia
67–	20	Luke & Biker #2 look at each other	Luke, Leia, Biker #2
67–	22	Luke leaps toward Biker #2	Luke, Leia, Biker #2
67–	28	Luke & Leia being chased by Bikers 3 & 4	Luke, Leia
67–	30,31	Luke & Leia side by side, Leia pulls ahead	Luke, Leia
67–	33,34	Luke drops back between Bikers 3 & 4 & fires	Luke
67–	55	Biker fires & hits Leia's bike	Leia, Biker
67–	63	Luke chases Bike #3	Luke
67–	66,72	Biker #3 bangs into Luke	Luke, Biker #3
91–	2	Wicket speeds thru forest on bike	Wicket

91–	5	Wicket is chased by Bikers	Wicket
93–	1	Wicket's bike is hit	Wicket
93–	2	Wicket grabs vine	Wicket
115–	68	Wicket lands on Biker	Wicket, Biker
115–	35	Bikers knocked off by vine	2 Bikers
115–	58	Bikers hit by rocks	Biker #1
119–	16	Biker Lassoed	Biker
115–	56	Ewoks fly over Bikers	Biker #1 & #2
67–	26	Luke & Leia chase Biker #1	Biker #1
67–	59	Biker sees tree	Biker
67–	17	Biker #2 looks at Luke & Leia	Biker #2
67–	38	Biker #3 looks at Luke & Leia	Biker #3
67–	45,47,51	Biker #1 looks for Leia	Biker #1
67–	54	Biker #1 pulls gun & aims at Leia	Biker #1
67–	57	Biker looks for Leia	Biker
67–	83	Biker aims for Luke	Biker
91–	3	Bikers in pursuit of Wicket	Biker
115–	33a	Bikers pursuing Ewoks	Biker
67–	39	C.U. Bikers foot	Biker
67–	7	Leia's Bike Guns fire	Leia

DAY 5	119–	9	Walker head turns toward logs	
	119–	10a	Walker hit by logs, Walker pilots adjust controls	2 Walker pilots
	119–	30	Ewok peers thru cockpit window	Ewok, 2 Walker pilots
	119–	33	Ewoks drop into cockpit	Walker pilot, 2 Ewoks
	115–	28	Walker pilots aim for Ewoks	2 Walker pilots
	115–	45	Walker pilots vibrate from boulder	2 Walker pilots
	119–	8b	Walker pilots manuever toward noise of Logs	2 Walker pilots
	119–	35	Ewoks pilot Walker while Chewy looks thru hatch	Chewy, 2 Ewoks
	119–	31	Chewy yanks walker pilot out of hatch	Chewy, Walker pilot
DAY 6	115–	57	Teebo & others drop rocks while flying	Teebo
	115–	65	Wicket flies toward Biker	Wicket
	115–	59	Teebo hit while flying	Teebo, 2 Ewoks

The bluescreen work is tedious and time-consuming. It is slow going, and the actors, the director, and the crew inch their way through the scenes.

Richard Marquand talks about the bluescreen filming. "I enjoyed the bluescreen work, I must say. It is ridiculous—but I actually enjoyed it very much. Again, this sequence—the Endor speeder bike chase—had been storyboarded and had also been videotaped based on the storyboards, so that we really did know what the bike chase was going to look like very early on. And we knew what moments of drama we needed in it. For my homework, I had actually written out a sort of list of what happens during the bike chase.

"So, in the studio, Mark is up on one of these speeder bikes and there are these enormous wind fans going. And the lights are set to show a sense of flickering light, as if we're moving through the forest at 200 miles an hour. It's very noisy. I'm yelling the action at him. Mark does this very, very well, so he's reacting to what I'm telling him is happening. 'Now you're coming around the corner. Now you're coming near a tree. And it's coming closer and you bank to the right and you come around the tree, and oh, what a relief.' And I'm going on like this as loudly as I can. Then we shot front shots and close-ups. Close-up, close-up . . . side shots, close-up, close-up, rear shots, close-up, close-up . . . other direction. And you just keep on shooting and shooting and shooting."

What is it like working with Carrie on the bluescreen scenes?

"Carrie finds the bluescreen work hard. There's nothing to concentrate on. I do think it's a miracle that anybody can do it. You've got nothing to relate to at all. There's a bluescreen behind you, you are on this bike, you've got me yelling at you and just a camera a few feet away—no actors, nothing. It's very difficult, but she does it quite well."

Wednesday, May 12

Richard Marquand has gone back to Crescent City overnight for the second unit shot of the Endor forest Imperial Bunker blowing up.

At ILM they are now well into the speeder bike battle sequence. "Luke and Leia chase bikes. Luke leaps off. Luke lands on Biker 2. Biker 1 pulls gun, fires, and hits Leia's bike."

Catering has become very "up market" on the set at San Rafael. In addition to coffee and doughnuts, there are strawberries, quiche, and cinnamon bagels. Mark Hamill is still excited as he climbs off his bike and reaches the ground. "I can really be there driving those bikes. I see it in my mind, I know how it's going to look...and then they say technicians, and it's a very odd feeling. Like re-entering the atmosphere from outer space. For a moment, you feel pretty silly, actually, being up there in the helmet, doing all that. I don't care about my reading of the line—how was the swaying?"

Monday, May 17

A continuation today of EXT. ENDOR FOREST—BIKE CHASES. Then, later this afternoon, everyone is hoping to begin the scenes that are labeled: EXT. ENDOR FOREST—BIKERS CHASE EWOKS. The call sheet for today looks like this:

1ST UNIT   CALL SHEET   Day of Shooting [53]

Show: BLUE HARVEST	Shooting Call 8A	Producer H Kazanjian	Date MONDAY, MAY 17, 1982

LEAVE HOTEL/CORTE MADERA 7a - REPORT TO ILM 7.15a
LOCATION: ILM BLUE SCREEN, SAN RAFAEL, CALIFORNIA

Director R Marquand

SC. NO.	SET DESCRIPTION	D/N	PAGES	LOCATION
67pt.	EXT. ENDOR FOREST - BIKE CHASES (to complete)	D	5/8	SAN RAFAEL
	Storyboard Nos: 20, 22, 23, 28, 31, 41, 52,			
	55, 24, 31A, 70, 76, 78, 72, 9, 34, 63, 66.			
	30A, 16, 78, 83, 33.			
	Character Nos: 1, 2, 4, 5, 6, and Extras			
91pt., 93pt., 115pt.	EXT. ENDOR FOREST - BIKERS CHASE EWOKS			SAN RAFAEL
	(See: Tuesday, May 18 Advance)			
	Character Nos: 3, 9 and Extras			

ADVANCE

DAY/DATE	Scenes	pages	location
Saturday, May 15 & Sunday, May 16	** REST DAYS **		
Tuesday, May 18:	Sc. 91pt., 93pt., 115pt. BIKERS CHASE EWOKS		ILM
	Storyboards #s: 91-2,91-5,91-3,93-1,93-2,115-6B,115-33A.		
Wednesday, May 19:	Sc. 115pt. & 119pt. WALKER FIGHTING EWOKS		
	Storyboard #s: 115-35,115-58,119-16,119-9,119-10A,115-45,119-8B,229-31		ILM

NOTE: The entire company-cast and crew alike-should be aware that the SET IS CLOSED. No visitors! No husbands,wives,children or friends will be allowed to visit the set.

Conditions:	Cover Set:								
Cast and Bits	Part Of	Lv. Hotel	Makeup	On Set	NO	Crew		HOTEL	to ILM
								LEAVE	REPORT
1. Martin		7.15a	7.30a	8a	3	Director	7a		7.15a
2. Caroline		6.45a	7a	8a	1	Unit Spvsr	↓		↓
3. Kenny	WICKET	8a	8.15a	9a					
4. Peter		W/N			1	Cameraman ILM			7.15a
					1	1st Asst. Dir.	7a		7.15a
5. Henson	Stuntman/Arranger	7a	7.15a	7.30a					
6. Skeaping	Dbl. Martin	↓	↓	↓	1	2nd Asst. Dir.	7a		7.15a
7. Green	N.D. Ewok	8a	8.15a	9a	1	Script Sup.	↓		↓
8. Morris		↓	↓	↓	1 + 1				
					2	Prod. Asst. 1 @	8.45a/		7a-7.]
					2	Cam. Op ILM			7.15a
					2	Cam Asst ILM			7.15a
					1	Mixer			↓
					1	Sound Crew			↓
					1	Makeup	8.30a		6.45a
Stand-ins	Extras		Report To	On Set	3	Creature MU			7.15a
					1	Hairdresser	7a		7.15a
Extras/ As 1. Scooter Bikers and then				6	Costumers (1+5)	7a		7.15a
As 2. Walker Pilots				1	Gaffers			7.15a
.... As 3. Wicket Dbls...........								
*PLEASE NOTE THAT THERE SHOULD BE NO *				1	Grips			7.15a
SMOKING ON THE ILM STAGE. THANK YOU.				10	Stagehands (ILM)			
********************************				1	Prop Crew	7a		
Note: Kenny, Green, Morris & Cox arrive				4	Special FX (ILM)	↓		↓
SFO on Saturday May 15 on Republic # 785								
at 10.57a				1	Painter	7a		7.15a
J. Tebrooke (W/robe) also on same flight				3	Construction	↓		↓

TRANSPORTATION Per J. Feinblatt						
All calls per Cptn unless otherwise noted						
						Dept.	SPECIAL INSTRUCTIONS

SPECIAL INSTRUCTIONS
ALL DEPTS: The viewing of dailies is restricted. Please check with the Production office before attending a screening.

Sp.Fx. Sc. 115pt. Wicket on bike
Stunts Semi Flying
Stunts Martin jumping from bike to bike

⋆ THIS FILM IS STRICTLY CONFIDENTIAL!
DO NOT DISCUSS YOUR WORK WITH OUTSIDERS

Tuesday, May 18

Today is a continuation of the bikers chasing the Ewoks. Kenny Baker is playing an Ewok, and there is also a stunt double for Kenny on hand. The mornings begin very early—they are in make-up by 7:15 and expected on the set by 7:45.

Richard Marquand related the following story about filming one segment of the chase. "I finally used a stunt Ewok. It was pretty dangerous on that bike. When you've got quite small hands, you can't even grip the handlebars very well. Kenny was terrific. And he really tried, but I was worried for his safety. So finally I asked a stunt person to wear the same costume for the sequence. There's a great moment in the whole chase which we devised way back in August, where, when the Ewok first steals the bike, he takes off so fast that he is just holding on with his hands, and his legs are flying out behind him, sort of flapping in the wind. To do this, we stood the bike up on its rear end and had the stuntman in the Wicket costume hold on; then he is hanging there and sort of kicking his legs. The effect is wonderful. Then we turn the film horizontally and you see him just streaming out like a banner—hanging on to the handlebars. It was terrific. Dino De Laurentiis, in memory of his late son, gave a rotating camera base to ILM. We used it to show the little Ewok losing complete control of the bike—where he actually spins it. It suddenly goes completely over and he scrambles to get on top of it, and then it rights itself again and he's scrambling to regain his balance the other way. And we used this spinning camera for that effect, which is fabulous."

It should be a delightful scene on screen and perhaps even one of the high points of what promises to be one of the most exciting segments of a movie already filled with exciting segments.

Thursday, May 20

Tonight it will be over. There is certainly an air of sadness on the set about the whole thing finally coming to an end, but there is also a sense of relief over today's proceedings.

Today the Ewoks are flying in their hang gliders. The gliders, suspended from the ceiling in front of the giant bluescreen, are magnificent-looking pieces of primitive technology. They are about 20 feet across and about 8 or 10 feet tall and look as if an Ewok could actually swoop down from the top of a ten-story-tall redwood tree and fly around the Endor forest in one of them. The Ewoks don't get properly airborne until 13 minutes before lunch. Again, this is careful, slow-moving filmmaking, and the morning is spent in preparation for the shots.

The Daily Production Report, filled out at the end of the day, is anticlimactic. It says that the company was dismissed at 6:30 P.M.** (The two asterisks are explained down toward the bottom of the report by the simple line "End of ILM Bluescreen with Actors.") The final report looks like this:

By the time they called a halt at 6:30 this evening, they had completed 23 takes on ten different sets. This will be a total of about 30 seconds on the screen.

How does this last day on *Jedi* compare with the last day of shooting on the other two movies? On Friday, July 16, 1976, the *Star Wars* crew had been tinkering with some retakes on the sequence of Princess Leia and the hologram, which R2-D2 shows to Luke and Ben Kenobi; they had also worked on the detention area cell block scene and could manage only 20 seconds of total film time completed. That was well below the one-and-a-half-minute daily average that they had achieved over the whole picture.

On the day *Star Wars* wrapped, Robert Watts, then Pro-

DAILY PRODUCTION REPORT

Unit POST PROD. ILM

	SHOOTING SCHEDULE AND STATUS										For Remarks and Delays See Reverse Side	NUMBER OF DAYS ON PICTURE INCLUDING TODAY									
	1st Unit	Rehearsal	Pre-Prod.	Travel	Holi-day	Lay-off	Re-takes	2nd Unit	Post-Prod.	Total		Shoot-ing	Rehear-sal	Pre-Prod.	Tra-vel	Holi-days	Lay-off	Re-takes	2nd Unit	Post-Prod.	Total
No. Days Scheduled	92			3	3	6		26		122										4	4
No. Days Revised																					

Date **Thursday, May 20, 1982**

Producer **HOWARD KAZANJIAN**   Director **RICHARD MARQUAND**   Unit Director _____

Working Title **BLUE HARVEST**   Prod. No. _____

Picture Started **1-11-82**   Scheduled Finish **5-6-82**   As Revised _____   Status **On schedule**

Sers (Set No.) **EXT. ENDOR FOREST - EWOKS FLYING/ILM BLUE SCREEN**

Location **SAN RAFAEL, CALIFORNIA**

Crew Call **7a**   Shooting Call **8a**   First Shot **11.47a** Lunch **12p** till **1p**   Dinner **-** till **-**   Last Shot **6.30p**

Company Reported To ☒ Studio ☐ Location   Company Dismissed At **6.30p ****   ☒ Studio ☐ Location ☐ Headquarters

After Lunch Shot **2.30p**   After Dinner Shot **-**   Last Bus Arrived At HOTEL **7.30p**

SCRIPT SCENES AND PAGES		MINUTES	SETUPS	ADDED SCENES	RETAKES				
	Scenes	Pages					Pages	Scenes		
Orig Script	132		Prev. 79.15	Prev. 1613	Prev. 3	Prev.				
Next Revised To			Today .30	Today 10	Today -	Today				
Taken Prev.			Total 79.45	Total 1623	Total 3	Total				
Taken Today			Scene No. Sc. 115pt.							
Total To Date			23 printed takes							
In the Taken			Added Scenes							
Schd. for Today			Retakes							
			Sound Tracks			Stills				

FILM FOOTAGES (for ILM Main Unit & Post Prod. shoot only)						EXTRAS USED
RES & NG	PRINT	TOTAL EXPOSED	IDENT.	WASTE	S/ENDS	A · Auto Allowance
580	6055	6635	TODAY	0		MU · Makeup Hairgoods
6174	54278	60452	PREVIOUS	170		WA · Ward Allowance
6754	60333	67087	TOTAL	170		MP · Meal Penalty
						TT · Travel Time

PLAYERS — CAST — WEEKLY — DAILY								No.	Rate	Adj	OT	Misc
Start · S Worked · W Finished · F Hold · H Rehearse·R Test·T Travel·TV Bkf'st Served · B	Time In	Time On Set	Time Dis-missed	Arrive hotel	Looped To	B		1	EWOK/LITTLE PERSON			
1 PETER MAYHEW	TV-F							*	GREEN @ \$100. per day			
2 KENNY BAKER	W	7a	7.20a 6.30p	7p								
3 TONY COX					\$200.							
4 JACK PURVIS												
5												
6 Cast lunch 12p - 1p												
7												
8								*	Green recd. an additional			
9									\$100. for today's work			
10									i.e. \$200. total for today			
11												
12												
13 ** END OF ILM BLUE SCREEN WITH ACTORS												
14												
15												
16												
17												
18												
19												
20												
21												
22												
23												
24												
25												
26												
27												
28								Standins		Meals		
29								1	Other		12p To 1p	
30									Waivers			
31									Total Atmos.		To	
32								Remarks				
33												

Executive **ROBERT L. BROWN**   Assistant Director _____

duction Supervisor, signed the production report noting that "with the exception of the above, all the scheduled scenes have been completed." The above contained 134 outstanding items to take home to the newly formed ILM group in California.

Shooting on *The Empire Strikes Back* had somehow been extended to Monday, September 24, 1979. Perhaps they all needed the weekend to prepare themselves for Scene 33, Exterior Plain of Hoth—cutting open the Tauntaun's belly. When that scene was shot, Director Irvin Kershner wasn't even there, nor was Harrison Ford present—just his gloves, worn by someone else.

Almost six years after *Star Wars*, on the set of *Jedi*, George Lucas stood in the shadows at the back of the ILM shooting stage in San Rafael and watched his Ewoks being unharnessed. There are approximately 500 special-effects shots, composed of about 2,000 separate elements, and a year of post-production still to go.

He gave a deep, involuntary sigh. "The easy part is over."

CHAPTER 13

GEORGE LUCAS

On Saturday night, June 26, 1982, the 20-year high-school reunion for the Downey High School Class of 1962 was held in Modesto, California. In the natural order of things, Downey and its 585 graduates, all now nudging forty, would have passed into a kind of decent obscurity, except for a five-word movie slogan that helped turn a modestly budgeted movie into a world-wide attraction.

"Where Were You in '62?" was the rallying cry of *American Graffiti*—the first of a string of megahit movies made by a bearded, bespectacled, and rather shy filmmaker named George Lucas, who was graduated from Downey High in 1962. He was the boy from the walnut ranch on the edge of town who had cracked the Hollywood moviemaking system; but in truth, few of the insurance executives, teachers, doctors, and lawyers gathered for the reunion remembered that much about their now-illustrious colleague. Although, as the Mistress of Ceremonies said, "He must have been more in tune with those times than I was!"

In the 20 years since high school, George Lucas has made a virtue of—and a considerable fortune by—being in tune with the times. Three of the top box-office champions of all time are his. *Star Wars*, *The Empire Strikes Back*, and *Raiders of the Lost Ark* have passed into the vernacular.

The fact that George Lucas had decided to attend the reunion in Modesto was a two-fold surprise. First, as Executive Producer of *Jedi*—the third and latest *Star Wars* movie—he had supervised the shooting in London, Yuma, Arizona, and Crescent City, California, and was now working 12 hours a day, six days a week, editing the complex special-effects footage for the movie; while in another cutting room at the Lucasfilm facility in San Rafael, *Jedi*'s British director, Richard Marquand, was editing the live-action footage. Second, his announced intention to attend the reunion brought about quite a bit of publicity, and George Lucas generally shies away from personal publicity.

An event that would not get much publicity was scheduled to take place about a week later. That was the annual Lucasfilm Ltd. employees' Fourth of July picnic, which would be held at George Lucas' 3,200-acre Skywalker Ranch in Marin County. A company yearbook had been assembled and printed and would be handed out to everyone who attended. It contained pictures, and short bios of all the employees; on page 8, following a message from President Robert Greber and a short pictorial history of Lucasfilm, there was a 73-word biography:

GEORGE LUCAS: Chairman of the Board
HOMETOWN: Off Hwy 99.
FAMILY: Growing.
SCHOOLS: Downey High, Modesto Junior College, University of Southern California.
INTEREST: CBS Evening News, Sixty Minutes.
SIGN: Taurus.
EMPLOYMENT HISTORY: 1966 turned down at Hanna Barbera Productions, 1967 turned down at Cornell Wilde Productions, 1968 first script rejected by United Artists (THX 1138), 1979 second script rejected by every major and minor studio (AMERICAN GRAFFITI), 1971 went into business for myself.

Therein lies not one but several stories!

Born in 1944 in Modesto, California, George Lucas was the only boy in a family of four children. His father owned a stationery supply and office furniture store in town and spent Sundays taking care of the walnut ranch. "My family came from nowhere—four generations in California and before that 100 years in Arkansas and another 100 years in Virginia. And that's it. Nobody knows where we originally came from. Obviously, from some criminal or somebody who got thrown out of England or France. It's great not to have been born a prince. I appreciate that. I realize some people have disadvantages to start with, but the biggest disadvantage is the frame of mind you are in. Anything is possible in this country."

Comic books and cliffhanger serials were two of his earliest interests. "I read a lot of comic books, everything from Uncle Scrooge to Superman."

With the passing of time, the Lucas comic book legend— like so many "resource material" quotes—has gotten severely out of focus. "I actually stopped buying them regularly at the age of nine. I still have all the comic books I ever bought. They fit into one small brown cardboard box, and the face value could not have been more than $50, which I paid out of my own pocket money."

About movie serials, he says: "Some of my favorites were the Republic serials and things like Flash Gordon. There was also a television program called *Adventure Theater*, which came on at 6:00 in the evening. We didn't have a television set, so I used to go over to a friend's house and we watched it religiously every night. It was a 20-minute serial chapter, and the leftover minutes of the half hour were filled with Crusader Rabbit. I loved it. I was probably the last kid on my block to get a television.

"There were two theaters in Modesto that we'd go to. One was sort of the 'A' theater and the other the 'B,' and I would go to the movies maybe once every other week."

Even the official Lucasfilm fact sheet allows that its founder was "never a good student." "My father thought that I would never amount to anything." But it wasn't going to the movies that was keeping him from making good grades in high school. "From about the time I was twelve or thirteen years old until eighteen, I was totally involved in cars. Sports cars mainly, but also dragsters. I wanted to be a race car driver in the worst way. I was a real car fanatic. I ate it. I slept it. I lived it. I had a small Fiat modified for racing and won a couple of trophies—hoping for the day when I could compete with the big cars."

Three days before graduation, Lucas was making a right turn into his parents' driveway from Sylvan Road when a classmate's almost new Impala slammed into him at 90 miles an hour. "I should have been killed—but I wasn't. I was driving with a roll bar and a racer's seat belt. For some reason, the seat belt broke during one of the rolls, and I was thrown clear just before the car pretzeled itself around a tree. If I had stayed in, I would have been dead. I'm living on borrowed time. No bones were broken, but my lungs were crushed, and that put an end to a racing career.

"While I was lying in the hospital I got to thinking about my future—whether auto racing was a prudent way to pursue my life. As a result, I sort of buckled down and decided to do something else.

"I wanted to be a commercial artist; a cousin of mine was a commercial artist for *Post Magazine* at the time. I really wanted to go to art school, but my father wouldn't pay for that because he didn't think it was a very solid career, so I went to junior college as a social science major. Anthropology, philosophy, sociology—I've always had a very strong interest in those fields. My minor at the time was English.

"I had become interested in cinematography during the two years at junior college in Modesto. A friend of mine had an 8mm and a 16mm camera, and we just had fun doing stop-frame animation. I made a short film on some other guys who were racing sports cars at the time. I met Haskell Wexler through a friend, a mechanic, who was doing some work on one of Haskell's race cars. He encouraged my filmmaking.

"Plus, my best friend was going to USC and said to me, 'Why don't you come? They have a cinema course here that's really easy. Anybody can get through.' I knew my dad wouldn't pay my way if I enrolled in the art department, but he would send me to what he called a 'regular college.'"

Film school proved to be the absolute right choice for George Lucas. "The first thing you learn is that there are no rules—moviemaking is making the impossible happen. Everybody has a favorite period in his life—high school, pre-high school, college, after college. I would have to say that film school was my favorite period. I was free and I was on my own and I had everything to look forward to. I was doing what I wanted to do and learning a tremendous amount. The cinema department at that time at USC was very exciting. There were a lot of other students there who were also mad about making movies. We were hoping to break into the film business and were all sort of idealistic and ambitious."

It would, however, take them the better part of a decade to make their mark in the commercial cinema. "I went first of all as a photographer. I wanted to be a cameraman, but at film school you have to do something of everything. Scriptwriting classes were the worst of times. I did terribly. I hated stories and I hated plot, and I wanted to make purely visual films that had nothing to do with telling a story. It's hard to explain. I didn't have a natural feeling for plot and scripts and whatnot. I just didn't find them that interesting. I guess that's in the nature of certain people. I enjoyed more visual, abstract ideas rather than stories. I was more interested in film—pure film. I was a difficult student. I got into a lot of trouble all the time because of that attitude. My first films were very abstract tone poems. It's not that I didn't want to work with actors; actually, I took a couple of years of drama. I not only had to work with actors, but I had to act myself, which was a terrifying experience!

"The film students were like foreigners living in a strange land and all speaking the same language, all of us banding together to beat on the doors of Hollywood. We would share resources. If you needed something, a friend would tell you whom you could get it from. And we all looked at one another's work, mostly at student film festivals." During this period Lucas met and formed an enduring friendship with Steven Spielberg. And it was at the 1967–68 Third Annual Student Film Festival that he received the Best Film Award for his most ambitious film school production, the 20-minute futuristic electronic labyrinth: *THX 1138:4EB*.

He did some work on the outer fringes of the film industy—as a cameraman for graphics ace Saul Bass, and on a series of United States Information Agency documentaries. "My first job in Hollywood actually was working for the United States government, cutting a film on President Johnson's trip to Asia, with Verna Fields as the supervising editor." Then George Lucas took up two separate short-term scholarships. First, as one of four students invited to make a documentary on the making of Carl Foreman's movie *MacKenna's Gold*, and second, an $80-a-week Samuel Warner scholarship to go to Burbank and watch other Hollywood movies being made.

The Lucas short, titled *Desert Poem*, turned out to be very similar to its title, rather than an exposition of the rough-and-tumble adventure story of *MacKenna's Gold*. By all accounts it was, and remains, the favorite of Carl Foreman. The Warner scholarship was good for six months. "Usually the experience didn't lead anywhere. I arrived just at the time when Warner Brothers had been sold to Seven Arts, and the only film being made was *Finian's Rainbow*. What I really wanted to do was be transferred to the animation department, which was empty. I figured that I would get a chance to find some film somewhere and use one of the idle animation cameras to make a movie."

The director of *Finian's Rainbow* was a young, film-school-trained director named Francis Ford Coppola. He heard that his trainee was champing at the bit and made him a promise: "If you stick around on the picture, I'll give you some things to do." Lucas' first assignment was to come up with one good idea a day. (That soon evolved into more than just "some things to do.") "I would also get involved in editing and special effects—which I knew a bit about.

After a while Francis began to rely on me as a sort of sounding board to try his ideas out on or as someone to help come up with solutions to technical and editorial problems."

Although Francis Ford Coppola had been five years ahead of Lucas in film school—and the first student ever to move in among the Hollywood heavyweights—the dream they shared, of making good movies, was only just short of obsessive, though they go about achieving that dream in different ways.

"Francis and I are about as different as night and day, which is why we get along so well. He is very adventurous and daring and bold. I am basically conservative, and plodding and careful. Francis concentrates on writing, story, actors; he comes from a theatrical background. I concentrate on camera, editing, and the technical side of film. Francis likes to jump off cliffs; I hug the ground."

The *Finian's Rainbow* arrangement segued right into the next Coppola project, *The Rain People*.

"My job on *The Rain People* was essentially the same," Lucas remembers. "I was a jack-of-all-trades—assistant art director, assistant cameraman, assistant director, assistant general catch-all. It was a very small crew, and whatever needed to be done, I did. I was also working in the morning on writing a revised and expanded version of *THX*. I would get up at 4 o'clock, write for four hours, and then go out and work on the production."

It was during the filming of *The Rain People* that the notion of forming a company called American Zoetrope came up. Lucas had always maintained "what a great thing it would be if you could just take the film school environment and transfer it to a professional setting with all the same camaraderie and interplay. Francis was the President and I was the Vice-President, and we started this little production company in an old warehouse in San Francisco. Warner Brothers eventually decided they would finance it—mainly because of *Easy Rider*. It had been a big hit. We said we were a crazy group of young filmmakers who were going to do great things in the film business, and they decided to bankroll us. I had already written the screenplay for *THX*, so it ended up being the first project of American Zoetrope."

Making *THX* became a baptism of fire for both Lucas as a director and American Zoetrope as a company. "I became a director out of self-defense as an editor. I was fortunate to get tied up with Francis. He said, 'Look, if you are going to direct, first you're going to have to be a writer.' So he forced me to write that first screenplay, which was pretty awful." Another writer was brought on board, and credit for the final shooting script was shared by Lucas and his old chum Walter Murch. The 95-minute film was shot in 40 days on a budget of $750,000. It was shot in the San Francisco Bay Area, using the then brand-new and unopened *BART* subway system for its surrealistic locations.

"The camera work was very flat, very two-dimensional, stylized, graphic. I was trying for a naturalistic look that was almost documentary in terms of lighting." Lucas turns to the subject of directing. "Once I started directing big productions, I didn't enjoy it, because of the fact that directing isn't hands-on work. I like hands-on. I actually like to cut film. Besides writing and directing, I was the lighting cameraman, and the editor—so it was a hands-on movie."

The crunch came on what Coppola and Lucas have both called Black Thursday. "Francis had borrowed all this money from Warner Brothers. [*Apocalypse Now*, in its then form, was part of the *THX*/American Zoetrope deal.] When the studio saw a rough cut of *THX* and saw the scripts of the other movies we wanted to make, they said, 'This is all junk. You have to pay us back all the money you owe us.' That is the reason why Francis did *The Godfather*—he was so deeply in debt he didn't have any choice."

THX was well received critically, but it did not make very much money at the box office. "If *THX* wasn't successful, it wasn't really that people perceived it as being flawed—the flaws were intentional. Often, we were trying things that could not possibly work. We would say, 'This is an interesting idea—either it's going to work or it isn't, but let's try it.' Later, in *Star Wars*, I had much less of that. I mean, *Star Wars* is a very safe movie—it's all designed.

"I was left high and dry. *THX* had taken three years to make and I hadn't made any money on it. My wife Marcia was still supporting us as a film editor; and after struggling to get *Apocalypse Now* off the ground, I thought: Well, I'll do the rock and roll movie—that's commercial." The rock and roll movie was to be known as *American Graffiti*. "The title first came up when I was doing one of my term papers at school. The name just floated into my head, and I wrote it down in a notebook. When I started writing the film, I was thumbing back through those notes and happened to spot *American Graffiti*.

"After *THX*, everybody had been accusing me of being a cold, arty director who could only do science fiction. Francis was giving me a hard time too, and he kept telling me to make something 'warm and human' to prove I wasn't a cold guy. You want warm and human, I thought; right, I'll give it to you.

"It is much harder to do a second film than it is to make your first film. Because *THX* was a strange movie, I really was unwelcome in the film business, and it took a long time before I was able to get *American Graffiti* off the ground."

The version of the *American Graffiti* screenplay that finally caused a nibble of interest at Universal Studios was crafted by Lucas and screenwriter friends Willard Huyck and Gloria Katz. (Huyck and Katz have recently finished the script for the new Indiana Jones adventure.) There were conditions to Universal's interest, however. The project had to have at least one big name—either a well-known actor or a bankable producer. "They gave me a list of names, and Francis' name was on the list. *The Godfather* was about to be released, and the whole town was abuzz. You could see what they were thinking—'From the man who gave you *The Godfather*.'"

Universal finally okayed a $750,000 budget with a 28-

day shooting schedule. It was the same size budget as *THX 1138*, but with a 12-day shorter shooting schedule.

Lucas found the whole shooting of the movie "a rather horrendous experience. I found myself saying, 'I really don't like directing. This is no fun. What I like is editing. That is a time when I can really sit back, lose track of time, and enjoy myself. Directing is very difficult because you are making a thousand decisions—there are no hard, fast answers—and you are dealing with people, sometimes very difficult, emotional people.' I just didn't enjoy it, so I was going to retire from that . . ."

American Graffiti touched a chord. Teenagers started to cruise again, which hadn't happened for years in some parts of the country. "After the film came out in 1973, I got so many letters from kids who said they had been lost, that they didn't know what being a teenager was all about until they saw *American Graffiti*. Being a teenager had meant smoking pot, hanging out, being mellow. But suddenly they saw the teenage years as being made up of more simple things like chasing girls, having fun, and goofing off. It was then I realized that in *THX* I was trying to get people to believe in an idea—and move them with an idea. It was a very pessimistic film, saying how awful things were.

"I began to think that in order to do anything in film that will have social repercussions—you have to make an optimistic movie that gives people hope. That way things CAN happen."

In January of 1973, six months before *American Graffiti* was due to be released, there was very little for George Lucas to be optimistic about. "I really didn't make very much money doing the film. It took two and a half years, and I averaged about $7,000 a year. At that point I was $15,000 in debt, and Universal hated the film so much they were thinking about selling it to TV as a movie of the week. So I thought, I'll whip up that treatment—the one that was to be my second deal at United Artists—my little space thing."

His "little space thing" began as a 14-page outline. "I

wanted to do a modern fairy tale—a myth. One of the things that occurred to me was that I had seen the Western movie die. We hardly knew what had happened—one day we turned around and there just weren't any Westerns any more. A director like John Ford grew up with the West, the very tail end of it, and he was out there when there were cowboys and shootings in the street. In a way, that was his *American Graffiti*.

"I didn't want to make a *2001*. I wanted to make a space fantasy more in the genre of Edgar Rice Burroughs. I wanted two ships flying through space shooting at each other—that was my original idea. You had never really seen a space dogfight in the movies up to that point, except maybe in a Flash Gordon, where you had all those funny little spaceships shooting Roman candles at one another. In those movies it was always one ship sitting here and another ship sitting there, and they shot these little lasers at each other, then one of them disappeared.

"The biggest problem was writing it—getting what was in my head onto a piece of paper and making it work to my satisfaction. Some people have the talent and some people don't. I knew, in the screenplay, that I wanted some funny dialogue and I wanted a certain character to be warm, yet somehow I couldn't seem to get it to happen.

"I looked at lots of movies—all kinds. Everything: Flash Gordon, spy movies, westerns, Samurai movies, Errol Flynn movies, space movies, science-fiction movies. At one point both Ben Kenobi and Princess Leia were going to be Japanese.

"I wanted everything in the movie to appear very used, very beat-up-looking. I was going for a kind of art deco underpinning to a gritty frontier Western town. With the Death Star, I was looking for something very practical and very technical without making it enormously expensive."

Lucas was contractually obligated to show his next project to United Artists and to Universal. Both studios turned a blind eye to the possibilities of *Star Wars*. Twentieth Century-Fox was prepared, however, to risk $10,000 for development money, and Lucas and his producer Gary Kurtz walked away with a 15-page-memo deal. Paradoxically, by the time the final Fox contract was initialed, *American Graffiti* had been released and, after a slow start, became a huge success, elbowing its way onto the list of the top 20 most profitable pictures of all time.

They decided to shoot the movie in England for two reasons: the large amount of stage space needed to build a galaxy was readily available and the local labor was dependable; and crews and raw materials were less expensive than in California.

This, however, was a vastly more complex project than anything Lucas had worked on before. "*American Graffiti* had maybe 40 people on the payroll, including the cast; *THX* had about the same. You can control a situation like that. On *Star Wars* we had over 950 people working for us, and I would tell a department head something and he would tell another assistant department head, who would then tell some other guy; by the time it got down to the end of the line, it was not there. It was gone. I spent my time yelling and screaming at people, something I had never had to do before.

"*Star Wars* was a great challenge to everybody who worked on it. As a realist, I feel that it fell much shorter than anything I have ever tried, and for that reason, it was much more disappointing. It was my first experience with REAL special effects. I had worked in opticals and animation and stuff like that, but not in the area of the real, problem-solving special effects that were generated by *Star Wars*. But, considering that we were breaking new ground and doing a lot of experimentation at the same time—in terms of technology and actual filmmaking—we did a fairly good job. The analogy that I would make is this—you are looking to run a two-minute mile, and everybody knows you are not going to make it. If you are looking to run a three-minute mile, you might do it. And if you fall short, you are not going to fall nearly as short of your goal as you do when you are trying to do it in two minutes.

"I certainly fell short of what I wanted to do in *Star Wars*, and nothing will change that. When I finished the film and saw the first cut, my only opinion was: I did a terrible job—but it works. It doesn't work very well—but it works. And that was reconfirmed when I saw the trailer for the first time. The trailer is more like the movie I set out to make—spaceships flying around and monsters and craziness. When I saw *Star Wars* at a preview, though, I realized that no matter how far short I thought it fell, the film did work for an audience."

On the night *Star Wars* opened on Hollywood Boulevard, George Lucas was sitting across the street in the Hamburger Hamlet. "I was mixing sound on the foreign versions of the film. I had been working so hard that, truthfully, I forgot the film was being released that day. My wife was mixing *New York, New York* at night in the same place we were using during the day, so at 6 P.M. she came in for the night shift just as I was leaving. There was a huge line around the block at the Chinese Theater. I remember saying, 'What's that?' I had completely forgotten, and I couldn't really believe it. I had planned a Hawaiian vacation as soon as we were finished, and I'm glad I wasn't around for all the craziness that took place after that.

"*Star Wars* nearly broke me. I'm not a good general. You start carving out little toy soldiers, and you get good. You get so good you start a factory, and now you have lots of guys in there carving toy soldiers. Only they are not as good, and you become frustrated. It was time I started listening to my own advice—the theme of my films: 'Anyone can do it!'"

In Hawaii at the same time was Director Steven Spielberg. While the *Star Wars* box office boiled over back home, the two directors built sand castles and tossed around an idea for a movie that Lucas had originated several years before. It was to have all the excitement, action, and flavor of the old Saturday afternoon serials they both loved. It was later christened *Raiders of the Lost Ark*. Other projects were going forward. A Spielberg protégé, writer Larry Kasdan, had turned in the first draft of the Indiana Jones story and had been hastily recruited into the "kitchen cabinet" to work on the screenplay for *Star Wars* Episode V, *The Empire Strikes Back*. The original writer on *Empire*, Leigh Brackett, had died suddenly.

Producer Gary Kurtz recalls: "During *Star Wars*, when we were feeling very optimistic, we'd sit around and talk about how nice it would be to do another movie if this one were successful. At the time, however, we had no idea if there was a market for it or not—it was just speculation. After the opening, we talked very seriously about going on with the next portion of the outline, which turned out to be the Empire story. It was about three months after the *Star Wars* release that we began thinking seriously about getting into production."

After a careful screening process (little is now ever left to chance after one or two personnel problems on *Star Wars*)—and to most people's surprise—Irvin Kershner was assigned to direct *The Empire Strikes Back*.

It was his ten-year-old son who tuned Kershner in to the *Star Wars* appeal. When they both went to see the film on its initial release, Kershner found himself watching his son's reaction more than what was happening on the screen. "At first his mouth dropped open in amazement, and he looked bewildered. Then he began laughing and was on the edge of his seat the whole time. I wondered why he was so excited. Gradually I got caught up too."

"A fair description of the plot," in writer Kasdan's words, "is to say it's the second act of a three-act drama. It's a second act in terms of plot complications and character development. I think one of the things that's different about *Empire* is that you might not come out whistling. The title tells you what the movie is about—the Empire is angry this time."

Carrie Fisher, who was only nineteen when Princess Leia first tangled with the forces of darkness in *Star Wars*, observes that "basically *Empire* has romance, minor tragedies, and characters working more off one another. Sure, it's a fairy tale just like the first one, but it has an added dimension."

With the guidelines firmly set in the original, and with most major problems in the areas of special effects, props, and set construction apparently solved, the shooting of *Empire* should have been simple. It wasn't. *Empire* ended up an expensive 55 days over schedule. Still, it recouped its investment within three months of the opening. Sequels traditionally attract about 65 percent of the original business, but in some territories *The Empire Strikes Back* recorded a bigger gross than *Star Wars* and, in due time, became the number two box-office champion right behind *Star Wars*. *Empire* received 14 Academy Award nominations and carried off six Oscars.

Despite his very substantial personal income, the Lucas lifestyle is modest. He waited several years before purchasing his first Dino Ferrari—used. "People have the perception that money will make everything wonderful—it doesn't make anything wonderful. You can live in a nicer house and choose what you want for dinner. But if your Mercedes has a dead battery, it's even more frustrating than your Chevy having a dead battery. When you're rich, everything is supposed to work."

With the various Lucasfilm Ltd. technical departments now consolidated in San Rafael, it was inevitably time for its founder to turn his thoughts to the third story in the saga. "*Jedi* is the final chapter of the second trilogy—the conclusion of the conflict between Luke and Darth Vader. It resolves the situation once and for all."

If production continues at its present pace, with a new *Star Wars* episode being premiered every three years, the final tale will not be unveiled until the year 2001, but already George Lucas is wondering aloud whether he has not already devoted too much time to the three films. "I've got ideas for the seventies and eighties, and I haven't even been able to deal with them yet!"

Should George Lucas need any confirmation that he has spent the last eight years wisely and well, there is a piece of *Star Wars* folklore that should help. At the end of a 1980 preview of *The Empire Strikes Back* in New York City, an unidentified man stood up in the packed audience and shouted across the auditorium, "Start Part Three!" The person who later claimed credit for this exhortation was none other than Dr. Isaac Asimov, himself a three-time Hugo winner and the acknowledged twentieth-century grand master of science fiction.

CHAPTER 14

"Special effects don't make the movie, and they are only important to tell the story and to give the characters credibility," says George Lucas. "If the characters are not there or the acting isn't good, the movie will fall apart. It can't sustain itself. People think these are special-effects movies. I would say the effects contribute maybe 15 to 20 percent to the enjoyability, effectiveness, and popularity of the movie—at the most. Even in *Star Wars*.

"If you start developing computerized backgrounds, hopefully that will be a way of bringing down the cost. But in reality, if things are done right, the films won't look any different from the way they look today. With these systems available, there will be a lot of filmmakers moving in. You'll have tiny figures walking around in giant and beautiful sets, which will be boring; the films will be a failure, and everybody will say: 'Computer movies are not commercial.'"

Lucas emphasizes his point again.

"The whole thing relies on the actors. I would say the acting and the story are at least 75 percent of the film. Just that. If you can't get that 75 percent, if you don't have good performances and a good plot, you will never get the film to run on the 25 percent that is left. No matter how brilliant a director you are, how fantastic the special effects, how beautifully it is photographed, how wonderful the music is, it will not work as a popular movie running on 25 percent."

Although moviemaking is a group endeavor, it still relies heavily on one man's vision. George Lucas in many ways crystallizes the Henry David Thoreau preference: "I would rather sit on a pumpkin and have it all to myself than be crowded on a velvet cushion." The Lucasfilm pumpkin has ripened and multiplied into five elegant but unobtrusive buildings in the industrial section of San Rafael, a town of about 45,000 people. The migration of like minds north includes such film names as John Korty, Michael Ritchie, Francis Ford Coppola, Phil Kaufman, Hal Barwood, Matthew Robbins, George Lucas, and Gary Kurtz. John Korty remembers: "In the old days people would treat me as if I were crazy, because I was making films in San Francisco. Now they ask how they can get in on it too."

George Lucas tried to explain his reasons for going it alone to *Fortune* magazine after *The Empire Strikes Back* had consolidated the *Star Wars* success. "The idea was to invest my money where I could get the highest return. I decided I had the most faith in my own films. Business is a necessary evil for me now. I'm trying to turn the system around. The studios use films they don't have the vaguest idea how to make in order to earn profits for their shareholders. I'm using my profits to make films." Making those films includes, of course, all the careful and arduous postproduction work that ILM has to do.

The most common question to any film technician who has worked on the actual shooting of a *Star Wars* picture is: "Why do we have to wait so long to see it?" As if, once the final foot of film from the locations had passed through the laboratory, all that remained was for the filmmaker to sign a few last checks, tape the relevant pieces of film together, and send the movie off to the movie houses.

In the summer of 1982, Howard Kazanjian explained: "The very first thing we start—the day after wrapping the picture—is developing the screen credits, which are usually late to the lab anyway. Once you go into post-production, you have to think about sound effects editors, dialogue cutters, ADR people, reserving looping stages and scoring stages. We have a lock set for *Jedi* for November 2, when we bring in John Williams to see the film.

"There will be 900 to 1000 individual shots still to go into the picture, with probably 2,000 different elements created by ILM to make up 500 of those shots."

There are no signs outside the Industrial Light and Magic building announcing what goes on inside. The giveaway, once the visitor is safely inside, is the distinctive Top-Hatted Illusionist logo which is on the wall behind the reception desk. In its seven years of operation, ILM has assembled a work force from many different areas. George Lucas explains ILM's way of operating. "We are trying to bring in outside projects so that in between our films we can keep everyone here working. The situation for having a permanent staff on special effects is very unique."

ILM General Manager Tom Smith presently allocates up to a quarter of the division's annual budget for research and development. This is a necessity because techniques are accelerating so quickly that everything ILM is working on now could be obsolete by the end of the decade. For the next several months, however, ILM will be working on the project it was set up to work on—*Star Wars*; specifically: *Jedi*. Often, ILM will be working six to seven days a week, in order to finish on time.

In the summer of 1982, the pitch is high and steady at the daily production meetings. At 8:29 A.M. precisely, the building's loudspeaker system announces, "Meeting in one minute." The small screening room where the meetings are held is filled to standing room with the 40 necessary people in attendance. The room is papered with several hundred storyboards in various shades of pink, blue, yellow, and white. There is one empty seat, second row center. It is reserved for George Lucas.

Production Supervisor Rose Duignan, sitting on a stool at the front of the room, moves the business along briskly. She reprimands the day crew for not slating their elements (identifying the shots) correctly and adds an admonition—part humorous, part serious—not to film spacecraft that aren't in the movie! The subject of strobing (intermittent flashings) on the movieola sparks a lively couple of minutes of discussion on the efficacy of two- and three-bladed projector shutters.

There is also, it seems, a kleptomaniac at large in the building. Tools have been "borrowed" in the dead of night and not returned; *Raiders* hats, patches, posters, and even some Hollywood trade papers have taken a walk from the model shop. The best suggestion is to set a trap. But the final decision is deferred, with the last speaker hoping aloud that the thief doesn't steal a spaceship. Visual Effects Supervisor Richard Edlund observes evenly, "The whole place is like a toy chest anyway."

Richard Edlund has been paying the price of three Oscar wins in six years with a greatly increased schedule and new demands on his time. He has come straight from the airport after delivering a lecture in London to a society of British cinematographers. Right now, he is more interested in viewing yesterday's work, which occupies the second half of the meeting that traditionally starts at 8:45, when George Lucas walks through the door.

Special effects are shot in extremely short spurts, generally lasting only between two and six seconds. They are projected on the "rock and roll" projector principle. This means lacing up the piece of film in a continuous loop which is then run forward and backward again without interruption—thereby allowing the technicians to watch all the shots several times over a short period of time and to detect any inconsistencies.

George Lucas arrives and the meeting begins. Today's agenda consists of: first, a super-fast traveling shot along a surface tunnel on the Death Star; and second, a steadicam (a gyroscopically balanced camera) test in the redwoods to simulate a speeder bike traveling at top speed, which will just pass muster if the wires are Vaselined out or etched out frame by frame, using the rotoscope system. "Better than building a forest ourselves," observes Howard Kazanjian to no one in particular. He probably means cheaper as well!

Richard Edlund is unhappy with a shot of the Rebel fleet

massed in space. He suggests a retake because the key light which is used to give the spacecraft shape and more dramatic dimension is awry. Finally, the meeting disperses with the kind of jovial self-criticism usually found on grade-school report cards: "Quite good, but can do better."

For Richard Edlund, it is very much a matter of professional pride. "The pictures we are making here are seen by many millions of people, so naturally we don't want something going out that doesn't look good. If we see the mistake and have time, we correct it. Anybody here will tell you that most of the pictures he's worked on have flaws that make him cringe. There are certain shots that I just want to hide my eyes from. I see them, and I ask others of my peers—the effects community—if they noticed; but they don't see them! That makes me feel better, but not good!"

Twenty-four hours later, General Manager Tom Smith was congratulating his print department on producing the Rebel fleet retake so swiftly. "We redid the shot and saw it first thing this morning. George looked at it and said it's too long on the screen, so we're shooting it over again today. That's not something you can foresee—you plan as best you can. It is the same in principal photography; you don't budget a film expecting to get everything right on the first take."

Tom Smith talks about *Jedi* and ILM: "Right now, the whole building is on a 50-hour week. Eventually we will also have three crews working at night. We have about 120 people, and I don't think we are going to get any larger than that. Since *Empire*, we have developed more independence on the part of the crews."

How, exactly, is ILM organized?

"During *Empire*, Richard Edlund was the Supervisor of Special Effects and had everyone working for him. Now the administration is handled from the production department by Rose Duignan and three coordinators. Each coordinator has a supervisor of special effects working with him or her, and each supervisor runs two camera teams. Effectively, we have six outfits out there shooting.

"George keeps insisting that there won't be any more special effects in *Jedi* than there were in *Empire*. But I can already see that the new ones are going to be more complicated. What will probably happen—as the effects start rolling in—is George's appetite will increase.

"From the technical angle, two things have changed: we have doubled the capacity of the optical department to two printers and two processors, and we have now developed the go-motion system to a point where it can do remarkable things. We have devices that move an object during the exposure, which induces a blur in the picture and makes it look as if the object is actually moving. So what began with the Tauntaun in *Empire* and continued with the monster in *Dragonslayer* is now going to reach fruition in *Jedi*."

What lies in the future?

"In the next five or ten years I see a tremendous revolution in special effects. Computers are going to play an increasing role in what we do. We gave a demonstration of this in *Star Trek: The Wrath of Khan*. In the film you see a video representation of what they call the Genesis effect. It is a fantastic image where we start in space looking at a moonlike object. The camera tracks rapidly toward it as a small probe hits the planet. The planet bursts into flames, and the camera begins orbiting around the planet. Slowly, the flame transforms the planet into a habitable earth while the camera continues tracking through mountains and over lakes and so on. A shot that would have been totally impossible by any other means was pulled off with a computer—and every single image in that sequence was a digital image. There is not a real set anywhere. It's all on disk!"

What other changes does he see?

"What will happen is that the modelers will be building images by watching a cathode ray tube and moving new electronic images into position on the cathode ray projection. They will fashion a model in two dimensions or from two perspectives and electronically rotate it; then you will be able to see it from all angles. Also, the optical department will be able to take ten or fifteen elements that the cameramen and modelers have made, AND the motion that is taking place, and composite them all onto one screen. The way it is done now is that you send it to the optical department, where it is run through machinery, then developed, then printed, then projected, and on and on and on. With the new techniques, everything will be done at once.

"In the future, someone like George Lucas or Steven Spielberg will just be able to sit down at a screen and see it all happening. It will get to a point where the creative filmmaker will have his hand on the joystick and be able to make the world move the way he wants it to move."

Joe Johnston has now worked on four of Lucas' movies. He had wanted to be an oceanographer until he was deflected by the art classes he took at Pasadena City College into an art program. This eventually led him into industrial design, where he worked on "watches, seats for buses, things like that. A lot of people I went to school with had gone into the movie business—John Dykstra and about five or six others. One of them, Bob Shepherd, was working on *Star Wars*. He just put out the word he was looking for people, and I went to talk to him." Joe Johnston has now been with Lucasfilm for seven years. "We design a lot of the *Star Wars* hardware here that is built in England and eventually used in live action—like the skiffs, the Sail Barge, and the Imperial walkers. For the first six or twelve months of the production, we're doing pure design, and that's really the fun part.

"I did some *Star Wars* model building, but it wasn't the heavy construction. I just kind of added parts to a lot of the models between design work and storyboard stuff.

"On *Empire* everything was preplanned. Our storyboards even had frame counts on them with the precise number of frames needed for each individual shot. The film was going to be cut precisely. We knew beforehand, for instance, that Shot M154 called for 112 frames. There is obviously flexibility in that, but you know pretty much whether it's going to be a one-second or half-second shot. It required a lot of thought, but it worked out nicely. We have found that it's easier to start with the effect and then work that into the live action, rather than getting stuck with something they design and build in England that you have to try and reproduce over here.

"It seems to be more difficult to do a film like *Jedi*. The shots are more complex, there are more of them, and they involve things we haven't really tried to do before, but that is the best way to learn. *Empire* made *Star Wars* look easy; *Jedi* makes both of them look easy. I don't know where we could go from here!"

Another member of the team is Ralph McQuarrie. He strolled into the motion picture business after having been a leading illustrator with the Boeing Aeronautics Company, Litton Industries, and Kaiser Graphics. His artist's impression of the Apollo activities on the dark side of the moon gave millions of television viewers an accurate idea of the mission's progress when the live camera transmission was blocked out.

"I was hired initially to give George Lucas a chance to get as close as he could to the ideal look for things he had been dreaming about getting into his films. Actually, George could have done any or all of the conceptual sketches himself, because he draws quite well. But George concentrated more on ideas and let me get them into shape because I have a greater facility for drawing and painting. He wanted me just to support his first script with visuals. He felt it was the kind of script that people weren't very impressed with. The idea seemed kind of funky. The scope of *Star Wars* was so vast that George felt he could use a few of my paintings to convince the people at Fox that his movie idea would be interesting. They listened to his presentation, looked at my four or five paintings, and were convinced enough to give him sufficient money to finish the script and for me to do some more paintings."

Three men share the Visual Effects credit for *Return of the Jedi*. They are: Dennis Muren, Ken Ralston, and Richard Edlund. All are veterans of several Lucasfilm and Industrial Light and Magic projects.

Dennis Muren's first film, shot with a 16mm camera during a summer vacation, used stop-motion and special effects. It obtained a regular theater circuit release as an independent motion picture. After his work on *Jedi*, he will have worked on all three of the *Star Wars* movies. He was also effects director of photography on *Dragonslayer*, supervisor of special visual effects on *E.T.* and has also worked on many television commercials.

Ken Ralston has kept busy at ILM working as effects cameraman on *Empire*, supervisor of visual effects on *Star Trek II: The Wrath of Khan*, and he has worked on special effects on both *Dragonslayer*, and *Poltergeist*.

An impressive Viking figure in modern dress, Richard Edlund has worked on *The China Syndrome*, and *Poltergeist*, and he won Academy Awards for his work on *Star Wars*, *Empire*, and *Raiders*. During an interview with San Francisco journalist Peter Stack, he tried not to lose the writer in a welter of technical data or futureworld sorcery. "I'm not like an actor who can talk about how I prepare emotionally for a role . . . so what I end up talking about is how we make movies, even with the most sophisticated technology, out of chewing gum and baling wire. Most people would be amazed to find out how many thumbtacks and clothespins hold things together. As hard as anyone tries to make celebrities out of us special effects guys, the truth is, we are like cottage industrialists, locked up in our workrooms, devising this or that. We're true lab rats, most of us . . . we never see any sunlight . . . always fiddling around with gimmicks, with gadgets, with strange concepts. It's surprisingly unglamorous!"

How did they revive the use of the VistaVision camera?

"The VistaVision system had been developed in the 50's by Paramount and Technicolor and was short-lived. A tremendous amount of money had been spent to develop it. Cameras and later equipment were all sitting around, a movement on the screen, an effect that would cost 25 or 30 thousand dollars to build from scratch, we could get for a thousand bucks.

"On *Empire* we probably broke records for the number of elements deposited in a specific scene. They are flying in, out, and around . . . asteroids are tumbling through space, some just barely missing the camera. There are shadows playing across the faces of the asteroids that go off into the distance, so you don't have the effect of just nothing but a background card with space painted on it in the background. In this one particular shot there were approximately 20 separate photographed elements. That doesn't include the animation and rotoscope work that went into it as well. Probably 100 pieces of film or more were generated through the process of putting that one composite together.

"Since *Empire*, we have done *Raiders*, *Dragonslayer*, *Poltergeist*, *Star Trek*, and *E.T.* Naturally, in doing other projects you learn things, even though they are only indirectly applicable. Whenever anybody here embarks on a project, he puts 150 percent of his effort into it. On the *Star Wars* movies we don't say, 'No, George, we can't do it.' I don't believe anything is impossible in effects, provided you have the time and money. The degree of success will hinge on the money. And even if you have enough money, you may not have enough time. We are not in a situation where we can command whatever we want to happen. You can't wish it done, you have to do it—so therefore, we have to compromise.

"I think George Lucas is the quintessential effects director in films. He knows how far we can go, he knows how much of it to use. The best effect that can be done on film will die if you leave it on the screen two seconds too long. You start seeing the frayed edges and all the problems. We're trying to trick people all the time; that's our job. If your ten-year-old goes to the theater and something doesn't look right, he immediately notices. He doesn't have to have any kind of education other than watching film since he was old enough to look. If our shot has a flaw in it, he'll pick that flaw out—and it has distracted him from the drama at hand!"

Edlund pauses a second, then adds, "And we have let the director down."

The Lucasfilm post-production division, called Sprocket Systems, is very definitely a State of the Art facility. It is dedicated to pushing the limits of film editing and sound-track recording to the upper limits, while keeping the cost down to viable limits.

If there is a genetic strain in the Sprocket Systems' approach to film editing, sound design, and computer development, it is, according to General Manager Jim Kessler, to "avoid the idea of 'This is what we used to do.' We have been involved with *Jedi* since January 1981. We will be involved beyond the release date to probably July of 1983 in order to do all the foreign language mixes. Our main focus is on sound and trying to upgrade the original recording at the production level. So any sound post-production processing that takes place is really only an enhancement of the original, as opposed to a fix-and-patch job. We're trying to get beyond the level of survival, which was just attempting to get dialogue and sound effects audible, and reach into new dimensions."

Kessler continues: "Today films are done in a piecemeal fashion. But back in the thirties, the studios controlled all facets of a film and we are determined to get back to that. One reason is lower cost. You make fewer mistakes, and you provide a better finished product. It may sound contradictory, but it means taking a passive and, at the same time, an aggressive role. We are attempting to have some effect on the film production level, and also some effect in the presentation—to make the theater owners, producers, and distributors a little more aware that the sound of film isn't yet totally explored. And we are doing that mostly by demonstration—through the work we've done here.

"In five to ten years' time, we should be back in the thirties. Our philosophy is one of being a post-production division that does sound work at the end, but we are developing our staff and organization to become designers of sound at the same time."

Ben Burtt was the man with the tape recorder who started it all, immediately after the July Fourth holiday weekend, back in 1975. This was two years before Sprocket Systems got going in earnest. George Lucas remembers hiring Burtt. "Usually Walter Murch worked with me. He was the genius whom I went to school with and who had done the sound work in all my movies. But he was committed to Fred Zinnemann and *Julia* at the time as an editor. He was also working on *The Godfather*, and with Carroll Ballard on *The Black Stallion*. So we decided to go back to USC. We went to the sound department there and asked the instructor, who is a friend of ours, 'Where's the next Walter Murch?' They sent us Ben Burtt."

Lucas continues: "We went over some of the sound effects for *Star Wars*. There were several categories that I wanted him to do. One was animals. Another was to collect all kinds of dialects plus transportation sounds, like those of jets, trains, cars—any kind of sound that could be used for a laser gun—weird zaps and cracks, things like that. Those were the main areas. So Ben spent two years developing sound effects—he did all the ray guns, spaceships exploding, and toward the end he worked for three or four months on Artoo. I said I wanted to have *beeps* and *boops*. Well, it is easy to say that, but it's another thing to take those *beeps* and *boops* and actually make a personality."

Ben Burtt couldn't agree more. "It started out very slowly. We'd get one or two words a week that we liked. George would come back on Friday, and I'd say, 'Well, I've gotten the first two words out of Artoo, the first two sentences in that reel. Now here are possible ones for the third and fourth.' I would plan ten alternatives for each one and we would discuss it. It became a very nitty-gritty thing.

"Anything which required characterization was the hardest, because you had to relate to the storyline. We had Artoo talking to Ben Kenobi. You have to be on a level with Alec

Guinness, come up with a character responding to him that's going to make him look good, and not seem silly. So in a sense you have got to achieve a performance with Alec Guinness or Tony Daniels through sound, which is not easy; that is what I struggled with the most. George pushed a great deal of that, and many times I think I stopped too early. I was sort of satisfied with what I had, but he wasn't. I'd work for a long time on something I thought was just perfect, and he'd say, 'No, no it's not any good.' And I'd be crushed and upset and resentful.

"In the beginning George particularly did not want anything electronic in the picture, except maybe robot language. Electronic sound had been, in a sense, a cliché in science-fiction movies. He wanted to avoid that and have as many organic sounds as possible. Real sounds that existed and could be recorded somewhere in the world, wherever they might be. That's why I spent so much time just roaming around, looking and listening at factories, Army bases, and train tunnels. I started for the company with absolutely nothing—literally. I was handed a microphone and a portable Nagra, and I operated out of my apartment living room very much on my own for a year. So I collected sounds and a weekly paycheck. Now the library has grown, over the six years I've been here, to some 600 tapes on the shelf. A very good collection in that it represents a lot of high-quality recordings done in stereo."

Will the sound department become a separate entity?

"We're not in the business of supplying sound to other people; the library is full of ideas and raw material, and we are expanding it constantly. We do use some things more than once or dust down an old sound and add something new to it. Most often I'm trying to create a new sound for each thing, right from the beginning. On the third film, I do go into material that we have stockpiled, but there are probably 500 to 600 new things we have to record just for *Jedi*.

"My very first assignment was to come up with a voice

for the Wookiee. The only thing they said was, 'We have this giant creature who is like a big teddy bear. He's a good guy, but sometimes he's ferocious. We need a nonhuman voice for him that's really believable, but not recognizable as a known animal.' In a film like *Star Wars* you are creating a total fantasy world. Nothing really exists. None of the equipment makes any sound during filming, or the sound it does make isn't the right one. All the sets look great, but they are totally dead. The whole movie is comic-book. It needed really energetic sounds that were visceral."

What about the spaceship sounds in the movies?

"I wandered around Los Angeles International Airport just recording landings in different areas. But the most interesting stuff came from a place in Burbank that built and tested jet engines. They've got the isolated engine sitting in a wind tunnel, and they run it up and go into a lot of different maneuvers. You can't ordinarily record a jet engine that stationary. I would bring the microphones into their test chambers and get a variety of motors—everything from 747s down to helicopters and turbines. Although in the end, the most frequent spaceship sounds are not engines at all, but rather are sounds like the TIE fighters flying by—which was an elephant screaming, slowed down and stretched out electronically."

What about some of the other ships?

"I also went on a hike to a mountain in the Poconos in northern Pennsylvania which has a huge radio tower on the top. The wind is very strong there and it creates an eerie singing-in-the-wires kind of sound. My wife had been there as a kid, and she told me about it. It was hard to record but was ultimately used for the Y-Wing spacecraft and the sort of howling sound they have.

"Since I've been hired to spend more time on a film than the average sound editor does, I've taken on different responsibilities. So we use the term 'sound design.' When I first made contact with the business, sound was, by necessity, one of the last steps in production and consequently had the minimum amount of time, minimum amount of

money left over—and patience on the part of the producers—to allow someone to do the job properly. The way
most sound tracks are done is to divide up the work among
a large group of people, almost in an industrial fashion,
where several reels of the picture will go to editor A, several
to editor B—and there will be maybe no communication
between them at all.

"We share some of those problems at times. But at least
we have a small group of people responsible conceptually
for what is happening, so you get more of one person's
vision. You don't need 25 or 50 people; you only have them
in order to get it done in time. With our system, one person
can do more and more in terms of editing, cutting, and
mixing."

How about the sound in *Jedi*?

"*Jedi* is a continuation of things we've done. We do have
many more characters doing a lot more talking, and they
can't have perfectly ordinary voices—that part is more complicated. We have new environments, new spaceships and
battles. I would say most of the creative pressure on us is
the fact that we want to outdo ourselves.

"I'm working on what I call the all-alien version. Every
character speaks another language—one you won't understand. It's an extreme approach to see what happens in
certain scenes and whether you can still understand the
action. With the Ewoks, for example, a lot of information
is conveyed through body language, and sometimes it is
more interesting that way."

How is the sound plant at Lucasfilm?

"Compared to most sound-editing operations, we are
somewhat innovative in our technology, but it's all using
equipment that is found elsewhere in the world. We've
stolen a few ideas from video editing, a few from music
recording, and we are doing a light editing now on tape
without going to sprocketed film. Doing it this way allows
one person to read more. The more you work with a new
system like this, the easier it is to detach yourself from some
of the traditions. I spend about 25 percent of my time ex-

perimenting, at least during the early phase, which won't happen once we get a cut of the picture together. We occasionally come up with ideas like this 24-track business we are using now, with time codes that interlock tape machines and film—that's new. And the successful ideas we'll use on *Jedi*. It wasn't until *Jedi* that I really had the clout to say, 'Let's try an idea I have on the production side,' and people were willing to listen. I had never been on the set of any picture prior to *Jedi*, so I had something to learn. I went with the expectation that maybe I could find solutions to some of the problems we've had in the past. A lot of new ideas were tried, and many of them failed instantly. I think we have ended up with something a little better than we've had in the past, but not a huge percentage."

While Ben Burtt remains the roving reporter of Lucasfilm, nipping off to spend a week on a Navy destroyer recording every *snap*, *crackle*, *pop*, and *ping*, someone has to stay behind to mind the shop. Tomlinson Holman is mild mannered and bespectacled, a highly qualified man who was hired, among many other things, to take the kinks out of the new Sprocket multimillion dollar high tech dubbing facility in San Rafael.

The Brave New World of computers is just one of the mandates of a gentleman named Ed Catmull. "Three years ago George Lucas wanted to bring high technology into the film industry, so he went out on a search, and I was the one who got picked.

"George didn't want to put any pressure on me, but he wanted to bring in high technology. He wanted it done on *Jedi*, and he wanted it done right. There were three areas that were important to him. The first was computer control to assist in the film editing. In that process, one transfers the video image and edits on video where the computer can keep track of the cuts. It allows for strong film quality with the convenience of video. The second was audio. George wanted the computer to be used to make it easier to edit the sounds. Those two were vital; the third was pure graphics.

"On *Empire* the number of sound reels per film reel is 70. There were 12 film reels for that production, so there were about 800 sound reels. And George likes to change things—that's what editing is all about. He also wants the people working there to be responsive. Well, it's pretty hard to be responsive when you have got 70 reels to cut—to find them and to keep up with what's going on. As you go through the stages of the premix and mix, if you decide to make a change, it becomes a big deal. The sound editors work night and day three weeks before the film goes into release; then the director looks at it and makes changes. Make changes? It's due in the theater!"

What is the goal, then, of all the computer work?

"Our goal is doing things so the creative people never have to make the same decision twice. You want to make sure that if you tighten something up—lose a couple of frames—the other things such as ambient sounds all stay at the same level. You only have to concentrate on the fact that you have removed something. That's actually easy. If you have to add something, that is more difficult; but there are processors capable of doing all of this."

CHAPTER 15

By the fall of 1982, the people at Industrial Light and Magic and at the Sprocket Systems had all their energies focused on finishing post-production on *Jedi*. There were also many additional editors and technicians who had been hired to do specific jobs on the movie. Deadlines on the production schedule were coming up daily, and the train that Kazanjian referred to back in January—before the movie started—was still barreling down the track.

In October, Howard Kazanjian surveyed his production schedule outline (Appendix #1) and pronounced the picture right on target in terms of the release date—that is an unchangeable date.

But there was nothing to worry about. Originally, October 4 had been set as the date for "Sound Efx Editor begins to EOP." Translated: Sound Effects Editor begins and works to the end of picture—or right up to the sneak preview. The film now is visually near enough to completion so that the task of getting all the sound on the track can begin. All the special effects may not be completed, but the filmmakers have the temporary composites in and they know what the film is going to look like, so the sound must begin.

Next, the Foley Walker editors begin. Foley Walker involves all the minimal background sound effects. If the actors are walking down a gravel path and the sound track needs the sounds of their feet crunching on the gravel, then gravel is laid out in a sound studio and someone actually walks on it. The sounds are recorded and then inserted into the sound track. This procedure also applies to other background effects such as a door opening, or a glass being set down on a tabletop, or the noise of clothing in motion; in short, all the minor background sounds that must accompany the action on screen.

Sound effects don't seem to have changed that much over the years. Somehow, with all the technological advances in moviemaking, one assumes that most of the sounds are recorded on the spot and that only a slight number of sounds must be added later. But the dialogue is the important sound that is recorded during a take, and everything else is adjusted or inserted. The sound effects department does have a vast sound library, so they don't always need to record a new effect; but for *Jedi*, and the other *Star Wars* movies, they are creating a new world, so many of the sounds are new.

The next step is a fine cut of the picture when ILM is supposed to have all the temporary composites done. Once the temporary composites—those pieces of mock-up film that show what will eventually be there—are inserted, the big date, LOCK PICTURE, is reached. This is it; this is what *Jedi* is going to look like—unless, of course, someone decides that it still needs just a bit of tinkering. Now, at least, there is a black and white print of what they think the movie is going to look like.

The LOCK PICTURE designation is made essentially for the music sound track and sound effects. John Williams has to have a final version from which to start writing the music because everyone has to go to London at the beginning of January and record the music with the London Symphony Orchestra. At the point of lock picture, Marquand, Lucas, and Burtt will sit down with John Williams and go over the print scene by scene and say: Here is a high point; here is a lull; here is an explosion; the music should build here; and so on—until they all have a feel for the moods and changes of the potential score.

Williams and his people time the scenes to the second in order to start thinking of the way to fit the music to the visuals. Williams gets a sense of the pacing, the beat of the movie, and those wonderful new melodies start going round and round in his head. Kazanjian explains: "If you don't lock the picture, and Johnny's writing for a certain number of seconds and a certain number of frames and we change something—then it's all out of whack. What we're going to do when Johnny's here is give him two reels to take back to L.A. to work on. Then, two weeks later, we're going to give him two more reels, and so on, until he's written the music for the whole movie." By giving Williams two reels at a time, they are, in essence, setting several "lock picture" dates—one for each segment of the film—thereby making up for being a little behind schedule.

Now, after all of that, Kazanjian explains that the "lock picture" is not absolute, because if a few minor changes in the film have to be made after Williams has recorded the score, the Music Editor for the movie, Ken Wannberg, who has worked on the other *Star Wars* movies and who is also a composer can come in and stretch the music out to fit a changed scene, or condense it to fit a shortened scene. What is beginning to emerge from talking with Kazanjian about his outline is that the dates are dates to shoot for, dates that have to be respected, but there is almost always time to make a few small changes in the film.

With the new theater and sound system that have been installed in the Sprockets building at the San Rafael headquarters, Lucasfilm now has one of the best sound-editing systems in the world.

By the middle of November, more sound effects editors are at work. There is a person who has done all of R2-D2's sounds and is back working on him exclusively; another does Chewbacca. It takes maybe two weeks to get all of Chewie's dialogue perfectly recorded and on tape. Then the sound editor moves on to another chore, and all the dialogue editors begin work. There will also be about two weeks of looping done in Los Angeles with the principal actors. Lucasfilm, right now, simply doesn't have the space to do all the looping in San Rafael, so they go to the Goldwyn Studios. Eventually, at the Ranch, Lucasfilm, Ltd. will have the facilities for all aspects of the sound engineering. As each actor finishes his work on the looping in Los Angeles, the track will be sent back to San Rafael, and the editors will begin putting the sound onto the master track.

ADR is Automatic Dialogue Replacement. For looping, in the old days, the piece of film that had the snippet of dialogue on it was cut out separately and put on a continous loop so it would be run over and over again. ADR is all computerized, and the work is done on a print of the film. It is the laying in of synchronized words to lip movements on the screen. (In contrast, dubbing is putting in sounds that didn't exist before.)

Once the dialogue and additional sound effects are nearly completed—and the final mix is underway, and the negative is cut and assembled—the first "black track" of the film is made. A "black track" is simply a color-timed film without its optical sound stripping—literally a black track in lieu of stripping. This step precedes the more finalized "answer print"—color-timed footage with composite sound. Sometimes the black track is referred to as the first answer print.

If, for example, a section of the film is too dark, due to cloud cover or overcast weather conditions on the day of filming, the scene can often be color corrected in the laboratory. Kazanjian recalled just such a case while shooting in Crescent City. In one scene, Carrie Fisher was immersed in a bath of bright sunlight, and it was necessary for the lab to tone down this brightness and correct the color from a warm feeling to a more blue effect. Through a variety of methods the tones, hues, contrast and overall color density of the film can be altered—by the use of different film stocks with variable light sensitivity ratings (ASA), filters, gels, light levels, development time and solution. Scenes can be made warmer by adding a warm color, or colder by the addition of blue. Complexion tones of the actors' faces can also be changed somewhat.

Prior to the final printing process, color timers or graders "time" the black track picture. This is a method for selecting print lights and color filters to improve the densities and color renditions of the original footage.

The filmmakers have one week to tinker, and then the film is finished. The next thing that happens, after the prints are struck, is the opening — what everyone has been waiting for and the last date on the schedule: JEDI RELEASE.

The opening of the movie will take place simultaneously in England, Canada, and the United States. There will be 100 prints in the U.K. and Canada, at least 150 70mm prints in the U.S., and an additional 800 to 1,000 35mm prints in the U.S. There may be as many as 1,500 prints of *Jedi* in release all at once, but the final number hasn't yet been absolutely decided.

Return of the Jedi has gone from a short meeting in London in the spring of 1980 between Howard Kazanjian and George Lucas to a dramatic and exciting film showing in hundreds of theaters in many nations. What began almost ten years ago with George Lucas deciding to go back and work on his "little space thing" has spawned a new galaxy.

It is a galaxy filled with heroes and villains, characters who have become archetypes outside the world of movies. Luke and Leia and Han live here, as do Darth Vader and Jabba the Hutt. Names such as Yoda, Chewbacca, R2-D2, and C-3PO have become part of our lives, joined by Ewoks and Tauntauns. In this galaxy, we ride in X-Wing Fighters and Landspeeders, do battle with AT-ATs and Death Stars, and visit places like Tatooine and the Green Moon of Endor. It is galaxy of good and evil, of hope and desperation, and of the Force.

With the end of *Jedi*, we see the end of the triology that has given us this galaxy. But, like the best of tales, the people, the places, and the grand moments stay with us to reflect on and enjoy. And there is more to come . . . in a galaxy far, far away.

APPENDICES

Appendix #1. The Producer's Tentative Production Schedule, dated September 11, 1981

While several of the dates on this schedule were tentative and quite a few of the other dates were later adjusted, it is a comprehensive overview of the deadlines necessary for the making of *Jedi*.

Appendix #2. Map of EMI Elstree Studios

The proportions may not be 100 percent accurate on this map, but it is a quick reference for sound stages and buildings at the studio where all three *Star Wars* movies and *Raiders of the Lost Ark* have been filmed and where the next *Raiders* movie will begin shooting in the spring of 1983.

Appendix #3. *Blue Harvest* "One-Line" Redwoods Schedule

The one-line shooting schedule for the Crescent City shoot of the Endor forest scenes.

Appendix #4. One-line Shooting Schedule No: 3

This is a reference guide for the basic shooting schedule of *Jedi*. Again, some of the days were adjusted. If the production needed to move on to another set in order to stay on schedule or to make up some time, or needed an additional day on a certain set, then scenes were sometimes returned to later; or the second unit stayed on a set in order to catch up, while the first unit, in order to stick to the schedule, moved on.

Appendix #5. Complete cast and crew credit list

APPENDIX #1

REV 9—11—81

Tentative Production Schedule

1980

JULY	George Lucas starts first draft of screenplay
SEP	Stuart Freeborn begins developing creatures
OCT	Joe Johnston begins story boards

1981

FEB 28	George Lucas delivers script
MAR 3	U.K. Production Meeting
APR 1	U.S. Production Budget meeting
JUN 1	Lucas delivers second draft of screenplay
JUN 22	Monster shop begins
JUL 1	Model makers begin
	Richard Marquand to U.S.
JUL 13	Larry Kasdan script meetings begin
SEP 7	Marquand returns to U.K.
SEP 14	Kasdan delivers script
SEP 16	Howard Kazanjian to U.K.
NOV 16	ILM Model makers begin
DEC 19	Kazanjian returns to U.S.

1982

JAN 2	Kazanjian to U.K.
JAN 4	ILM begins shooting Space Battle
JAN 11	PRINCIPAL PHOTOGRAPHY BEGINS—U.K.
MAR 31	Move to U.S. locations
APR 1	Unpack—Line-up Yuma
APR 2–15	U.S. location—shoot Yuma
APR 16	Unit travel to Crescent City & Line-up
APR 17–30	U.S. location—Crescent City

MAY 1	1st Unit travel to U.K. & San Rafael
MAY 1–28	2nd Unit remains Crescent City
MAY 3–15	San Rafael blue screen & Rancor Pit
MAY 15	PRINCIPAL PHOTOGRAPHY FINISHES
MAY 28	2nd Unit finishes shooting
	ILM Bluescreen finishes
MAY 29	2nd Unit travel to U.K. & San Rafael
JUN 1	ILM begins Ground Battle & Barge sequences
JUN 23	1st Rough Cut
JUL 7	2nd Rough Cut
JUL 28	3rd Rough Cut
AUG 6	4th Rough Cut and SCREENING
AUG 11	Supervising Dialogue Editor begins
SEP 1	Sound Designer begins
SEP 30	Director's Cut
OCT 4	Sound Efx. Editor begins to EOP
	Sound Adm Asst. begins to EOP
	Technical Asst. begins to EOP
OCT 11	Foley Walker begins (10 weeks)
OCT 22	Fine Cut
OCT 29	ILM Finishes all temp composites
NOV 1	LOCK PICTURE
NOV 1–3	Spot Music
NOV 4	Make Sound Efx., B&W Dupes & Snd Xsfers for Sound Efx. Cutters
NOV 8	Sup. Foley Editor begins thru final mix
	Asst. Foley Editor begins thru final mix
	Sound Efx. Editors 2 & 3 begin to EOP
	Asst. Sound Efx. Editors 1 & 2 begin to EOP
	Print Library Editor begins thru final mix
NOV 15	Dialogue Editors 1 & 2 begin thru final mix
	Asst. Dialogue Editors 1 & 2 begin thru final mix
DEC 1	Re-Sync Editors 1 & 2 begin thru final mix
DEC 6	Sound Trans. Runner begins thru EOP
DEC 13	Foley begins thru EOP
DEC 25	CHRISTMAS DAY
DEC 27	ADR Looping begins
	Music Cutter begins
1983	
JAN 2	Kazanjian to U.K.
JAN 3	Music recording begins
JAN 10	U.K. ADR Looping
JAN 22	Music recording finishes
JAN 24	Pre-mix dialogue at Sprockets

JAN 31	Last ILM Finals in
	ILM can take outside work
FEB 7–18	S.F. Pre-mix sound efx
FEB 21	Final Picture Mix starts
FEB 21	Negative Cutting begins
FEB 23	4 Track Mix
MAR 11	1st Black Track
MAR 14	Timing Correction print
MAR 16	Interpositive in
	Internegative in
MAR 17	MPAA Code SCREENING
MAR 18	Negative cutting finishes
MAR 29	Canadian Censor Print
APR 1	Stereo Optical Mix
	JEDI in Can
APR 1	Mono mix (D/M/E)
APR 8	6-Track (M/E)
APR 11	70mm 6-Track Dolby Optical Track
APR 19	70mm printing
APR 29	Turn over all elements to FOX
MAY 10	Last day for 70mm striping/sounding
MAY 16	Last day to deliver prints
MAY 27	JEDI RELEASE

THE "STARWARS" SAGA CONTINUES
THE EMPIRE STRIKES BACK
EMI STUDIOS LAYOUT
(not to scale)

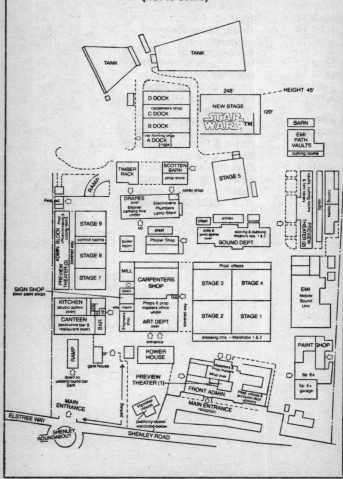

APPENDIX #3

BLUE HARVEST "One-Line"
REDWOODS
MAIN UNIT SHOTS

SC. #	Page Count	Description	Characters
65	1	SHUTTLE LANDING SITE: Heroes trek uphill. Spot Bikers lunch.	Luke, Leia, Han, Chewie, R2, 3PO, Rebel Troopers, Imperial Scouts.
66	1 3/8	BIKERS LUNCH: Heroes sneak attack, shootout, bike chase begins. (2 bikers emerge from far side?)	Luke, Leia, Han, Chewie, Imperial Scouts, Rebel Troopers, Stunts & Doubles.
71	1	BIKERS LUNCH: Luke returns to site, rejoins group. They go after Leia.	Luke, Han, Chewie, R2, 3PO, Rebels, (dead biker?).
72	2 7/8	LEIA'S CRASH SITE: Leia meets Wicket, fights scouts, bikes crash, heroes escape.	Leia, Wicket, 2 Scout Officers, (dead biker?).
74	6/8	LEIA'S CRASH SITE: Heroes find crash site & move on, looking for Leia.	Luke, Han, Chewie, R2, 3PO, Rebels, (dead biker?).

75	2 5/8	NET GAG: Heroes meet Ewoks via net trap.	Luke, Han, Chewie, R2, 3PO, Stunt Doubles, Teebo, Ewoks.
88	1	RIDGE OVERLOOKING BUNKER: Heroes spot scouts & bikes near bunker and plan strategy. 3PO translates to Wicket and Teebo, then Wicket runs off.	Leia, Han, Chewie, R2, 3PO, Wicket, Teebo, Rebel Troopers, Scooter Troopers.
89	2/8	NR. BUNKER: Wicket flipping bike switches.	Wicket, (scouts?).
90 (1,2)	2/8	RIDGE: Group watches Wicket, then start to move out.	Leia, Han, Chewie, 3PO.
91 (1,2)	2/8	NR. BUNKER: Scouts race toward Wicket just as he takes off on bike.	Wicket, Scouts.
92 (1,2,3)	3/8	POV – BUNKER: One Scout is left behind.	One scout.
		RIDGE: Group reacts to the situation. Han & Chewie go after the last guard.	Leia, Han, Chewie, R2, 3PO.
94 (1,2)	2/8	BUNKER: Rebels have stripped a scout and sneak into bunker.	Leia, Han, Chewie, Teebo, Scout, Rebels.
115 (1,2,3, 19,20,21,37, 38,41)	1 1/8	BUNKER: Heroes captured by Imperial Forces. Later, during the Ewok attack, they make it to the bunker door and try to hot wire terminal.	Han, Leia, Doubles, R2, 3PO, Teebo, Rebel Troopers, Scooter Troopers, Imperial Troopers, Ewoks, Walker.

119 (36,37, 38,39,40,41, 42,44,45)	1 1/8	BUNKER: Han & Leia are still trying to hot wire door, then the 2nd door closes. Battle raging all around. Leia gets hit.	Leia, Han, Chewie, Imperial Troopers, Rebel Troopers, Ewoks.
124 (1,2,3,4)	4/8	BUNKER: Chewie shows up in walker, tricks troopers. Heroes blow up bunker.	Imperial Troopers, Leia, Han, Chewie, Rebels, Ewoks.
131	1/8	NR. DESTROYED BUNKER: Heroes & captives witness the destruction of the Death Star... As it explodes in the sky.	Leia, Han, Chewie, R2, 3PO, Wicket, Teebo Rebels, Scouts, Imperial Troopers & officers, Ewoks.

MAIN UNIT PHOTOGRAPHY—REDWOODS LOCATION
Proposed start date 4/26/82 ???

SCHEDULE AS OF 4/5/82

Day 1	Biker's lunch	Sc. PT 65, 66 POV & EXT
Day 2	EXT. Shuttle Site EXT. Biker's Lunch	Sc. 65, 71
Day 3	LEIA's Crash Site	Sc. 72, 74
Day 4	"	"
Day 5	EXT Bunker	Sc. 88, 89, 91, 90, 92, 94
Day 6	"	"
Day 7	NET GAG	Sc. 75
Day 8	EXT BUNKER—Battle	Sc. 115, 119, 124, 131
Day 9	"	"
Day 10	"	"
Day 11	"	"

APPENDIX #4

STAR.WARS

REVENGE OF THE

J E D I

	ONE-LINE SCHEDULE No: 3	14th December, 1981.	
DATE:	SET:	SC. NOS:	PAGES:
Monday, 11th January:	EXT. TATOOINE LANDING AREA – SANDSTORM	44	2
Tuesday, 12th January:	EXT. JABBA'S PALACE GATE + INT. PALACE GATE + MAIN HALLWAY	6, 7, 15.	3.4/8
Wednesday, 13th January:	EXT. JABBA'S PALACE GATE + INT. PALACE GATE + MAIN HALLWAY	6, 7, 15. to comp.	—
Thursday, 14th January:	INT. EWOK VILLAGE SQUARE	78	3.3/8
Friday, 15th January:	EXT. EWOK VILLAGE SQUARE	78 contd.	—
Saturday, 16th January:	NO SHOOTING		
Sunday, 17th January:	NO SHOOTING		
Monday, 18th January:	EXT. EWOK VILLAGE SQUARE	132	7/8
Tuesday, 19th January:	EXT. EWOK VILLAGE SQUARE	132 contd.	—
Wednesday, 20th January:	INT. EWOK CHIEF'S HUT	79	1.4/8

	ONE-LINE SCHEDULE No: 3	14th December, 1981.	
DATE:	SET:	SC. NOS:	PAGES:
Thursday, 21st January:	INT. EWOK CHIEF'S HUT	79 contd.	—
Friday, 22nd January:	EXT. EWOK VILLAGE SQUARE	80	3.6/8
Saturday, 23rd January:	NO SHOOTING		
Sunday, 24th January:	NO SHOOTING		
Monday, 25th January:	INT. JABBA'S THRONE ROOM	8	1.6/8
Tuesday, 26th January:	INT. JABBA'S THRONE ROOM	11	3.5/8
Wednesday, 27th January:	INT. JABBA'S THRONE ROOM	11 contd.	—
Thursday, 28th January:	INT. JABBA'S THRONE ROOM	13	3.5/8
Friday, 29th January:	INT. JABBA'S THRONE ROOM	13 contd.	—
Saturday, 30th January:	NO SHOOTING		
Sunday, 31st January:	NO SHOOTING		
Monday, 1st February:	INT. JABBA'S THRONE ROOM	16, 17pt., 19.	2.1/8
Tuesday, 2nd February:	INT. JABBA'S THRONE ROOM	16, 17pt., 19. contd.	—
Wednesday, 3rd February:	INT. JABBA'S THRONE ROOM	21	1.5/8
Thursday, 4th February:	INT. BARGE — OBSER- VATION DECK	23, 25, 27 31, 34.	2.6/8
Friday, 5th February:	INT. BARGE — OBSER- VATION DECK	23, 25, 27, 31, 34. contd.	—
Saturday, 6th February:	NO SHOOTING		

	ONE-LINE SCHEDULE No: 3	14th December, 1981.	
DATE:	SET:	SC. NOS:	PAGES:
Sunday, 7th February:	NO SHOOTING		
Monday, 8th February:	INT. BARGE – OBSER- VATION DECK	23, 25, 27, 31, 34. contd.	—
Tuesday, 9th February:	INT. BRIDGE VADER'S STARDESTROYER	59, 61, 62pt., 64, 106.	1.7/8 3/8
Wednesday, 10th February:	INT. REBEL CRUISER MAIN BRIEFING ROOM	54	3.6/8
Thursday, 11th February:	INT. REBEL CRUISER MAIN BRIEFING ROOM	54 contd.	—
Friday, 12th February:	INT. REBEL CRUISER – BRIDGE	85, 101, 113, 121, 84pt., 86pt., 99pt., 103pt., 112pt., 117pt., 125pt., 129pt.	1.7/8
Saturday, 13th February:	NO SHOOTING		
Sunday, 14th February:	NO SHOOTING		
Monday, 15th February:	INT. REBEL CRUISER – BRIDGE	85, 101, 113, 121., 84pt., 86pt., 99pt., 103pt., 112pt., 117pt., 125pt., 129pt.	
Tuesday, 16th February:	INT. DUNGEON CORRI- DOR + CELL	9, 12, 14.	1.6/8

	ONE-LINE SCHEDULE No: 3	14th December, 1981.	
DATE:	SET:	SC. NOS:	PAGES:
Wednesday, 17th February:	INT. DUNGEON CORRI- DOR + BOILER ROOM	10	1.5/8
Thursday, 18th February:	INT. DEATH STAR – MAIN DOCKING BAY	4, 69, 95.	1.7/8
Friday, 19th February:	INT. DEATH STAR – MAIN DOCKING BAY	48	1.3/8
Saturday, 20th February:	NO SHOOTING		
Sunday, 21st February:	NO SHOOTING		
Monday, 22nd February:	INT. DEATH STAR – MAIN DOCKING BAY + CORRIDOR	47, 70, 126A, 127.	1.6/8
Tuesday, 23rd February:	INT. DEATH STAR – MAIN DOCKING BAY	127 contd.	—
Wednesday, 24th February:	INT. DEATH STAR – MAIN DOCKING BAY	127 contd.	—
Thursday, 25th February:	INT. DEATH STAR – EMPEROR'S ROOM	52, 73.	2.2/8
Friday, 26th February:	INT. DEATH STAR – EMPEROR'S ROOM	96, 107, 114.	3.6/8
Saturday, 27th February:	NO SHOOTING		
Sunday, 28th February:	NO SHOOTING		
Monday, 1st March:	INT. DEATH STAR – EMPEROR'S ROOM	118, 122.	2
Tuesday, 2nd March:	INT. DEATH STAR – EMPEROR'S ROOM	118, 122 contd.	—
Wednesday, 3rd March:	INT. DEATH STAR – EMPEROR'S ROOM	118, 122 contd.	—
Thursday, 4th March:	INT. DEATH STAR – EMPEROR'S ROOM	118, 122 contd.	—
Friday, 5th March:	INT. DEATH STAR – EMPEROR'S ROOM	118, 122 contd.	—

	ONE-LINE SCHEDULE No: 3	14th December, 1981.	
DATE:	SET:	SC. NOS:	PAGES:
Saturday, 6th March:	NO SHOOTING		
Sunday, 7th March:	NO SHOOTING		
Monday, 8th March:	INT. YODA'S HOUSE	50	2.6/8
Tuesday, 9th March:	INT. YODA'S HOUSE	50 contd.	—
Wednesday, 10th March:	EXT. DAGOBAH – YODA'S HOUSE + X-WING	51	3
Thursday, 11th March:	EXT. DAGOBAH – YODA'S HOUSE + X-WING	51 contd.	—
Friday, 12th March:	INT. RANCOR PIT + HOLDING TUNNEL	17pt., 18pt., 20pt.	2.1/8
Saturday, 13th March:	NO SHOOTING		
Sunday, 14th March:	NO SHOOTING		
Monday, 15th March:	INT. RANCOR PIT + HOLDING TUNNEL	17pt., 18pt., 20pt.	—
Tuesday, 16th March:	INT. RANCOR PIT + HOLDING TUNNEL	17pt., 18pt., 20pt.	—
Wednesday, 17th March:	INT. RANCOR PIT – BLUE SCREEN	17pt., 18pt., 20pt.	—
Thursday, 18th March:	INT. RANCOR PIT – BLUE SCREEN	17pt., 18pt., 20pt.	—
Friday, 19th March:	INT. IMPERIAL LAND- ING PLATFORM LOWER DECK	81pt., 82.	3
Saturday, 20th March:	NO SHOOTING		
Sunday, 21st March:	NO SHOOTING		

	ONE-LINE SCHEDULE No: 3	14th December, 1981.	
DATE:	SET:	SC. NOS:	PAGES:
Monday, 22nd March:	INT. IMPERIAL LAND- ING PLATFORM LOWER DECK	82 contd.	—
Tuesday, 23rd March:	INT. BUNKER CONTROL ROOM	97, 104, 123.	1.1/8
Wednesday, 24th March:	INT. BUNKER CONTROL ROOM	97, 104, 123.	—
Thursday, 25th March:	INT. DEATH STAR CON- TROL ROOM	3, 108.	7/8
Friday, 26th March:	INT. COCKPIT MILLEN- NIUM FALCON	84, 86, 99, 103, 112, 117, 125, 129, 85pt., 101pt., 113pt., 121pt.	3.4/8
Saturday, 27th March:	NO SHOOTING		
Sunday, 28th March:	NO SHOOTING		
Monday, 29th March:	INT. COCKPIT MILLEN- NIUM FALCON	84, 86, 99, 103, 112, 117, 125, 129 contd. 85pt., 101pt., 113pt., 121pt.	—
Tuesday, 30th March:	INT. COCKPIT IMPE- RIAL SHUTTLE	2, 56, 60, 62, 130pt.	3.1/8
Wednesday, 31st March:	INT. COCKPIT IMPE- RIAL SHUTTLE	2, 56, 60, 62, 130pt.	—
Thursday, 1st April:	INT. REBEL CRUISER – MAIN DOCKING BAY	55	5/8

COMPLETION OF STUDIO SCHEDULE

APPENDIX #5

Directed by .... RICHARD MARQUAND
Produced by .... HOWARD KAZANJIAN
Screenplay by .... LAWRENCE KASDAN
and GEORGE LUCAS
Story by .... GEORGE LUCAS
Executive Producer .... GEORGE LUCAS
Co-Producers .... ROBERT WATTS, JIM BLOOM
Production Designer .... NORMAN REYNOLDS
Director of Photography .... ALAN HUME B.S.C.
Edited by .... SEAN BARTON, MARCIA LUCAS,
DUWAYNE DUNHAM
Visual Effects .... RICHARD EDLUND A.S.C.,
DENNIS MUREN, KEN RALSTON
Costume Designers ..... AGGIE GUERARD RODGERS,
NILO RODIS-JAMERO

Mechanical Effects
Supervision .... KIT WEST
Make-Up and
Creature Design .... PHIL TIPPETT,
STUART FREEBORN
Sound Design .... BEN BURTT
Music by .... JOHN WILLIAMS

Set Decorators ..... MICHAEL FORD, HARRY LANGE
Conceptual Artist...................... RALPH McQUARRIE
Art Directors................ FRED HOLE, JAMES SCHOPPE
Assistant Art Directors............... MICHAEL LAMONT,
JOHN FENNER, RICHARD DAWKING
Set Dresser .... DOUG VON KOSS

Construction Manager ....BILL WELCH
Assistant Construction Manager ....ALAN BOOTH
Construction Supervisor......................ROGER IRVIN
General Foreman.............................. BILL IIAMS
Construction Foremen ...... GREG CALLAS, GUY CLAUSE,
              DOUG ELLIOTT, STAN WAKASHIGE
Paint Foreman ....GARY CLARK
Sketch Artist................................ROY CARNON
Scenic Artist .... TED MICHELL
Decor and Lettering Artist ....BOB WALKER
Set Draftsmen................................REG BREAM,
        MARK BILLERMAN, CHRIS CAMPBELL
Production Buyer........................... DAVID LUSBY
Construction Storeman................. DAVID MIDDLETON

Location Director of Photography ....JIM GLENNON
Additional Photography ....JACK LOWIN
Operating Cameramen .. ALEC MILLS, TOM LAUGHRIDGE,
               MIKE BENSON
Focus Pullers .... MICHAEL FRIFT, CHRIS TANNER
Assistant Cameramen ..LEO NAPOLITANO, BOB LA BONGE
Second Assistant Cameramen.. SIMON HUME, STEVE TATE,
        MARTIN KENZIE, MICHAEL GLENNON
Gaffers ....MIKE PANTAGES, BOB BREMNER
Aerial Photography ....RON GOODMAN,
              MARGARET HERRON
Helicopter Pilot .... MARK WOLFE
Key Grip .... DICK DOVA SPAH
Best Boy ....JOE CROWLEY
Dolly Grip ....CHUNKY HUSE, REG HALL
Matte Photography Consultant..... STANLEY SAYER, B.S.C.
Rigging Gaffers ..... CLARK GARLAND, TOMMY BROWN

Chief Make-Up Artists ....TOM SMITH,
              GRAHAM FREEBORN
Make-Up Artists ..... PETER ROBB KING, DICKIE MILLS,
           KAY FREEBORN, NICK DUDMAN
Chief Hairdresser.................. PATRICIA McDERMOTT
Hairdressers............. MIKE LOCKEY, PAUL LE BLANC
Chief Articulation Engineer .... STUART ZIFF
Assistant Articulation Engineer ....EBEN STROMQUIST
Armature Designer ....PETER RONZANI

Plastic Designer . . . . RICHARD DAVIS
Sculptural Designers . . . . . CHUCK WILEY, JAMES HOWARD
Key Sculptors . . . . DAVE CARSON, TONY McVEY,
DAVE SOSALLA, JUDY ELKINS,
DEREK HOWARTH
Chief Moldmaker . . . . WESLEY SEEDS
Moldmaker . . . . RON YOUNG
Creature Technicians . . . RANDY DUTRA, KIRK THATCHER,
DAN HOWARD, JAMES ISAAC,
BRIAN TURNER, JEANNE LAUREN,
RICHARD SPAH JR., ETHAN WILEY
Creature Consultants . . . . JON BERG, CHRIS WALAS
Production/Creature Co-Ordinator . . . . PATTY BLAU
Latex Foam Lab Supervisor . . . . TOM McLAUGHLIN
Animatronics Engineer . . . . JOHN COPPINGER

Wardrobe Supervisor . . . . RON BECK
Costume Supervisor . . . . MARY ELIZABETH STILL
Wardrobe Mistress . . . . JANET TEBROOKE
Shop Manager . . . . JENNY GREEN
Jeweler . . . . RICHARD MILLER
Creature Costumers . . . . BARBARA KASSAL,
EDWINA PELLIKKA, ANNE POLLAND,
ELVIRA ANGELINETTA

Property Master . . . . PETER HANCOCK
Assistant Property Master . . . . CHARLES TORBETT
Property Supervisors . . . . DAN COANGELO,
BRIAN LOFTHOUSE
Property . . . . HOLLY WALKER, IVAN VAN PERRE
Propmakers . . . . BILL HARGREAVES, RICHARD PETERS
Master Carpenter . . . . BERT LONG
Master Plasterer . . . . KENNY CLARKE
Master Painter . . . . ERIC SHIRTCLIFFE
Supervising Rigger . . . . RED LAWRENCE
Supervising Stagehand . . . . EDDIE BURKE
Sail Co-Ordinators . . . . BILL KREYSLER,
WARWICK TOMPKINS
Sails Engineering . . . . DERRICK BAYLIS, PEGGY KASHUBA

Production Sound . . . . . . TONY DAWE, RANDY THOM
Boom Operators . . . . . DAVID BATCHELOR, DAVID PARKER

Sound Assistants .... SHEP DAWE, JIM MANSON
Audio Engineers .... T.M. CHRISTOPHER,
CATHERINE COOMBS, KRIS HANDWERK,
K.C. HODENFIELD, HOWIE, TOM JOHNSON,
BRIAN KELLY, JAMES KESSLER,
SUSAN LEAHY, ROBERT MARTY,
SCOTT ROBINSON, DENNIE THORPE,
JOHN WATSON
English Lyrics by .... JOSEPH WILLIAMS
Huttese Lyrics by .... ANNIE ARBOGAST
Ewokese Lyrics by .... BEN BURTT

Re-Recording Mixers .... BEN BURTT,
GARY SUMMERS, ROGER SAVAGE

Music Recording .... ERIC TOMLINSON

Orchestrations .... HERBERT W. SPENCER

Supervising Music Editor...... KENNETH WANNBERG

Re-Recording Engineer .... TOMLINSON HOLMAN
Assistant Film Editors .. STEVE STARKEY, CONRAD BUFF,
PHIL SANDERSON, NICK HOSKER,
DEBRA McDERMOTT, CLIVE HARTLEY
Sound Effects Editors................. RICHARD BURROW,
TERESA ECKTON, KEN FISCHER
Dialogue Editors . LAUREL LADEVICH, CURT SCHULKEY,
BONNIE KOEHLER, VICKIE ROSE SAMPSON
Assistant Sound Editors......... CHRIS WEIR, BILL MANN,
GLORIA BORDERS, SUZANNE FOX,
KATHY RYAN, NANCY JENCKS,
HELEN CEASMAN

Production Supervisor .... DOUGLAS TWIDDY
Production Executive .... ROBERT LATHAM BROWN
Unit Production Manager .... MIKI HERMAN
Assistant Production Manager .... PATRICIA CARR
Associate to Producer................. LOUIS G. FRIEDMAN
First Assistant Director/
Second Unit Director .... DAVID TOMBLIN
Second Assistant Directors .... ROY BUTTON,
MICHAEL STEELE, CHRIS NEWMAN,
RUSSELL LODGE

Production Assistant .... IAN BRYCE
Production Co-Ordinator .... LATA RYAN
Co-Ordination Assistants .... SUNNI KERWIN,
                                        GAIL SAMUELSON
Script Supervisor .... PAMELA MANN FRANCIS
Location Script Supervisor ....BOB FOREST
Stunt Co-Ordinator .... GLENN RANDALL
Stunt Arranger .... PETER DIAMOND
Casting .... MARY SELWAY BUCKLEY
Location Casting ....DAVE EMAN, BILL LYTLE
Assistant to Mr. Kazanjian .... KATHLEEN HARTNEY ROSS
Assistant to Mr. Bloom .... JOHN SYRJAMAKI
Assistant to Mr. Lucas............................JANE BAY
Choreographer ....GILLIAN GREGORY
Location Choreographer.....................WENDY ROGERS
Production Controller .... ARTHUR CARROLL
Production Accountant..............MARGARET MITCHELL
Production Accountant......................COLIN HURREN
Assistant Accountants.................. SHEALA DANIELL,
                                        BARBARA HARLEY
Location Accountants............... DIANE DANKWARDT,
                                        PINKI RAGAN
Transportation Co-Ordinator.............. GENE SCHWARTZ
Transportation Captains...................JOHN FEINBLATT,
                                        H. LEE NOBLITT
Studio Transportation Managers ....VIC MINAY,
                                        MARK LA BONGE
Location Contact ....LENNIE FIKE
Still Photographers .... ALBERT CLARKE,
                                        RALPH NELSON JR.
Unit Publicist .... GORDON ARNELL
Assistant Publicist...........................JUNE BROOM
Research................................DEBORAH FINE

PRODUCTION AND MECHANICAL EFFECTS UNIT

Special Effects Supervisor............. ROY ARBOGAST
Special Effects Foreman ....WILLIAM DAVID LEE
Special Effects Floor Controller ....IAN WINGROVE

Senior Effects Technician .... PETER DAWSON
Chief Electronics Technician .... RON HONE
Wire Specialist............................. BOB HARMAN
Location Special Effects .... KEVIN PIKE, MIKE WOOD

MINIATURE AND OPTICAL EFFECTS UNIT
INDUSTRIAL LIGHT AND MAGIC

Optical Photography Supervisor ... BRUCE NICHOLSON
Effects Cameramen...DON DOW, MICHEAL J. McALISTER,
BILL NEIL, SCOTT FARRAR,
SELWYN EDDY III, MICHAEL OWENS,
ROBERT ELSWIT, RICK FICHTER,
STEWART BARBEE, MARK GREDELL,
DAVID HARDBURGER
Assistant Cameramen........ PAT SWEENEY, KIM MARKS,
ROBERT HILL, RAY GILBERTI,
RANDY JOHNSON, PATRICK McARDLE,
PETER DAULTON, BESSIE WILEY,
MARYAN EVANS, TOBY HEINDEL,
DAVID FINCHER, PETER ROMANO
Optical Printer Operators....... JOHN ELLIS, DAVID BERRY
KENNETH SMITH, DONALD CLARK,
MARK VARGO, JAMES LIM
Optical Line-Up............ TOM ROSSETER, ED L. JONES,
RALPH GORDON, PHILIP BARBERIO
Lab Technicians....... TIM GEIDEMAN, DUNCAN MYERS,
MICHAEL S. MOORE

Art Director-Visual Effects .... JOE JOHNSTON
Production Illustrator .... GEORGE JENSON

Stop Motion Animator .... TOM ST. AMAND

Matte Painting Supervisor ...... MICHAEL PANGRAZIO
Matte Painting Artists....... CHRIS EVANS, FRANK ORDAZ
Matte Photography ...... NEIL KREPELA, CRAIG BARRON

Chief Model Makers .... PAUL HUSTON,
CHARLES BAILEY, MICHAEL GLENN FULMER,
EASE OWYEUNG

Model Makers .... WILLIAM GEORGE, MARC THORPE,
SCOTT MARSHALL, SEAN CASEY,
LARRY TAN, BARBARA GALLUCCI,
JEFF MANN, IRA KEELER,
BILL BECK, MIKE COCHRANE,
BARBARA AFFONSO, BILL BUTTFIELD,
MARGHI McMAHON, RANDY OTTENBERG

Modelshop Supervisors .... LORNE PETERSON,
STEVE GAWLEY

Animation Supervisor .... JAMES KEEFER
Head Effects Animators................... GARRY WALLER,
KIMBERLY KNOWLTON
Effects Animators .... TERRY WINDELL, RENEE HOLT,
MIKE LESSA, SAM COMSTOCK,
ROB LA DUCA, ANNICK THERRIEN,
SUKI STERN, MARGOT PIPKIN

Supervising Visual Effects Editor .... ARTHUR REPOLA
Visual Effects Editors...................... HOWARD STEIN,
PETER AMUNDSON, BILL KIMBERLIN
Assistant Visual Effects Editors...... ROBERT CHRISOULIS,
MICHAEL GLEASON,
JAY IGNASZEWSKI, JOE CLASS

General Manager, ILM .... TOM SMITH
Production Supervisor .... PATRICIA ROSE DUIGNAN
Production Co-Ordinators .... WARREN FRANKLIN,
LAURIE VERMONT
Administrative Staff .... CHRISSIE ENGLAND,
LAURA KAYSEN, PAULA KARSH,
KAREN AYERS, SONJA PAULSON, KAREN DUBÉ
Production Assistants .... SUSAN FRITZ-MONAHAN,
KATHY SHINE
Supervisor-Still Photography .... TERRY CHOSTNER
Still Photographers .... ROBERTO McGRATH,
KERRY NORDQUIST
Electronic System Designers .... JERRY JEFFRESS,
KRIS BROWN
Electronic Engineers...................... MIKE MacKENZIE,
MARTY BRENNEIS

Computer Graphics . . . . WILLIAM REEVES, TOM DUFF
Equipment Engineering Supervisor . . . . GENE WHITEMAN
Machinists . . . . UDO PAMPEL, CONRAD BONDERSON
Apprentice Machinists . . . . DAVID HANKS, CHRIS RAND
Design Engineer . . . . MIKE BOLLES
Equipment Support Staff . . . . WADE CHILDRESS,
                    MICHAEL J. SMITH, CRISTI McCARTHY,
                                         ED TENNLER
Supervising Stage Technician . . . . TED MOEHNKE
Stage Technicians . . . . PATRICK FITZSIMMONS,
              BOB FINLEY III, ED HIRSH, JOHN McLEOD,
                        PETER STOLZ, DAVE CHILDERS,
                          HAROLD COLE, MERLIN OHM,
                        JOE FULMER, LANCE BRACKETT
Pyrotechnicians . . . . THAINE MORRIS, DAVE PIER
Steadicam®Plate Photography . . . . GARRETT BROWN
Ultra High Speed Photography . . . . BRUCE HILL
                                        PRODUCTIONS
Color Timers . . . . JIM SCHURMANN, BOB HAGANS
Negative Cutter . . . . SUNRISE FILM INC.
Additional Optical Effects . . . . LOOKOUT MOUNTAIN FILMS,
              PACIFIC TITLE, MONACO FILM LABS,
    CALIFORNIA FILM, VISUAL CONCEPTS ENGINEERING,
        MOVIE MAGIC, VAN der VEER PHOTO EFFECTS

EWOKS

MARGO APOSTOCOS
RAY ARMSTRONG
EILEEN BAKER
MICHAEL H. BALHAM
BOBBIE BELL
PATTY BELL
ALAN BENNETT
SARAH BENNETT
PAMELA BETTS
DAN BLACKNER
LINDA BOWLEY
PETER BURROUGHS

DEBBIE CARRINGTON
MAUREEN CHARLTON
WILLIAM COPPEN
SADIE CORRIE
TONY COX
JOHN CUMMING
JEAN D'AGOSTINO
LUIS DE JESUS
DEBBIE DIXON
MARGARITA FERNANDEZ
PHIL FONDACARO
SAL FONDACARO
TONY FRIEL
DAN FRISHMAN
JOHN GAVAM
MICHAEL GILDEN
PAUL GRANT
LYDIA GREEN
LARS GREEN
PAM GRIZZ
ANDREW HERD
J. J. JACKSON
RICHARD JONES
TREVOR JONES
GLYNN JONES
KAREN LAY
JOHN LUMMISS
NANCY MACLEAN
PETER MANDELL
CAROLE MORRIS
STACY NICHOLS
CHRIS NUNN
BARBARA O'LAUGHLIN
BRIAN ORENSTEIN
HARRELL PARKER JR.
JOHN PEDRICK
APRIL PERKINS
RONNIE PHILLIPS
KATIE PURVIS
CAROL READ
NICHOLAS READ

DIANA REYNOLDS
DANIEL RODGERS
CHRIS ROMANO
DEAN SHACKENFORD
KIRAN SHAH
FELIX SILLA
LINDA SPRIGGS
GERARLD STADDON
JOSEPHINE STADDON
KEVIN THOMPSON
KENDRA WALL
BRIAN WHEELER
BUTCH WILHELM

Mime Artists	FRANKI ANDERSON, AILSA BERK, SEAN CRAWFORD, ANDY CUNNINGHAM, TIM DRY, GRAEME HATTRICK, PHIL HERBERT, GERALD HOME, PAUL SPRINGER
Stunt Performers	BOB ANDERSON, DIRK YOHAN BEER, MARC BOYLE, MIKE CASSIDY, TRACY EDDON, SANDRA GROSS, TED GROSSMAN, FRANK HENSON, LARRY HOLT, BILL HORRIGAN, ALF JOINT, JULIUS LEFLORE, COLIN SKEAPING, MALCOM WEAVER, PAUL WESTON, BOB YERKES, DAN ZORMEIER

Thanks to the U.S. Department of Interior
Bureau of Land Management and National Park Service
Photographed in Buttercup Valley, Death Valley
and Smith River, California
and EMI-Elstree Studios, Borehamwood, England

Cameras and Lenses by Joe Dunton Cameras Ltd.
Aerial Camera Systems by Wesscam Camera Systems (Europe)
Lighting Equipment and Crew from Lee Electric Ltd.

Production Vehicles Courtesy of GMC Truck and Oldsmobile
Location Service by Cinemobile
Air Transportation by PAN AM
Rerecording at Sprocket Systems
Music Recording at Anvil-Abbey Road Studio
Special Visual Effects Produced at Industrial Light and Magic,
Marin County, CA

Color By Rank Film Laboratories® Prints by Deluxe®
Recorded in DOLBY℗
A Lucasfilm Ltd. Production
A Twentieth Century-Fox Release
Music Performed by the London Symphony Orchestra
Original Soundtrack on RSO Records and Tapes
Novelization from Ballantine Books
TM & © Lucasfilm Ltd. (LFL) 1983
All Rights Reserved

CAST

MARK HAMILL	as Luke Skywalker
HARRISON FORD	as Han Solo
CARRIE FISHER	as Princess Leia
BILLY DEE WILLIAMS	as Lando Calrissian
ANTHONY DANIELS	as C-3PO
PETER MAYHEW	as Chewbacca
SEBASTIAN SHAW	as Anakin Skywalker
IAN McDIARMID	as the Emperor
FRANK OZ	performing Yoda
DAVID PROWSE	as Darth Vader
JAMES EARL JONES	as the Voice of Darth Vader
ALEC GUINNESS	as Ben (Obi-Wan) Kenobi

Supporting Cast

R2-D2	KENNY BAKER
Moff Jerjerrod	MICHAEL PENNINGTON
Admiral Piett	KENNETH COLLEY
Bib Fortuna	MICHAEL CARTER
Wedge	DENIS LAWSON
Admiral Ackbar	TIM ROSE
General Madine	DERMOT CROWLEY
Mon Mothma	CAROLINE BLAKISTON
Wicket	WARWICK DAVIS
Paploo	KENNY BAKER
Boba Fett	JEREMY BULLOCH
Oola	FEMI TAYLOR
Sy Snootles	ANNIE ARBOGAST
Fat Dancer	CLAIRE DAVENPORT
Teebo	JACK PURVIS
Logray	MIKE EDMONDS

Chief Chirpa	JANE BUSBY
Ewok Warrior	MALCOM DIXON
Ewok Warrior	MIKE COTTRELL
Nicki	NICKI READE
Stardestroyer Controller #1	ADAM BAREHAM
Stardestroyer Controller #2	JONATHAN OLIVER
Stardestroyer Captain #1	PIP MILLER
Stardestroyer Captain #2	TOM MANNION
Jabba Puppeteers	TOBY PHILPOTT, MIKE EDMONDS, DAVID BARCLAY
Puppeteers	MICHAEL McCORMICK, DEEP ROY, SIMON WILLIAMSON, HUGH SPIRIT, SWIM LEE, MICHAEL QUINN, RICHARD ROBINSON

Lucasfilm
Administration
1- 415-
662 - 1800

Lucasfilm
Personell Dept.

PO Box 2009

San Rafael California
~~~~~~~~~~
94912